Routledge Handbook of Sports Sponsorship

The *Routledge Handbook of Sports Sponsorship* provides a comprehensive guide to the successful management of sport sponsorship. Covering the development of an appropriate sponsorship strategy and the implementation of the sponsorship operation, this book offers detailed guidelines for sports organizations.

The text also offers the first clear review of the legal issues associated with marketing, copyright and contracts in print, television and radio sponsorship, and contains a wealth of sport-specific case studies. It includes:

- sports marketing and management theory illustrated with real-world examples;
- an overview of the roles of the key stakeholders such as event organizers, commercial sponsors, athletes, the media, service providers and public authorities;
- thorough explanation of the legal issues involved in sports sponsorship;
- a major international sports sponsorship case study examined in full from concept stage to post-event analysis.

The *Routledge Handbook of Sports Sponsorship* is essential reading for students and a valuable reference for professionals in sports law, sports management, sports marketing and brand management.

Alain Ferrand is Head of the Department of Sports Management at the University of Lyon, and an Associate Professor at the University of Turin and the Scuola Dello Sport, Rome. **Luiggino Torrigiani** is President of LT and Partners Sports Management Consultancy, based in Lausanne. **Andreu Camps i Povill** is Professor and General Director at L'Institut Nacional d'Educació Física de Catalunya, Barcelona, and a practising sports lawyer.

Routledge Handbook of Sports Sponsorship

Successful strategies

Alain Ferrand, Luiggino Torrigiani
and Andreu Camps i Povill

Translated by Pierre-François Lalonde
and Elizabeth Christopherson

LONDON AND NEW YORK

First published 2006 in French language edition

This edition first published 2007
by Routledge
2 Park Square, Milton Park, Abingdon, Oxon OX14 4RN

Simultaneously published in the USA and Canada
by Routledge
711 Third Avenue, New York, NY 10017

Routledge is an imprint of the Taylor & Francis Group, an informa business

© 2007 Alain Ferrand, Luiggino Torrigiani and Andreu Camps i Povill

Typeset in Sabon by
Book Now Ltd

British Library Cataloguing in Publication Data
A catalogue record for this book is available from the British Library

Library of Congress Cataloging in Publication Data
A catalog record has been requested for this book

ISBN10: 0–415–40110–0 (hbk)
ISBN10: 0–415–40111–9 (pbk)
ISBN10: 0–203–96782–8 (ebk)

ISBN13: 978–0–415–40110–4 (hbk)
ISBN13: 978–0–415–40111–1 (pbk)
ISBN13: 978–0–203–96782–9 (ebk)

Printed and bound by CPI Group (UK) Ltd, Croydon, CR0 4YY

Contents

Figures and tables

Figures

Tables

Acknowledgements

This book is the result of a friendship and matching of complementary experiences. With special thanks to Prof. Ian Henry for his collaboration, and Liz Christopherson and Pierre-François Lalonde for the translation from French to English. Beyond the method, we hope you will enter the sponsorship spirit.

Abbreviations

CNOSF	French National Olympic Committee
CSR	Corporate Social Responsibility
DNS	Domain Name System
EC	European Community
FFVB	French Federation of Volleyball
FIFA	Fédération Internationale de Football Association
FIVB	International Federation of Volleyball
ICANN	Internet Corporation for Assigned Names and Numbers
IOC	International Olympic Committee
NF	National Federations
NOC	National Olympic Committee
OCOG	Organizing Committee of the Olympic Games
OG	Olympic Games
ROI	Return On Investment
SNOC	Slovenian National Olympic Committee
TOP	The Olympic Partner Programme
UCI	International Cycling Union
UEFA	Union of European Football Associations

Introduction

In the media, sponsorship is often approached from the standpoint of its economic impact. Certain sponsorship figures are, indeed, spectacular. According to a study carried out by the World Federation of Advertisers (WFA), the worldwide range of estimates for total sponsorship investments is 33.2 billion dollars. The forecasts regarding market development trends projected a budget of 49 billion dollars for 2006. Although it is difficult to precisely quantify the importance of sponsorship, to the extent of its forming an integral part of the marketing strategy of companies, it should be stressed that investments with regard to sponsorship are continually rising. Indeed, global investments increased from 7.7 billion dollars in 1990 to more than 28 billion dollars in 2002. The investments made by companies have multiplied by a factor of 3.7 during the course of the past 12 years and one can estimate that the annual increase is approximately 10 per cent. This increase, however, is not homogeneous. There are great differences that exist between countries, sports and associated events.

The development of sponsorship methods is equally notable at the strategic level, as well as at the operational level. In a little less than 20 years, the focus of sponsorship has shifted from the valuation of brand exposure (e.g. jerseys, boards, etc.), to the sponsor's brand activation by focusing attention on the organization's relationship with the people interested in the event. In this context, the target is to deliver a tangible benefit to the target group by providing them with enjoyment, information, entertainment, etc. According to the IEG (2004) sponsorship report regarding sponsorship and marketing expenditure in North America, companies spent 38.4 billion dollars (that is, 16 per cent of the total) in sponsorship operations and 191.6 billion dollars (83.2 per cent of the total) for marketing. In addition, if one considers the relationship between the expenditure directly linked to sponsorship and that linked to activation (e.g. television sponsorship, special operations, etc.), one notes that the latter was three times higher than the former (28.8 billion dollars compared with 9.6 billion dollars). Table 0.1 represents the breakdown of the spending allocations for sponsorship in North America in 2002. It should be noted that the contract now accounts for only 25 per cent of the total expenditure related to sponsorship operations. The sponsors have thus learned how to benefit from a sponsorship operation by enhancing it through advertising (35 per cent), publicity (20 per cent), hospitality (public relations) (10 per cent) and so forth.

Table 0.1 Expenditure related to sponsorship operations in North America in 2002

Means	Percentages
Sponsorship contract	25%
Advertising	35%
Promotion and specific operations	20%
Hospitality and public relations	10%
Other	10%

Source: Adapted from IEG sponsorship report (2004) and the DMA Group

The data testify to a progression in strategy (the assessment of the results and assortment of opportunities, in association with the strategy of a company, search for synergy with the other proceedings of marketing, etc.), as well as the implementation of these programmes (e.g. follow-up operations, programmes of activation integrated into the proceedings of marketing, etc.). In addition, the growing economic impact of sponsorship represents an indicator of the intensifying social impact of sporting events and the progression of the marketing strategies that relates to them. Thus, in this introduction we first define the foundation of such marketing strategies in order to establish them within a system. Subsequently, we will specify the objectives and the positioning of this book.

Sponsorship is based on an exchange process between two parties

The exchange is a process that consists of obtaining something from someone in return for something else. In the context of sponsorship, this presumes four conditions.

- An organization that seeks sponsors must conceive a sponsorship offer in connection with the rights which it holds.[1]
- The offer must represent value for the potential sponsor (company, local authority, etc.).
- The organization must be able to deliver this provision of services specified in the exchange.
- The potential sponsor must be free to accept or decline the offer (the transaction may involve an exchange of product and/or a provision of a service).

These relations are summarized in Figure 0.1.

In this context, the rights holder (regardless of whether he or she manages the process without calling on an agency) must be able to analyse the expectations of potential sponsors, in an effort to design and commercialize an offer that is likely to satisfy them and outperform competition. This phase enables the following important points to be made. It is consistent with Kotler and Armstrong's (2004) marketing management principles:

- the various stages of the procedure for the two involved parties – diagnostic analysis, strategy design, planning, implementation and assessment;
- pursued objective – the satisfaction of partners;

Figure 0.1 The relationship between the rights owner and sponsor

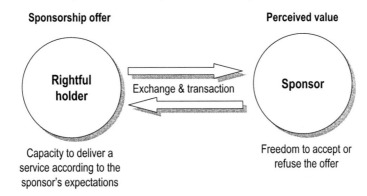

- the included extent of ideas and services;
- the extremely competitive environment;
- the economic and/or social value of the exchange.

From a marketing standpoint, the value is tied to the ability of the sponsorship service offer to satisfy the sponsors' expectations and objectives. It could be economic (e.g. to increase awareness, strengthen or modify image, develop sales, stimulate distribution network, etc.) and/or social (e.g. promoting corporate policy, reinforcing internal cohesion, etc.).

As previously noted, the provision of a service in the field of sponsorship calls for possessing marketing rights related to the use of an event's brand and athletes' image, and to the display of commercial brands in the public sphere, etc. In this context, it is necessary to point out that no organization holds the marketing rights of sport in general or in a particular sport. Indeed, sport is a social practice that can develop outside all institutional contexts. The practice of sport becomes institutionalized insofar as an assembly is structured around a mission. This mission is embedded deep within the statutes of sports organizations. Hence,

> the Olympic spirit is a philosophy of life, paying tribute to and uniting qualities of the body, will, and spirit into a balanced unit. Uniting sport to culture and education, the Olympic spirit strives to create a lifestyle based on finding happiness through the joy of effort, in the educative value of setting good examples and the respect of universal fundamental ethics principles (IOC 2006).[2]

Consequently,

> the Olympic movement brings together all those who accept to be guided by the Olympic Charter and who recognize the authority of the International Olympic Committee (IOC), namely the International Federations (IF) whose respective sport is on the program of the Olympic Games, the National Olympic Committee (NOC), the Organizing Committee of the Olympic Games (OCOG), athletes, judges and referees, associations and clubs, and at last all the organizations and institutions recognized by the IOC (ibid.).

Thus, the determination of members to develop a certain sport (indeed a certain notion of sport) transforms into the creation of an organization in charge of setting the sphere of activity. The organization thus becomes the owner of its own brand as well as that of other events it organizes.

The social impact of a sports organization and its events will depend, in particular, on the following factors:

- the power and legitimacy of the sporting organization (e.g. is it the French Volleyball Federation with its 100,000 licensees or only one of its clubs with its 100 members?);
- the characteristics and number of people who participate in the event (e.g. is it just a friendly tennis match or a tournament gathering the ATP top 100 players?);
- the power and the legitimacy of the stakeholders[3] involved (e.g. are they small clubs, local sponsors or are they national teams, with large TV coverage and worldwide sponsors?);
- the venue where the event takes place (e.g. is it a football match between two American Major League Soccer teams, or a Ligua match at Camp Nou in Barcelona?);
- the importance of the outcome (e.g. is it the Athletics Regional Championship finals or the World Championship finals?);
- the media coverage of the event (e.g. is it global, such as for the Olympic Games, or local, as for a regional competition?);
- The impact on the territory (e.g. is it a one-shot event like a Davis Cup competition or is it a recurrent event such as the London marathon involving each year local and regional institutions, volunteers, etc.?).

Sports sponsorship exists within a global system

The institutionalization of sport leads it to develop within a global system. This system joins together a more or less significant number of stakeholders. These correspond to the persons or entities in relationship with the organization and the events it organizes. There are internal stakeholders (i.e. athletes, clubs, employees, politicians, etc.) and external stakeholders (i.e. communities, media, sponsors, public opinion, etc.). Sponsorship is, therefore, not simply a bilateral relationship between the rights holder and the sponsor, but rather a multilateral relationship, involving a significant number of stakeholders in this system. Figure 0.2 presents the global system in which the event-driven system is located, which we chose to develop, for the most part, by taking into account its social impact.

It is a complex system in which stakeholders are interdependent. Thus, the audience of an event influences the value of a sponsorship proposition. An athlete who does not participate in events covered by the media will find it difficult to have media exposure. A sports federation will have a weak social impact if the events it organizes do not involve the clubs and if the events are not associated with the region. The global system, as a whole, consists of three systems: the event-driven system in itself, the sporting system and the system relating to the region in which it is held. These three systems interact, taking into consideration the associations which exist between the groups of interests. Consequently, sponsorship should be managed within the framework of a systemic approach.

Figure 0.2 The three systems interacting in event sponsorship

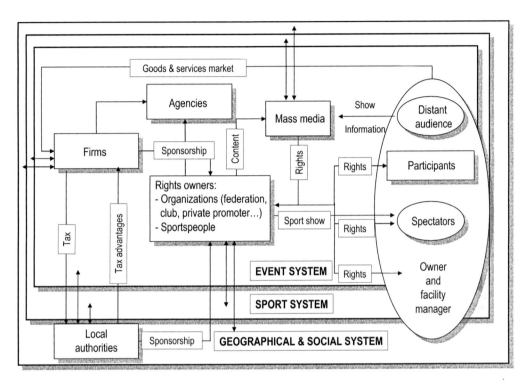

The event system

It is an event-driven system because of the energy it transmits. The main stakeholders are rights holders, participants, audience, media, sponsors and agencies.

Rights holders

Depending on the individual case, these rights are held either by an association or a company. It implies that athletes and sporting groups possess their own rights. Rights holders can, in certain situations, elect another entity to market their rights and/or organize an event.

Audience

The audience is extremely influential on the level of impact of the sponsorship operation. The audience is made up of a direct audience (i.e. participants, spectators, judges, etc.) and an indirect audience (i.e. viewers, listeners, readers, Internet users, etc.) The most important expectations of the audience relate to the sports event, entertainment, excitement, search of information, etc.

Media

The media are the audience amplifier. Contrary to popular belief, the media do not construct the event, since in most cases they will 'cover' the event only if a sufficient number of 'clients' are interested. In the context of a sponsorship operation, it is increasingly essential to have an agreement between the rights holder, the media and the sponsors.

Sponsors

Sponsors will often compete for visibility in the stadium, or on athletes' apparel, yet they are learning to be partners. In effect, sponsorship operations are business-to-business opportunities for sponsors.

Agencies

There are various types of agencies which one can categorize according to their principal objective – consulting firms in sport marketing, search firms for sponsorship, etc. Their general role is to liaise between the rights holders and the sponsorship companies.

Local authorities

The state, regional and local authorities could be deeply involved in the events system. For the Olympic Games, all cities who submit an application to host the games must have the complete backing of their local and national governments. At the local level, sport requires facilities which may belong to local communities. Local authorities, subsequently, have communication strategies leading them to seek a return on investment. Furthermore, this operation supports the opportunity for the establishment of sponsorship companies within the local authority's territory.

Apart from public interest, stakeholders get involved in a sponsorship operation because they believe it contributes to the success of their strategy. These participants have progressively begun to understand that these operations give them the opportunity to work on collaborative programmes which would enable them to increase the value of their return on investment.

The sports system

The nature of the event determines the nature of the stakeholders involved in the sports system. First of all, this system involves participants who are specific to the club and federation sports system. It is established within a traditional hierarchy – international federation, national federation, league and club. Secondarily, the system is made up of public or semi-public sports management organizations, ministries and local structures. Their number and characteristics greatly influence the social impact of the event.

The geographical and social system

The event and its stakeholders are located within a geographical and social system. This relationship can be tight, taking into account the fact that the sport constitutes a vector of economic and social development, or loose when it consists of an event organized by a commercial body which does not seek a long-term impact on the region. For example, Sport Canada[4] stressed the fact that hosting of international sport events brings direct and significant benefits across a broad range of government priorities. Economic benefits

> include job creation, particularly in the small and medium-sized business sector, regional development, increased tourism, increased exports, enhanced infra-structure and increased tax revenue. Social benefits range from unique work experiences including training and youth participation, to volunteer promotion and increased emphasis on fitness and health.

Consequently, sport is a tool for sustainable development.

Implementing a sponsorship management method allowing stakeholders' expectations to be fulfilled

As we mentioned, each stakeholder has a strategy, objectives to obtain (whether they are commercial or institutional) and more or less precise expectations concerning the provision of a service in itself. Although certain objectives are at times conflicting, stakeholders are collaborating more and more by setting up systemic marketing programmes. This is a continuous process consisting of engaging in activities and programmes of cooperation and collaboration involving partners and users, whose aim is to create or increase the economic and/or social value of the unit, at a reduced cost.

The organization in charge of delivering a service must deploy a quality management procedure. The procedure aims at mobilizing the whole organization in an effort to meet expectations, at the best cost, with the purpose of ensuring the lasting satisfaction of the stakeholders. In its most elaborate form, sponsorship is nothing more than the use of quality management principles within a systemic marketing framework. This translates to implementing methods and tools which make it possible:

- to identify which stakeholders attach value to the event (or to that which is sponsored);
- to select stakeholders in connection with the mission sought after by the rights holder;
- to conceive the most competitive offer likely to satisfy the expectations of all targeted stakeholders;
- to deliver a satisfactory service to the stakeholders, even exceeding their expectations.

This requires the relationship between the stakeholders concerned to be managed within a legal framework. Derbaix *et al.* (1994) point out that sponsorship is not possible if an event cannot be regulated. An event comes with a rights holder and it ought to be managed and protected like a brand.[5] As previously noted, the rights holder must verify beforehand that the promised offer of service to the sponsor will be deliverable. This offer often involves other participants such as athletes, media partners, etc. It is therefore advisable, prior to designing any sponsorship strategy and, more importantly, commercializing any offer, to define and secure relationships between the parties concerned at the legal/judicial level.

To define and secure relationships between stakeholders

The relationship between the rights holder and the sponsor is formalized within the framework of the contract. The quality and the security of the delivered service depend on the control of a certain number of external factors to this relationship. It is necessary to analyse this system in order to define the legal articulation, thereby making it possible to control the critical factors, to guarantee the normal course of this partnership, without unforeseen incidents. Zero risk does not exist. This is why it is advisable to instigate the legal means to make it possible to react as soon as possible in the event of a problem.

Each organization and each event is unique, bearing in mind their distinctive features and the stakeholders involved. This specificity is reinforced by the marketing strategy, which has a twofold objective to contribute to the realization of the mission of the rights holder and to reinforce the perceived value of the marketing strategy within the market. It will be particularly important to give the event a distinctive identity, to position it with direct and indirect competition. In this context, the legal aspects must not only contribute to the success of the marketing strategy, but must also provide all the guarantees necessary. We pointed out earlier that an organization cannot take over a particular sport, but only its institutional framework. In this context, it will be appropriate to legally articulate the internal and external factors that customize the event and guarantee its differentiation. It is obvious that the legal mechanisms which make it possible to guarantee individualization and the property of the event must be protected by a legal order.

The world of sport is under the influence of two types of legal entity of differing nature:

1. the legal entity responsible for the sport emanating from the sporting structures (i.e. National Olympic committees, sporting federations, leagues, clubs, etc.);
2. the legal entity issuing from the power of public authorities, with competences and capacity to settle certain aspects in connection with, or related to sport. This is a public legal entity.

The convergence on the same social activity, a sporting event in this case, of two legal entities of a different nature, based occasionally on different legal principles having different manners of performing and different means at their disposal, makes the legal analysis of the sport very complex. A hypothetical proposition for uniform and constant solutions, valid at all times and in all places, is almost impossible and, in any case, simplistic and risky.

What is the intended readership?

This book is aimed at stakeholders of the three systems which we have presented here and at certain participants in relation to those systems.

More specifically it is aimed at:

* sports organizations seeking partners for themselves, their events and teams;
* event organizers;

- professional athletes;
- existing or potential sponsors;
- public authorities involved in sporting events;
- service providers in the field of sports marketing;
- academics and students in the fields of management, communication, marketing and sport management;
- any communications, advertising and production agencies interested in the topics developed.

At the sport organizations level, this work is more particularly intended for presidents, CEOs, general secretaries, marketing managers, sponsorship managers, communication managers, lawyers, etc., as well as people in charge of sporting events.

At the business and marketing agencies level, the book is particularly intended for heads of department, and for marketing, commercial, communications, financial, legal affairs, sponsorship, brand, product and distribution network managers.

What expectations do we wish to satisfy?

Expectations relating to the aforementioned stakeholders refer to competences of the strategic type and operational type. The strategic approach is the first phase. It makes it possible to analyse resources and competences in relation to the environment in which the organization is evolving, in order to react to the economic, legislative, competitive pressures, etc., and to benefit from opportunities. That notably allows us:

- to analyse the market evolution in a proactive way;
- to analyse event stakeholders' rights;
- to identify the most attractive offers and markets;
- to identify where the competition comes from and to outperform it;
- to find new opportunities;
- to identify and reinforce one's own competitive advantages;
- to position and structure the offer;
- to elaborate on the marketing mix in relation to the targeted segments;
- to design and work out the commercial informational support (document, PowerPoint presentation, multimedia presentation, etc.);
- to secure rights in relation to the brands;
- to define contractual relationships between stakeholders;
- to set objectives and to design a plan of action to obtain the objectives set forth;
- to determine the level of engagement of human and financial resources.

The strategic analysis calls for an analytic approach based on a collection of facts and a careful analysis of data. This analysis must be operationalized. In the sponsorship context, the rights holder (or their representative) will seek to achieve their commercial objectives through a personalized approach for each targeted partner. That will notably allow us:

- to get detailed information in order to choose targeted partners;

- to design a customized proposal;
- to debate the relevance of the association/venture (the match or fit);
- to propose activation strategies in connection with sponsorship operation;
- to implement a system for the return on investment of the sponsor;
- to define and negotiate contractual elements with the sponsor and the entire set of stakeholders involved (sponsors, media, licensing companies).

Given the positioning of this book in relation to the aforementioned expectations, we have structured this work into five chapters:

- Chapter 1 reveals the construction of sponsorship management principles from an analysis of its evolution over the past 30 years. Thus, during the 1980s, sponsorship came into view as an original communication technique that companies strove to integrate into their communications strategy. In the 1990s, it became a communication technique linked to the marketing-mix variables. Today, the goal is to activate the sponsor's brand in order to create a positive relationship between the brand and the targeted stakeholders in the system.
- Chapter 2 relates to the legal analysis of the design of a sporting event and the nature of rights which it is advisable to take into account. These are the rights related to the event's brand, the individual and collective image, the copyright and intellectual property, as well as Internet rights. It is a matter of defining and of securing the legal relationships between the stakeholders associated with the sporting event.
- Chapter 3 analyses the strategy and the implementation of sponsorship in relation to the process of persuasive communication. We analyse the stages of this process and develop an exclusive model to allow for conceptualization and then implementation of effective, persuasive sponsorship strategies.
- Chapter 4 expands on the legal and commercial aspects tied to sponsorship contracts. This relates to the general aspects of the contractual relation, the contracts relating to the audiovisual aspects, the licence agreements, the contracts of advertising exploitation, and the complex contracts which mix various aspects.
- Chapter 5 provides a case study of an event that could take place on a yearly basis in Paris in August. This project is called the 'Perrier Fluo Beach Volleyball Experience', and it is organized by the French Volleyball Federation. The case study will allow us to look at the event both from the events rights holder's standpoint (i.e. the French Volleyball Federation), as well as from the sponsor's standpoint (i.e. Perrier, which belongs to Nestlé Waters), in an effort to illustrate the strategic and operational implementation of this sponsorship plan.

1
Principles of sponsorship management

Over the course of the past 30 years, sponsorship has evolved immensely both at the strategic and operational levels. Analysis of the evolution of this market trend enabled us to identify three periods. Initially, sponsorship was conceived as a communication technique with potential for integration into the communication strategy of companies. The second defined period saw companies seeking to exploit synergies between their sponsorship strategy and other variables of the marketing mix in an effort to ensure the best possible return on investment. Currently, the sponsorship trend is twofold. On the one hand, the trend consists in integrating sponsorship in the various strategies of the company; on the other hand, it is based on leveraging the brand of the sponsor with the various targets of the company. Analysis of the current trend allows us to understand the basis and dynamics of sponsorship and it enables us to better control the strategic and operational stakes.

FIRST STAGE: EXPLORING AN INNOVATIVE AND ACTIVE COMMUNICATION TECHNIQUE

In the 1980s, we saw the rapid development of sporting events with the support of increased media exposure. Many companies dissociated themselves from traditional modes of communication by engaging in operations of sponsorship in order to develop a closer relationship with their targets, to enhance their public image and to increase their awareness (UDA 1986). The sponsorship market grew considerably as sporting organizations (i.e. federations, clubs, event organizers, etc.) sought sponsors. For the majority of companies, sponsorship emerged as a new source of financing. They focused on the sale of this new service but had not yet adopted a marketing approach. Most organizations did not have a notion of how to approach and negotiate with the sponsors, nor did they conceive of a sponsorship offer aimed at satisfying the expectations of the sponsors. Organizations disappointed many of their customers by failing to analyse the expectations of the sponsors and by not conceiving a strategy to satisfy these expectations.

Thus, after a phase of enthusiasm, decision makers started questioning the efficiency and the selection of sponsorship operations. During this 'learning' stage, the actors sought to understand this means of communication and rationalized their strategy better.

The strategic bases of sponsorship

Sponsorship is difficult to define due to the broad variety of situations characterizing this type of operation (Saporta 1985). Nevertheless, most authors who have defined sponsorship while testifying to their experience in this field focus on one of the aspects of this system of communication. In this very diverse context, we approach sponsorship from its three principal bases: a means of communication, an association of a company with a sporting or cultural event, and as an economic relationship between the sponsored entity and the sponsor. We will then go beyond the strictly operational perspective in an effort to understand the sponsorship procedures.

The association of a company with a sporting event, an athlete or a sporting team

In the majority of definitions, sponsorship is based on the concept of relationship and/or association. For example, Sahnoun (1986: 24) regards it as 'a tool of communication that makes it possible to directly link a brand or a company with a gravitational event for a given public'. According to Piquet (1985: 15), sponsorship 'refers to a particular system of communication implemented by a sponsor that aims at associating the sponsor's brand in the minds of consumers through the spirit of the sporting or cultural event'. Furthermore, the Howell report (1983), states that sponsorship is the 'support by a person or organization unrelated to a sport, sporting event, sporting organization, or a participant in a competition, for the mutual benefit of the two parties'.

The event, social in nature, provides energy to the system

These definitions highlight the great diversity in terms of potential sponsorship combinations. However, it is the event which provides energy to this system (see Figure 1.1). The

Figure 1.1 The event as a focus point for attracting the public

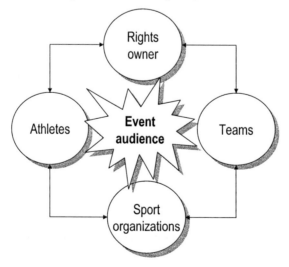

etymology of the term 'event' testifies that it is likely to have a strong impact on social groups. With this point of view, Piquet (1985: 104) considers that an 'event is primarily a gravitational social occurrence, a place where men and women gather in a sort of collective celebration to attend a sporting or cultural spectacle. The event is subjectively perceived as an opportunity for carrying out an achievement'. What would be the impact of the athletes, teams and sport without an event?

The sporting event has a socio-cultural anchor possessing an identity of its own. Bourdieu (1979), Pociello (1983) and Bromberger *et al.* (1987) studied in depth these particular social phenomena. They analysed the sporting event as a subject of social identity and as a vehicle of values and social representations. According to Bromberger *et al.* (1987), the differentiated characteristics displayed in a sporting event would incline specific groups of spectators to invest themselves in that event. Indeed, the distribution of individuals inside a stadium is a function of a complex combination of criteria where contrasting sociological universes emerge and where particular social identities are affirmed.

The social sharing of the emotions and interest for the event

Emotion is the cornerstone of an event. According to Maffesoli (1988: 68), 'the common sensitivity ... results from the fact that one takes part or relates, in the strict and perhaps mystical meaning of these terms, to a common ethos'. Thus, what is privileged is not so much that which each individual will voluntarily adhere to (contractual and mechanical perspective), but rather that which is emotionally common to all (significatory and organic perspective). It is thus a fundamental mechanism by which the sporting event produces an experience of identification within what could be called 'emotional communities' (Maffesoli 1988: 68). The sporting event is a socially shared mode of expression. It offers the optimal conditions essential for creating an emotional contagion. This mechanism operates on the spectators directly but also via the media, particularly through the most powerful of all: television. The use of live and elaborate technical means enables the producer to reinforce the spectacular side of a sporting competition. Television and in a broader sense, the media, make it possible to create virtual communities. In a society that is being increasingly dominated by communications, this offers a new means to provide individuals' participation in a relational and social existence.

The socio-emotional impact of a sporting event results in stimulating the interest of the direct or distant audience. In a broad sense, the audience of an event constitutes an important quantitative indicator. Interest is a dimension of commitment and is therefore a relevant indicator that enables appreciation of the social impact of an event. This interest can be distributed from the general scope to more specific provisions: for sport in general, a specific sport, an event, a team, or for an athlete, etc. From this standpoint, the Summer Olympic Games constitutes the events with the strongest impact worldwide (see Table 1.1).

The interest of the direct or indirect public depends on cultural factors. Thus, each particular sport, i.e. baseball, American football, cricket, rugby, etc., has a precise socio-cultural anchoring. In addition, certain characteristics either reinforce, or alternatively, attenuate the level of interest. At times, sporting organizations arrange the regulations and format of the competition in order to reinforce the interest of the public and to make the sport more appealing. For example, the International Federation of Volleyball changed its rules of the game for the Sydney OG.

Table 1.1 Comparative interests in viewing the Olympic Games on TV in 1999

Events	Interest (from 1 to 5)
Olympic Games	3.8
FIFA World Cup	3.1
IAAF World Championships in Athletics	3.0
Wimbledon Championships	2.6
FIA Formula One World Championship	2.4
Cricket World Championship	2.0

Source: Adapted from IOC (2000)

The uncertainty factor

The uncertainty of the sporting outcome is paramount since the interest and emotion vanish if the result is foreseeable. For example, when the winner of a football match is obvious, the spectators leave the stadium earlier to avoid traffic jams. By contrast, spectators or viewers remain focused on a game with a tied score, as a goal may change the end result of the game at any time. In 1991, the television audience record for a football match in France was surpassed during the finals of the European Cup, where Olympic Marseilles competed against Belgrade Red Star at Bari. No goal had been scored during allotted time and overtime. The viewer coverage total reached its maximum peak at the end of the overtime, during a penalty shoot out, with 18 million viewers. By contrast, the domination of Michael Schumacher and Ferrari during the 2002–3 F1 season caused a decline in the television audience. To restore the uncertainty factor and public interest in the Federation Internationale de l'Automobile (FIA) championship, the Formula One Constructors Association (FOCA) modified the rules of the competition.

A unique image

An image relates to the subjective representation that people have in relation to an event. The representation is socially shared given the social impact of the event. At the operational level, it is considered that the image of an event relates to all the connotations associated with that event. To assess the image of the Olympic Games, a survey was conducted on which words people associate with the Olympic Games.

Research carried out by the IOC shows that the words most often associated with the Olympic Games in 1998 and 1999 were as shown in Table 1.2. A content analysis of these terms reveals the image of the Olympic Games is structured into four dimensions:

- *Hope:* The Olympic Games are symbolic of the hope for a better world. The games set an example and lesson of discrimination-free competition.
- *Dream and inspiration:* The Olympic Games provide the inspiration essential to materializing personal dreams through the effort, sacrifice and determination of the athletes.
- *Friendship and fair play:* The Olympic Games offer tangible examples of how humanity can overcome political, economical and racial obstacles through the values inherent to sport.

Table 1.2 Words most often associated with the Olympic Games in order of importance

	Level of association
Friendship	8.40
Multicultural	8.39
Global	8.39
Participation	8.22
Peace-loving	8.10
Determination	8.00
Festive	8.00
Fighting to be the best	7.92
Patriotic	7.92
Celebration	7.80
Honourable	7.75
Dynamic	7.60
Fair competition	7.60
Modern	7.40
Unity respectful	7.20
Belonging to this world	7.20
Uncorrupted	7.10
Dignified	7.10
Trustworthy	7.00
Eternal	7.00

Source: Adapted from IOC (2000)

- *Joy through effort:* The Olympic Games celebrate the participation and the universal joy ensuing from individual efforts without concern for the result.

Definition and typology of sporting events

This set of characteristics positions the sporting event in the nucleus of the sponsorship system. Thus, the following definition is proposed: 'a sporting event is a powerful social act associated with a specific image, generating collectively shared emotions, and whose outcome is uncertain'.[1]

Note that its media strategies generally emerge from the aforementioned characteristics. Indeed, the media are interested in the events which mobilize an audience corresponding to their target market. The event generally consists of a 'pull' strategy, i.e. the ability to attract an audience. However, certain media sometimes use a 'push' strategy. In this latter case, the media push certain events onto their public while hoping to find an audience. The French channel Canal+ provides us with an example of a 'push' strategy, presenting its audience with American football and in particular the Super Bowl.

From a quantitative standpoint, sporting event differentiation is a function of the power and legitimacy of the rights holder(s), the audience size, the geographical impact, the sporting legitimacy, and the primary[2] stakeholders' alliances through relationship marketing programmes.

The criteria presented in Table 1.3 are proposed with a view to establishing a typology. This typology is illustrated based on three events with different characteristics: the Summer

Table 1.3 Dimensions relating to the typology of sporting events

Dimensions	Indicators
Power and legitimacy of rights owner(s)	Strong versus weak
Size of the audience	Major versus minor
Location of the audience	World, continental, national, local
Sporting legitimacy	Competition versus exhibition
Frequency	One shot, one-day recurring, multi-day recurring
Alliances of primary stakeholders	Strong versus weak

Table 1.4 Profiles of three differentiated events

Dimensions	Summer Olympic Games	2003 Street Hockey World Championship	English Premier League
Power and legitimacy of rights holder(s)	Strong	Weak	Strong
Size of the audience	Billions	Million	Hundreds of millions
Location of the audience	World	National and partially worldwide	European and partially worldwide
Sporting legitimacy	Strong	Medium	Strong
Frequency	Every 4 years	Every 2 years	38 days (one-day recurring) per year
Alliances of primary stakeholders	Strong	Weak	Medium

Olympic Games, the Street Hockey World Championship 2003 in Sierre (Switzerland) and the English Premier League (Table 1.4).

An active technique integrated into the communication strategy

In the early 1980s, marketing managers understood the benefit they could derive from association with a brand, a sporting event, an athlete or a team within an event, thus the use of the phrase 'event-driven communication'. However, sponsorship, as with advertising, is a tool integrated into the communication strategy of a company, which Brochand and Lendrevie (1989) describe as the entire set of major and interdependent decisions in relation to the main objectives and means of implementation to reach these objectives.

Figure 1.2 depicts the various phases of a communication strategy. There are three essential phases for implementing a communication strategy. The first phase consists of defining the objectives and which targets to reach. The second phase relates to the means of implementation to achieve the established goals. For this, it is necessary to consider the message to be transmitted, the chronology to be implemented and the required budget. The third phase relates to the results analysis.

As previously mentioned, sponsorship appeared as an innovative means of communication enabling a company to distance itself from the traditional and below-the-line advertising means. The strategy consisted in integrating sponsorship into the communication

Figure 1.2 Phases of a communication strategy

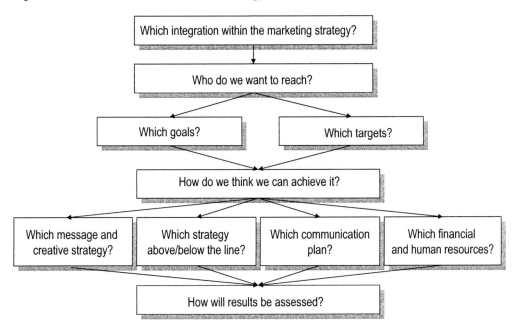

strategy of the company while distinguishing it from patronage. In this context, the approach was more focused on the objectives and targets, as well as on the most tailored option for sponsorship operations.

Targets

Since the event is a powerful social phenomenon for a given public, the sponsor targets its action of communication on the interested parties – that is, the 'stakeholders' introduced in Figure 1.3. In the middle, the participants and spectators are directly involved in the event. The distant audience is then tied to the event via the media. Furthermore, the event itself encompasses various organizations such as the organizer, local authorities, media, etc.[3] The periphery contains the public opinion, politicians, opinion leaders (pundits), suppliers, personnel of the organizations involved, etc.

A company aims at a certain number of targets, some of which are more important than others, such as its current and potential consumers, suppliers, company personnel, public opinion, local communities, business world, financial institutions, shareholders, media and distributors. Rarely does a company want to communicate with this entire set of targets all at once using only one sponsorship programme. Rather, sponsors establish priorities. A study by Crowley (1991) made it possible to identify four types of sponsors, each one with a distinct orientation towards each of the following:

- the consumer;
- company personnel;

Figure 1.3 The various stakeholders of a sporting event

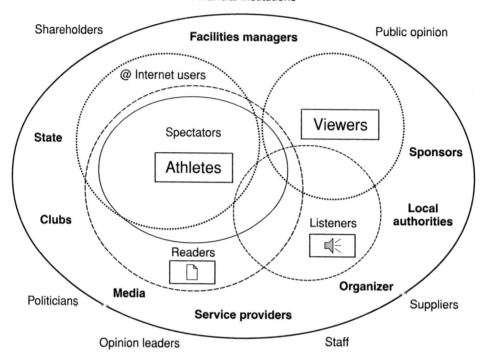

- public opinion;
- the business world.

Thus, to target an action of sponsorship properly, it is advisable to know the direct and indirect audience of an event thoroughly both from a quantitative and qualitative perspective, i.e. the socio-demographic characteristics, lifestyle, consumption habits, etc. Consequently, studies on audiences increased dramatically: TNS Sofrès, Sports Marketing Surveys, French Institute of Demoscopy, Sport Lab, Sport Research International, Eurodata TV, BVA, etc.

Sponsors analyse the compatibility of the audience of an event based on their communication and/or marketing targets.[4] This refers to one of the dimensions of the convergence analysis relating to the sponsorship offer (called 'fit'). The superimposing of the targets is illustrated by Figure 1.4.

Commercial communication and corporate communication

Sponsorship builds a relationship between a brand, a product, a service and potential or existing consumers, whereas patronage establishes a different type of relationship between a company and a set of stakeholders. The former relationship is homogeneous (brand/target), whereas the latter is heterogeneous insofar as it relates to three distinct entities,

Figure 1.4 Overlap between the audience of the event and the communication and/or marketing targets of the sponsor

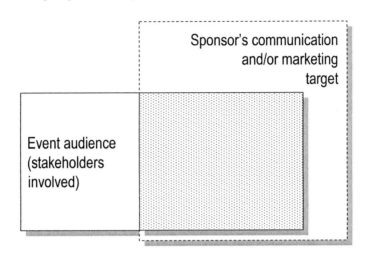

Sponsor's communication and/or marketing target

Event audience (stakeholders involved)

namely the marketing target interested in the products manufactured by a company, the economic community of this company (i.e. personnel, shareholders, suppliers, distributors, etc.) and the support community (i.e. all those people who are not an integral part of the first two publics, but who are nevertheless perceived by the company). These relationships require systems of communication.

Sponsorship and company patronage both aim at enhancing the brand awareness and image of a company. However, sponsorship is seeking to incite consumers to buy through commercial communication, whereas company patronage is seeking to enhance its social image with corporate communication. Firms are now considering their corporate social responsibility (CSR). In line with Bowen's principles (1953), Davis (1973: 313) defines CSR as 'The firm's consideration of and response to, issues beyond the narrow economic, technical and legal requirements of the firm … to accomplish social benefits along with the traditional economic gains which the firm seeks'. Commercial communication essentially aims at increasing the sales of a brand or a product, whereas corporate communication emphasizes the values and the financial and/or social performance of a company. Thus, the combination of these factors enables the company to act at four communication levels (see Table 1.5).

Based on this typology, commercial communication is a means used for the sponsorship of a brand or a product, whereas corporate communication is used within the framework of patronage either to enhance company values or to promote its management style. However, history shows that sponsorship was used very early on as a corporate means of communication. For instance, Elf Aquitaine conducted an action of sponsorship in the field of sailing with the twofold objective of promoting values relating to ecology and respect of the environment in addition to adhering to the values relating to the performance of that company. In the early 1980s, Elf's communication and public relations director stressed the fact that the company committed to that sport because it had to choose a sport that featured the image of the company as a firm which has an international image, not

Table 1.5 The four levels of communication

Commercial communication		Corporate communication	
Aims at promoting the performance of the product	Aims at managing the public image	Economic performance of the company	Corporate social responsibility performance of the company
Product presentation	Brand presentation	Financial communication	Communication of values
Tangible characteristics	The assumed territory of the brand	Financial and resource management of the company	Fundamental values of the company (e.g. identity, culture)

Source: Adapted from Ferrand and Pagès (1996)

evoking pollution, a 'marine' image, since Elf Aquitaine pumps most of its oil and gas resources from the sea and secured control over offshore technologies (Labro 1982).

In addition, institutional communication can have a positive impact on business by enhancing the internal atmosphere within the company or by improving relationships with suppliers and customers. Hence, the traditional dichotomy relationship of sponsorship/commercial and patronage/institutional appears to be outdated. In the 1980s, companies started adopting a fully integrated strategy of communication through sponsorship, patronage, publicity, public relations, etc.

Sponsorship objectives

The objectives of sponsorship depend on the purpose of the commercial or institutional communications. Thus, an outline of the objectives generally associated with these two types of communication will be presented.

Sponsorship and commercial communication

A commercially oriented sponsorship communication will seek to increase sales. However, the purchase or repurchase of a product or service is influenced by a great number of variables relating to the customer, the environment and the marketing operation. Specifically, sponsorship is used to increase the credibility and awareness of a brand, to enhance image transfers and to stimulate a distribution network or a sales force to develop business-to-business relations. Each aforementioned objective will now be examined.

Credibility-oriented sponsorship

Originally, the primary objective assigned to sponsorship was to increase the credibility of a company. Credibility-oriented sponsorship aims at associating the technical performance of a product or service with an event, either directly (e.g. sport shoes) or indirectly (e.g. information management). Sponsors opting for this type of sponsorship approach are typically amongst the 'official suppliers' sponsorship package category of an event. This type of sponsorship serves the product strategy of those companies that typically operate in the technical or technological spheres.

Brand awareness sponsorship

Awareness relates to the fame and recognition of a brand, product or service within a population. In a strict sense, awareness is the act of being recognized or quoted independently from the qualitative components of the image. It is a measure of the percentage of target customers who are aware of the object's existence. There are two types of awareness which are strongly correlated. Unprompted brand awareness corresponds to the percentage of people who are able to name a brand or event spontaneously in a given product or event category. It is an indicator of retention. For example, 'top of mind' refers to the brand which is most often quoted first. Prompted brand awareness indicates the percentage of people who are able to name a brand from a list relating to a category of product or service, while taking into account that the list also contains fictitious brands or certain brands that do not belong to the category. This indicator assesses the ability to recognize various brands, and it generates a higher number of responses than with spontaneous awareness surveys.

Image reinforcement and/or transfer through sponsorship

The term image corresponds to the set of associations relating to an entity (i.e. event, brand, athlete, etc.). In the context of an image transfer sponsorship, the sponsor's intention is to appropriate the image of a sporting event to its own brand, service, or product. The appropriation calls upon two procedures which will be analysed in detail in the following section. The first procedure consists in reinforcing associations shared by the sponsor and the sponsored entity. The second procedure consists in transferring specific features of the image of the sponsored entity to the image of the sponsor.

The image of a brand influences purchasing decisions, whereupon brand management is important from a strategic perspective. Figure 1.5 illustrates the management of the image within the framework of an operation of sponsorship. It relates to the mutual relationship between the image of the sponsor, its identity and the sporting entity image. This identity relates to the associations the sponsor would like to actively communicate to the target. The sponsor may wish to reinforce certain associations of its choice (e.g. being festive and reactive) and/or to create new associations (e.g. being ecological and close to nature). In this context, the strategists of a company can evaluate the appropriateness of an image transfer sponsorship operation by carrying out an analysis of fit relating to associations between the desired identity and the image of the event. They can share certain image features (e.g. festive) even though the sponsored entity may also possess specific features (e.g. ecological). It is thus possible from a strategic point of view to consider a reinforcement of common associations (i.e. festive in our example) as well as a transfer of associations specific to the sponsored entity (i.e. ecological in our example). In order to achieve this, the strategists will need to evaluate the acceptance and credibility of the association between their company image and that of the sponsored entity with the stakeholders. That evaluation can done by collecting the opinions of a focus group concerning the association between the sponsor and the sponsored entity (e.g. 'Do you think that sponsor X and the sponsored entity Y mesh well together?') and the image features to be transferred

Figure 1.5 The strategic diagnosis of image transfer sponsorship

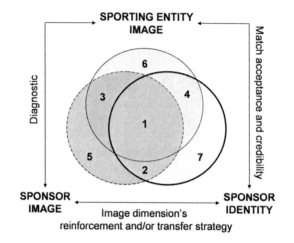

to the sponsor (e.g. 'What do you think about the association between following terms: sponsor X, entity Y and ecology?'). In this system there are seven possible consequences referring to the sponsor's image dimensions (see Figure 1.5):

1. potential reinforcement;
2. impossible to reinforce;
3. risky to reinforce;
4. potential transfer;
5. to phase out;
6. no interest for the sponsor;
7. impossible to transfer.

Mobilizing the distribution network

The sponsor can also mobilize its distribution network by associating it directly or indirectly with the sponsorship operation through, for instance, exhibitions, special operations and public relations. Peugeot, sponsor of the Roland Garros Tennis Tournament (i.e. the French Open), organizes 'Peugeot–Roland Garros Days' in cooperation with its dealers. The Peugeot–Roland Garros Days consist of a set of tournaments organized in France that are reserved for the customers of the dealers. Through this type of sponsorship operation, Peugeot also reinforces its partnership with dealers.

Stimulating the sales force

An event of interest to the sales force can be used as a support to stimulate the sales force through a sponsorship operation, thereby creating conditions for obtaining better commercial results. An emulation sponsorship operation may consist of organizing a competition amongst the sales force with a view to rewarding the best salespeople by inviting them as VIPs to the event of interest. Sponsorship operations whose aim is to stimulate sales forces can be coupled with operations to mobilize the distribution network which exploits the interest carried by the customers of the sponsored event. Combined operations provide salespeople with additional arguments contributing to increased sales.

Propagation of goodwill and positive attitudes

Goodwill attests to a favourable attitude towards a sponsor. Depending on the market, goodwill more or less influences purchasing decisions. It is rare for people to buy a brand to which they have an unfavourable attitude. Sponsorship aims at transferring the positive attitude people have to an event towards the sponsor, with a view to generating a feeling of gratitude in the targeted people, based on the fact that the involvement of the sponsor in the event contributes to the development of sport in general. During the Atlanta Olympic Games, a survey was conducted where 87 per cent of the respondents agreed with the statement 'sponsorship largely contributes to the success of the OG' and 55 per cent of them expressed a favourable attitude towards the official sponsors.

Developing business-to-business relationships

Public relations operations carried out in conjunction with the sponsored event constitute an effective way to develop business relationships between companies. Public relations operations are generally carried out in a prestigious and controlled environment where guests can entertain themselves, thus contributing to create privileged and individualized relationships. In the context of large events, most sponsorship packages include this type of service provision. However, it is necessary to keep in mind that the event must be attractive to the executives and managers. Additionally, the environment suggested must offer a fun and memorable experience to VIPs. Moreover, a public relations operation is one competitive advantage of sponsorship.

Increasing the sales

This objective constitutes the ultimate commercial goal of sponsorship. As previously mentioned, purchasing is influenced by a large number of factors, some of which relate to the marketing approach, whereupon it is difficult to isolate the impact of sponsorship on sales. Nevertheless, it is acknowledged that sponsorship contributes to sales development in the mid-term, with the possibility to evaluate the impact through particular operations. If, for instance, we combine a sponsorship operation with a sales promotion, we can evaluate the tangible benefits offered to consumers.

Sponsorship and corporate communication

Sponsorship can also be integrated with corporate communication strategies. Four categories of objectives enter into this scenario.

Developing social marketing programmes

Since the 1960s, corporations have realized that harmonious integration within a local community paves the way for establishing good relationships with citizens and institutional actors, thereby contributing to a positive climate inside the corporation by reducing conflicts. Social marketing is the application of marketing concepts and tools to programmes designed to influence the voluntary behaviour of target audiences where the primary objective is to improve the welfare of the target audiences and/or the society of which they are a part (Andreasen 1994). Major European soccer clubs such as FC Barcelona and AC Milan FCB have established foundations in order to finance these programmes in partnership with their sponsors.

Promoting corporate policy, reinforcing internal cohesion and motivating company personnel

These objectives are very important for a company. Sports sponsorship constitutes such a remarkable platform to create social bonds that a local basketball club sought to find one company sponsor per game. The company sponsor could invite its personnel and their families. They could relax and meet with managers, executives, and their respective families while enjoying themselves at a buffet dinner. Children had the opportunity to meet with players after the match and were allowed on the court for mini clinics and 3-on-3 matches. This type of operation allows for each individual to be acknowledged and have fun, which is good for business because it has a positive impact on the motivation of the personnel and on work relationships.

Enhancing personnel recruitment

Recruiting quality personnel is another key factor for a company as it directly influences the company's performance. As a result, companies must work on their corporate image. By way of illustration, ECCO, a European consulting company for temporary job placement, used its sponsorship involvement in the 'Masters Series' of climbing to recruit qualified personnel with a message focused on interconnectedness and leadership. Additionally, ECCO set up workshops on internal cohesion within the company to which it invited all its partners.

Companies combine commercial and corporate objectives

Sponsors have learned how to combine marketing or commercial and corporate strategies. Sponsors are supporting grass roots sports projects. The insurance and services company Norwich Union has been one of the major partners of British athletics since 1999, with £2m, or 20 per cent of the total deal, going towards development of the sport. In an interview (Gillis 2004: 39), the company's head of sponsorship, community and event management stressed the fact that the programme is a brand positioning tool: 'services are often perceived as faceless and uninspiring ... it is important for the brand to be seen as active in the community as part of our CSR. This is where our staff and policyholders live and work'.

The relational aspect of sponsorship has become increasingly important for companies needing attractive platforms to entice their customers, suppliers, prospective customers and partners, as well as for creating solid ties which go beyond mere commercial transactions. These strategies evolve with the objectives of the company through the life cycle of the product and according to the marketing plan. It may be necessary for a company to start by enhancing its brand awareness before working on its image, then stimulate its sales network, act on promotions in points of sale, improve its expertise, promote company values, develop customer loyalty, etc.

An impact-based economic relationship between the sponsor and the sponsored entity

Sponsorship implies an economic relationship between the sponsor and the sponsored entity regardless of whether it is tied to commercial or corporate purposes. The proper amount for this transaction can be an issue because the price of many sponsorship offers was established with a view to balancing the budget. Furthermore, sponsors were not able to fully appreciate the value of these services either because they were too emotionally involved, or they did not have the means to evaluate the impact of sponsorship operations. In recent years, it has been clearly established that the price depends on the impact of the sponsorship operation and that competitive markets generally pull prices downwards. In Chapter 3, we will look at the factors influencing the price of a sponsorship offer.

Two emerging questions: exploitation and effectiveness of sponsorship operations

Although certain decision makers in the 1980s engaged in operations of sponsorship that were often fuelled by a euphoric climate and their passion for the sport, the question of the effectiveness of this system of communication always arose. In an article published in the monthly magazine *Médias*, Field (1981) considered that sponsorship strategies were often implemented in an indistinct way, thereby making it risky for companies. In 1984, *Advertising Age* carried a review article by Walsh, who was arguably in full agreement with that paradigm. Similarly, Gross *et al.* (1987) investigated the measurement techniques American companies used to determine the effectiveness of sponsorship during 1985 and 1986. The investigation showed that approximately half of these companies did not assess the impact of sponsorship operations.

In 1987, the French monthly magazine *L'Expansion* published a sponsorship-related article by Rougé in its economics section expressing the malaise of the companies which had spent nearly two billion francs 'in an almost total fog'. In 1988, Bowey wrote the editorial for the congress of the European Society for Opinion and Marketing Research (ESOMAR) entitled: 'Sponsorship: effective or extravagant?' The same year, an article in a French review magazine paved the way for introducing more rationality in sponsorship campaigns (*Communication and Business* 1988).

Development of broadcasting sponsorship

This period of rationality in sponsorship coincided with the advent of broadcasting sponsorship, which consists of selling sponsorship of the transmission of a sporting event to an advertiser. The sponsor receives service provisions such as promotional trailers before the broadcast of the event, break bumpers and injection of their logo during breaks in the performance of the event, etc. This trend, which is expanding rapidly, is certainly irreversible given the commercial approach of television broadcasters. The growing share of private television channels, combined with the increasing competition between public and private TV networks to secure the audience, has led TV broadcasters to obtain the exclusive rights to the most popular sporting events (Figure 1.6).

In this context, it became extremely difficult to make a profit from advertising revenues alone because the advertising competition was intense. Subsequently, broadcasting sponsorship became a necessity. Sponsorship is recognized as a mean of communication offered to companies that can be used to promote their image. Unlike product placement, sponsorship has a different function from advertising screens and newspapers. Its official function is to represent the company sponsor. Consequently, on-site sponsorship came into existence. If a sponsor desired to promote its involvement in an event or to be associated with it, it would simply sponsor the televised transmission of the event. To prevent this 'ambush marketing' and to reinforce their impact, dominant sponsors invest in both on-site and broadcasting sponsorships. Ambush marketing focuses on non-sponsorship promotions coinciding with a given event, whereby it is possible to reach the very same audience interested in that sponsored event. Ambush marketing spurred the advent of events specially designed for the sponsors. Controlled events come with service provisions including the concept, organization and television broadcast.

This evolution was confirmed by the French Union of Advertisers' (UDA) bi-annual investigation carried out in 1990. The conclusion of the investigation was that sponsorship appeared as a new but unique mode of communication. Advertisers had learned how to deal with the peculiarities of sponsorship and when to make use of it. Today, sponsorship has an uncontested legitimacy, which is supplemented by the professionalism of advertisers. However, the rapid evolution of sponsorship slowed at the beginning of the 1990s due to a major restructuring in the sector.

Sponsors choose sponsorship to communicate a message while keeping an eye on the economic impact of the sponsorship operation. Company sponsors are essentially the

Figure 1.6 Two types of sponsorship

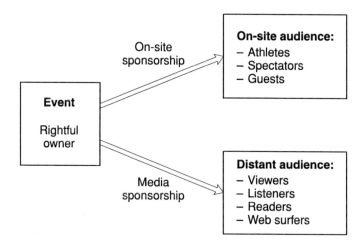

partners of sporting events and possibly sport in general. The event is the cornerstone of the sponsorship operation because it is the event that gets most of the visibility through media coverage. The media also contribute to the direct financing of the most important events by securing rights of transmission. Media financial involvement is increasingly consistent with the size of sporting events.

The increase in the rights purchased by broadcasters to transmit the Olympic Games constitutes another indicator testifying to the tendency that the inflation of those fees is tied to the increased size of the Olympic audience. Indeed, the broadcasting rights increased exponentially from 1.2 million dollars in 1960 to 900 million dollars in 1996.

The inflation in TV rights can be summed up with one word: profitability. The combination of broadcast sponsorship and large audience ensures profits which was good news for the Olympic Games. For example, 29.4 per cent of American households (82 million people) watched Tommy Moe winning the gold in the downhill at the Lillehammer Olympic Games on CBS in 1994. The Olympic Games' reach is comparable with that of the most important sporting event in the USA, the American Football Super Bowl, which reached 90 million viewers in 1993. The economic relationship between television and sport, mediated by the audience, has led broadcasters to programme the most popular sports to the detriment of other sports. Thus, in 1992, French television channels programmed two sports extensively: tennis (21 per cent) and football (16 per cent). Cycling came third with only 5.5 per cent of the time allotted to the transmissions of sporting events.

Broadcast sponsorship offers some advantages compared to on-site sponsorship:

- guaranteed exposure;
- branding opportunity;
- possible lower cost;
- better transfer in relation to the association with the event and unprompted brand awareness.

Heineken sponsored the broadcasting of the Rugby World Cup in England. The impact study by TSMS, a research agency specializing in the sponsorship and sports sectors, shows that the brand awareness of Heineken was greater than that of any other sponsor of the event. This leads us to believe that the reason Heineken was effective in its sponsorship operation was linked to the fact that it was the only company to sponsor the broadcasting of the event in England (Table 1.6).

SECOND STAGE: IMPROVED INTEGRATION WITH THE MARKETING MIX

According to a study carried out by Sponsorship Research International (SRI) in 1996, the world market of sponsorship was rebalancing. In the early 1980s, the United States' share of sponsorship-related expenditures represented more than 50 per cent of the global market. In 1994, their share had decreased to 34.8 per cent, while Europe accounted for 32.9 per cent of the world sponsorship market. According to Chris Jones, project manager with SRI, increasing sponsorship expenditures from Asia increased to balance the world sponsorship market of recent years, as Europe's and the United States' respective

Table 1.6 Unprompted brand awareness of the sponsors during the 1995 Rugby World Cup

Sponsors	Unprompted brand awareness (%)
Heineken	74
South African Airways	45
Cellnet	28
Sony	26
Coke	25
Citizen Watches	24
Famous Grouse	21
International Visa	17
Courage	17
Xerox	16
Toyota	13

Source: Adapted from TSMS

sponsorship-related expenditures declined. The sponsorship approach of the 1990s shows a better integration with the components of the marketing mix. The sponsorship communication approach became more fully integrated into the marketing approach, thereby creating the concept of 'Integrated Communications Marketing'. Imparting more rationality to sponsorship operations requires focusing more on the results, especially on the return on investment. Ultimately, sponsors banded together to counter the ambush-marketing strategies which had risen in the mid 1980s.

Interaction between sponsorship and marketing-mix components

Recent developments in sponsorship relate to the aim of sponsorship, but also to the relationship between sponsorship and components of the marketing mix. During the 1980s, sponsorship was incorporated into the communication strategy. Thus it appeared that sponsorship had a specific instrument resulting from a decision-making process similar to the one applied in advertising, public relations, etc. The position of Otker (1988) reflects the paradigm of the 1980s: 'commercial sponsorship consists of buying and exploiting the association with an event, a team, a group, etc. with a specific aim of marketing (i.e. communications[5])', thereby showing that sponsorship must contribute to the achievement of the marketing objectives. Hence, sponsorship began to evolve during the 1990s as sponsors learned how to develop synergies between sponsorship and components of the marketing mix.

The work of Dambron (1991) entitled 'Sponsorship and Marketing Policy' underscores the will to rationalize 'the existing relationship between sponsorship and marketing management' by focusing on the 'incorporating of sponsorship and components of the marketing mix, namely product, price, distribution, and communication'. Dambron's work is based on a qualitative investigation with large French companies, some of which are subsidiary companies of American or Japanese companies. His analysis reveals that the current challenge for sponsors and sporting organizations is to enhance the integration of sponsorship with the aforementioned components of the marketing mix (see Figure 1.7).

Figure 1.7 The interaction between sponsorship and the marketing-mix components

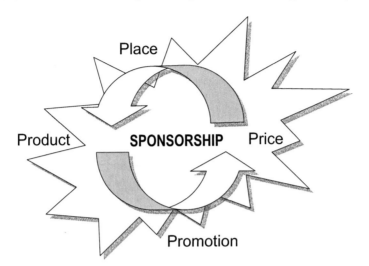

In this context Derbaix *et al.* (1994: 72) define sponsorship as 'a technique used by a company to create or support an independent socio-cultural event via media sponsorship in order to achieve marketing objectives'.

Sponsorship and the management of products and services

Sponsorship is likely to further the management of the products and services of certain companies when these products and services are directly or indirectly related to the sporting event. This approach correlates to the sponsorship category which aims at proving the quality and reliability of a product. Examples of this category, referred to as the official suppliers' category, abound in the technical and technological fields. It is also possible to demonstrate the credibility of new innovative technologies and, by extension, of product components.

Based on his analysis of sponsorship strategies in this field, Dambron proposes the following typology:

1. *Direct product demonstration.* A company employs a sponsorship operation to show and prove the quality and reliability of its products. By joining the F1 BMW-Williams team, Compaq built its image as a technology market leader. Compaq wants to demonstrate to the general public that it manufactures state-of-the-art products delivering high performance. Compaq's message is expressed in advertisements such as: 'In our world, wasting time is the only obstacle to success. By using Compaq's high performance Evo mobile workstation equipped with the Intel Pentium M processor, the BMW-Williams F1 team optimizes its tunings due to the Compaq technology and it gains invaluable tenths of seconds. To win a race, it is essential to save on time.'
2. *Indirect product demonstration.* A company's decision to engage in a sponsorship operation may be based on the need for further research and development or on the

issue of developing innovative solutions. This is also one of the objectives of the sponsorship operation in which Compaq engaged with the BMW-Williams team. Compaq's ongoing research process is reinforced through its slogan 'inspiration technology'.

3. *Product creation.* A company employs a sponsorship operation to create a new product within an existing product category or to expand its customer base. In 1989, Peugeot created the Roland Garros series with its flagship Peugeot 205 model. The idea was to capitalize on the sophisticated image of the Roland Garros event with a view to transferring the credibility of the event to the Peugeot 205 model, thereby segmenting the consumer market with a car expressing social status. The success of this composite brand name enables the car manufacturer to apply it gradually to its complete range of vehicles.

In the services category, the sponsorship operation is used to enhance the image of the company relative to the quality of its services by focusing on tangible aspects, reliability, responsiveness, customer care, empathy, etc. A good example of this is the sponsorship operation carried by UPS during the Olympic Games.

Sponsorship strategy and pricing policy

Sponsorship operations enable sponsors to channel the focal point of the direct and indirect public onto their products and services. Furthermore, price is a crucial factor influencing the purchasing decision. Sponsorship can be connected to the pricing policy in two ways. The first one relates to product placement, while the second is related to promotional strategies.

Sponsorship and product positioning

Sponsorship operations can allow sponsors to 'upmarket' their products or services. The purpose of product positioning is to shape consumers' beliefs with the hope consumers will ultimately differentiate the sponsor's brand from the brands of its competitors. Therefore, it is crucial to position the brand so it presents a clear and unique recognition in the mind of the consumer. According to Ries and Trout (1981: 23), product positioning has nothing to do with what you do to a product; it relates to what you do with the 'mind of your future customer, the prospective customer'. Thus, sponsors must seek to have their brands linked with wealthy social groups. Insofar as it is accepted in the public eye, it is possible to upmarket a sponsor's brand. Rolex used this strategy to upmarket its watches by associating with golf: this was the only way to rationalize the higher price of the Tudor branded watch, which is identical to the less expensive Submariner non-branded watch.

The Heineken group owns the Heineken, Amstel and Murphys brands. Heineken is expensive due to its pinnacle positioning, whereas Amstel is more popular and less expensive. Murphys, a dark ale, was never used to engage in a significant sponsorship operation. Sponsorship is an important part of the communication strategy of companies because it is an ideal platform to build a brand in various countries. In addition, a common passion for sport permits Heineken to bridge the gap with current and prospective customers, while facilitating trade agreements. The beer company manages its sponsorship strategy by adhering to the following three principles:

- no sponsorship of motor sports because of the risk of accident;
- no sponsorship of teams or athletes because the sponsorship operation impact often depends on their sporting results;
- event-driven sponsorship only.

Given the positioning sought for these two brands, Heineken limits its sponsorship to tennis, rugby and music events, while Amstel sponsors football, in particular the UEFA Champions League. Based on recent market studies demonstrating that the positioning of both event and brands has evolved, the company decided to substitute Heineken for Amstel for the 2005–6 season. This sponsorship-based example shows that the relationship between price management and brand positioning is substantial. Depending on the situation, a sponsor may choose to reinforce their brand positioning or to reposition it.

Sponsorship and sales promotion

Promotional strategies are directly related to the pricing policy. According to Dominitz and Tochon (1988: 26), promotions will have a 'direct influence on the purchaser by freeing him from his daily life while inviting him into an entertaining environment. Admittedly, promotions do not alter the customer's concern about the price, yet they stipulate, engross, and embellish its purchases'. Promotions generate consideration towards the brand. Sponsorship operations have the power to channel people's attention to the brand, thereby setting up a solid base for promotional operations. There are several promotional techniques: price reductions, free gifts, special offers, samples, exhibitions, tasting, contests and games, anthology, etc. Table 1.7 summarizes the sponsorship strategies for sales promotion.

This strategy can be used either with pinnacle or low-end products. As a low-end example, we can cite the Guy Laroche 'Drakkar Noir' perfume. The maker of this prestigious

Table 1.7 Sponsorship and sales promotion

Strategies	Examples
Pricing offers	Provide consumers with financial advantage such as: • Cash refund offers (rebates) • Special offers (e.g. price packs: consumers prefer immediate price reduction such as a reduced-price pack or banded pack offers)
Premiums (gifts)	Premiums provide incentives to purchase a particular product. Premiums can be: • Direct (e.g. with-pack premium) as when an additional article is offered free upon the purchase of another product • Deferred (e.g. free in-the-mail rebates) as when an additional advantage is offered but expected at a later time • Moral (e.g. charity) as when a percentage of the amount of the purchase is offered to a social cause
Free trials	The sponsor invites prospective customers to try a new product or service without cost or any purchase obligation
Samples	Offer of a free trial of a product or service provided to the public

Source: Adapted from Dambron (1991)

fragrance partnered with an offshore racing team. The partners chose a particular packaging with the inscription, 'Offshore Racing Team Limited Edition' and a drawing of an offshore race boat. This limited perfume edition was sold at a price 10 per cent lower than that of the traditional product.

Sponsorship and distribution channels

The distributor is no longer considered as a mere channel of distribution. The distributor now acts as a company equipped with its own strategy: Trade marketing is about integrating the strategy of the brand into the strategy of the company. In the context of a sponsorship operation, that may consist of (Table 1.8):

- a distribution network: trade partners used by the company to move products to end-users;
- a distribution channel: a network of trade partners and representatives of retailers sharing the same legal and commercial status and distributing a selection of products;
- points of sale (POS).

Sponsorship can be used to stimulate the actors of the distribution network, among which is the sales force. Insofar as the sales force has an interest in the sponsored event, athlete or team, the sponsorship operation can be used to activate the emotional link, thereby motivating the sales force. To achieve this, a large variety of means can be used, such as invitation to the event, public relations operations, and participating in a peripheral event.

Sponsorship can also be used to recruit a sales force. In this context, sponsorship makes it possible to motivate, increase awareness and mobilize the various actors of a distribution network. The atmosphere and mood created through the sponsorship operation are more important than the short-term financial results.

Table 1.8 Various means to stimulate points of sale (POSs)

Strategies	Examples
Creation of traffic	Organize raffles in which tickets are drawn to win free passes to the event or to win products of the sponsor
	Free gift or passes with minimum purchase
POS advertising	Using the symbols of the event to promote the products of the sponsors
	Can be tied to a sales promotion by using an end display or a promotional stand
Special activities at the POS	Athletes, organizers or products are used at the POS to enrich the promotion
	Product demonstrations
	Sales promotion
Organizing peripheral events	The sponsors' distribution network partners are invited to participate in an event (e.g. Peugeot organizes the 'Peugeot–Roland Garros Days' for its dealers. The event is a tennis tournament reserved for non-classified players, which Peugeot uses as a public relations operation)

Source: Adapted from Dambron (1991)

Integration of sponsorship and communications into marketing

Whereas the integration of the sponsorship strategy into the communications strategy was one of the stakes during the 1990s, the integration of the communications strategy into the marketing strategy remains the challenge in the new millennium. Schultz *et al.* (1993) pointed out that integrating communications into marketing creates a major competitive advantage for organizations. The use of the term 'integrated marketing communications' (IMC) expresses the will to accomplish that challenge. According to Shrimp (2003), IMC constitutes the process of developing and implementing persuasive communication programmes tailored to consumers and prospective customers. The objective of IMC is to influence or act directly on the behaviour of selected communication targets. It is essential to view all the intermediaries of the distribution chain as carriers of information for future communications. Integrated communications marketing employs all the forms of communication deemed appropriate to reach the consumer and prospective customers. In summary, IMC:

- aims at influencing the target's behaviour and its attitude towards the brand, the firm or its products;
- employs all touch points existing between the company and the target to provide the right experience;
- is based on a solid knowledge of consumers and prospective customers;
- creates a synergy between the various tools of communications, the communication strategy and other components of the marketing mix;
- builds relationships between the company and its customers, suppliers and distribution network;
- stresses the importance of human resources in managing the process and the relationship with targeted stakeholders.

In the sponsorship context, it is important to remember that the objective is to influence the behaviour of the people belonging to the communication target. The objective is achieved when the targeted group purchases or repurchases a given product or service. Companies are indeed interested in having a cognitive impact (i.e. brand awareness, perceived quality, etc.) or a psycho-sociological impact (i.e. image, gratitude, etc.) on their targeted audience, provided that this impact results in a behavioural effect (i.e. purchase or repurchase) within a short- or mid-term period. Table 1.9 summarizes sponsorship and communication objectives. Sponsors have developed vast knowledge about their prospective customers, and in particular, regarding the purchasing decision-making process, in order to use the most tailored communications strategy. In the context of a sponsorship operation, the goal is to capitalize on the emotions generated by the event for creating an association with the brand. This process, which is part of the experiential marketing framework, will be illustrated later with Coca-Cola.

Sponsorship has made it possible for companies to communicate in an unobtrusive environment compared with the saturated media advertising environment. Sponsorship also makes it possible to reach communication targets at a reasonable cost. The challenge now is to integrate sponsorship programmes into the marketing strategy of the companies and evaluate the return on investment of these operations.

Table 1.9 Sponsorship and communication objectives

Domains	Objectives
Brand awareness	To improve the brand and/or product recognition
	To maintain brand awareness
Information and perceived quality	To propose new applications
	To demonstrate the product
	To show that the product meets expectations
	To gain the confidence of the purchaser
Image	To reinforce or create the desired associations
	To create a preference for the brand
	To reposition the brand or the product
Recall	To point out the next purchase or consumption opportunities
	To showcase the distributors
Persuasion	To encourage customer loyalty
	To entice an immediate purchase
	To facilitate a discussion with a salesperson

The importance of the return on investment

The rationalization of sponsorship inevitably implies an analysis of the impact of the sponsorship operation in an effort to determine the return on investment (ROI). A 1994 study carried out by the French monthly magazine *L'événementiel* reveals more information about how companies control their sponsorship operations:

1. Large French companies with over three years of experience in sponsorship primarily engaged in cultural events (50 per cent) and sports (43 per cent).
2. While 85 per cent of those companies' objective was tied to an image transfer, only 31 per cent carried out a survey to determine the impact of their respective sponsorship operation.

This study clearly indicates that French companies involved in sponsorship operations care about the ROI. In short, little effort (e.g. surveys) is made to assess the image of the company following the sponsorship operation, which is surprising given that a company's image is related to the main objective of sponsorship operations. Based on a comparison made in 1998 (Table 1.10), it appears there is reinforcement yet no radical change in the trend of evaluating sponsorship operations.

Depending on their objectives, companies carry out an in-house study or outsource it to a specialized agency. They retain the task of carrying out in-house studies for the gathering of specific information and for the impact on sales. Most companies outsource the analysis of media effects, image surveys and their portfolio to a specialized firm.

Event organizers tend to follow the same trend. Indeed, impact studies are useful to the organizer because they allow him/her to provide quantitative and qualitative information to sponsors in an effort to get their loyalty. Additionally, impact studies enable organizers to better target their search for sponsors and to provide commercial incentives to sponsors. Thus the International Olympic Committee carried out its first study in 1985. Since then, the studies have expanded considerably (Table 1.11).

Table 1.10 Comparison of evaluating methods used by French sponsors

Mediums	1992 (%)	1998 (%)	Increase (%)
Press book	88	90	2
Awareness or image study	53	60	7
Media impact analysis	46	58	12
Specific study related to sponsorship	29	33	4
Impact on sales	23	28	5
Specific barometer	15	21	6

Source: Adapted from UDA (1998)

Table 1.11 Research and studies carried out by the IOC

Olympic image	Year	Number of countries
Consumers' point of view (quantitative)	1985	4
Olympic Games sponsorship (qualitative)	1987	6
Olympic Games sponsorship (quantitative)	1988	4
Olympic Games sponsorship (quantitative)	1989–1992	3
Olympic Games sponsorship (quantitative)	1993–1996	3
Study relating to the Olympic rings	1995	8
Sponsor test	1995–1996	1
Research relating to Olympic Games marketing (qualitative)	1996	5
Research relating to Olympic Games marketing	1996	9
Atlanta Olympic Games (quantitative)	1996	1
Nagano Olympic Games (quantitative)	1998	1
Olympic image and projects of communication	1998	11
Olympic image and projects of communication	1999	7
Sydney Olympic Games (quantitative)	2000	1
Olympic youth	2000	1
Validation of the Olympic brand (collectively)	2000	10
Sydney brand (during the games)	2000	1

Source: Adapted from IOC (2002)

The evolving expectations of sponsors regarding the evaluation and the return on investment forced the development of measuring instruments. Although this aspect will be further developed in Chapter 3, it is noted that visibility and impact are the main two dimensions of such evaluation.

Havas Advertising Sports developed the Sports Metrix, a tool that has the capacity to analyse 10,000 newspapers originating from five continents. It can process information based on a linguistic model and evaluate the meaning of that information. The automatic press review makes it possible to select standard commodities and to detect trends. This tool can also be used to analyse the image of a sponsor, opinions about the positioning or reputation of a brand, past evolution trends, and the moves of competitors.

In 1994, ISL Worldwide created Sponsorship Research International (SRI), which analyses the media effects of sponsorship. SRI calculates the audience of an event; it measures the association between a sponsor and the sport or event it sponsors; and it evaluates the coherence between a sponsor and the sport or event the sponsor is associated with.

Sport Surveys Marketing, which was set up the same year, is an independent English company that specializes in the analysis of media effects. It links television effects with the measurement of the impact of the sponsorship operation through two specific indicators. The first indicator calculates the television airtime allotted to the sponsor in order to estimate the corresponding advertising equivalent. The second indicator determines unprompted and prompted brand awareness with a view to identifying potential purchasing intentions.

Developing brand equity

From a marketing point of view, it is impossible to ignore brands. The brand is valuable both for the sporting organization and the consumer. Kapferer and Laurent (1983) showed that consumers were more aware of a brand when there was a perceived risk in matters of proper choice, financial expenditure, safety, etc. Symbolic brands such as Nike and Adidas compete with Coca-Cola, Sony, Levis and other well-known brands. Major sporting events such as the Olympic Games, Football World Cup and organizations such as FIFA, NBA, Manchester United and Ferrari follow the same trend. These brands have achieved a certain degree of 'clout' which Aaker (1991) refers to as brand equity for their added value perceived in the market. Brand equity corresponds to all the assets and liabilities linked to a brand, including its name or symbol, which add to or subtract from the value provided by a product or service to a firm or its customers. The assets and liabilities underlying brand equity must be linked to its name and/or symbols (i.e. logo, packaging, colour, etc.). If a company changed its name or logo, all or part of its assets would be modified or perhaps lost, although certain components associated with the original brand could be transferred to the new name or new symbols of the brand. The assets and liabilities of brand equity are varied and they differ from one case to the next. Aaker (1991:16) categorizes brand equity into a set of five categories of brand assets and liabilities. These categories are:

• 'brand loyalty;
• name awareness;
• perceived quality;
• brand associations in addition to perceived quality;
• other proprietary brand assets – trademarks, patents, channel relationships, etc.'

In the framework of sponsorship, various aspects of brand equity are exploited. Earlier in this chapter, it was explained how a sponsor could benefit from a brand's popularity, image, perceived quality, and loyalty. To illustrate this point, an examination is presented of the French football club, l'Olympique Lyonnais (Table 1.12), winner of four consecutives championships in France (2001–5) with the largest budget (€112 million) of the French Premier League.

The development of brand equity cannot be achieved without legal protection. This legal aspect became paramount due to the advent of ambush marketing.

Table 1.12 Sponsorship opportunities tied to various aspects of l'Olympique Lyonnais brand

Goals	l'Olympique Lyonnais (OL)	Sponsorship opportunities
Brand awareness	Ranked 2nd in a prompted brand awareness test, behind l'Olympique de Marseille Scored 100% in an assisted brand awareness test with French football fans Despite a good performance in the Champions League, it still has a weak brand awareness at the international level	It has strong brand awareness in France yet weak brand awareness internationally. Therefore, it mainly attracts sponsors whose aim is to target football fans within the French market
Loyalty	27,000 season ticket holders (in a stadium of 41,000 seats) with an 80% loyalty rate An average of 35,000 spectators during the 2004–2005 season	Solid results that offer 'trade marketing' opportunities which aim at increasing visits to the sponsor
Image	Fans develop a mental image of the club around the following aspects: • an important, ambitious club • will and courage • enjoyment and frustration • the city of Lyon	Appealing for a sponsor willing to promote entrepreneurial values, although the emotional components are rather weak
Perceived quality	Fans have the following impressions regarding the brand image of the club: • good sporting results, but could be better • well-managed club • modern facility • services are too expensive • lack of ambition towards recruiting players	The fans' perception of the club is favourable in an environment where certain managers take foolish risks, which is a positive argument for reassuring potential sponsors. However, the conservative management style of the club incites the frustration of supporters hoping for a winning team with star players
Other assets	Trademark OL is a partnership created in 1998 between the OL association (34%) and the sporting firm (66%) with powerful shareholders. Two groups of sponsors companies OL Television channel in partnership with TLM, a local television station broadcasting to Lyon and surrounding areas Two magazines	The current situation of the club is stable due to the effective management of the club. However, the regional corporate network limits partnership opportunities at the international level

Minimizing the risk of ambush marketing

According to Bayless (1988), ambush marketing is a strategy by which an organization indirectly associates with an event in order to obtain the same benefit as the official sponsor. The first occurrence of ambush marketing occurred during the 1984 Olympic Games with Eastman Kodak strategizing an association with the games, although Fuji had won the sponsorship bid to be the official sponsor. Kodak created this association when it sponsored the rebroadcast of the games on ABC, as well as the official movie of the American sports teams. During the 1988 Olympic Games, all the official sponsors saw at least one of their competitors use the ambush-marketing strategy. Wendy's ambushed McDonald's, American Express ambushed Visa, Quality Inns ambushed Hilton, and Fuji took revenge against Kodak which was then the official sponsor of the 1988 games. Fuji carried out a massive communication campaign associating it with the American swimming team and several American athletes. This phenomenon increased in the course of the Olympic Games. Sandler and Shani (1989) characterize ambush marketing as a planned effort (i.e. campaign) by an organization to indirectly associate with an event with a view to capture partial recognition and benefits conferred to the status of being the official sponsor. Their definition divulges the fact that ambush marketing is a meticulously designed strategy. Ambush marketing is rather expensive given the fact that it mostly relies on the media and, if possible, on the sponsorship of the television broadcast of the event. Furthermore, the main objective of ambush marketing is to create confusion in the minds of consumers in order to reduce the impact of the sponsorship operation of a competitor.

Consequently, the IOC has attempted to prevent ambush marketing since the latter could jeopardize the financing of the Olympic movement by undermining the confidence of company partners in the International Olympic Committee's marketing programme (TOP). According to the IOC, ambush marketing includes:

- the utilization of a means by a non-partner company for creating a false association with the Olympic Games;
- the violation of laws protecting the use of the Olympic symbols by a non-partner company;
- the intentional or involuntary interference of a non-partner company with legitimate marketing activities of the Olympic company partners.

Taking into account the threat caused by ambush marketing, the IOC took the following seven initiatives prior to the 2000 Sydney games.

1. Lobbying of the New South Wales government for the implementation of a specific legislation providing full protection for the Olympic brand, thereby setting restrictions regarding the sale of merchandise occurring in the street, aerial publicity over the city of Sydney, and unauthorized marketing operations. Subsequently, three acts were proclaimed, namely the Olympic Insignia Protection Act 1987, the Sydney 2000 Games (Indicia and Images) Protection Act 1996 and the Olympic Arrangement Act.
2. Control of marketing operations in the airspace over the city of Sydney.
3. Agreement with the World Federation of the Sporting Goods Industry (WFSGI) specifying the rules with regard to marketing.
4. New directives regarding the sale of tickets, the operations of public relations, and the promotions involving National Olympic Committees (NOCs).
5. An umbrella marketing programme specifying the rights and duties of the event and of the Olympic family for preventing the risks of conflicts between TOP partners belonging to different product categories.
6. Monitoring of ambush-marketing attempts in the media and on the Internet.

7. Ensuring that there is no publicity within the perimeter of the sporting venues.

The Olympic Games were the first victim of ambush marketing. During the 1990s, new methods of ambush marketing developed with large-scale events. Meenaghan (1994: 80–81) made a list of such methods:

- 'sponsorship of the broadcast of the event';
- 'choosing to be a minor sponsor of the event, yet launch massive advertisement campaign';
- 'buying as many advertising slots as possible in the broadcast of the event';
- 'engaging in operations of on-site promotion during the event';
- 'using photographs of recognizable venues, equipment, and/or symbols as background in an advertising campaign during the event'.

This is not an exhaustive list since creativity has no limits. In short, sponsors and organizations learned to defend against ambush marketing following the example of the IOC. Sandler and Shani (1989) and Meenaghan (1994) suggested the following actions:

- reducing the number of sponsor categories and maintaining consistency in these categories;
- devoting more effort and money to protecting the event and to promoting the official sponsors;
- bundling on-site sponsorship and broadcasting sponsorship;
- checking sponsorship rights carefully, exploiting the most secure one and taking legal action against ambush marketing.

The debate concerning ambush marketing has become intensive, given the number of sponsored events, teams, players, referees, etc. Nike's comment concerning its marketing campaign for the 1998 FIFA World Cup was highlighting the fact that the company was not trying to cash in on the event through ambush marketing. It was simply partnering with teams and players who took part in the World Cup, thereby legitimizing its presence in that event. Nike has set up a programme of communication focused on football, not on the World Cup. Consequently, over 250,000 people visited Nike's 'People's Republic of Football', opened by the Brazilian football team, and featuring interactive games, merchandise and soccer skills areas. Miniature cars emblazoned with Nike logos and filled with Nike players roamed the streets, stopping and offering free clinics. Advertising hoardings were everywhere. Six competing teams wore the Nike strip. According to the Sport+ Market study (1998) Nike generated a 32 per cent sponsor recognition rate. Furthermore, over two-thirds of British consumers failed to recognize or misidentified the Official World Cup Sponsors. Given such global competition, ethics in marketing should be discussed.

Greater sophistication of sponsorship implementation

Whereas the 1980s served as a learning curve in the sponsorship process for many actors, the 1990s led to the rationalization of the implementation of sponsorships. Arthur *et al.*

(1998) analysed the practices of companies in the area of sponsorship with a view to proposing an operational model for implementing and managing sponsorship. Their model is based on eight principles:

- Sports sponsorship must be carefully selected to ensure that the values and images of the sponsor are compatible with those of the sponsored entity.
- The sponsorship operation must be selected according to the required objectives.
- Sponsorship must be integrated in the communication strategy.
- Sponsorship must be evaluated efficiently.
- Sponsorship must be carried out following a precise contractual agreement.
- Sponsorship must be based on a long-term agreement.
- Sports sponsorship must seek protection against ambush marketing.
- Sponsorship must develop or enhance the sponsor's brand.

Among all these principles, the development of sponsorships has become increasingly important since the 1980s. Impact studies on sponsorship operations often yielded disappointing results for sponsors hoping to achieve unrealistic goals. As a result, Otker (1988) and others view sponsorship as the catalyst of an operation of communication, not its driving force. The notion of developing the sponsor was not evident then. The trend was more about developing the event (Piquet 1985) than about activating the sponsor's brand. Field experience showed that sponsorship needed to be developed through specific operations, thereby laying the groundwork for the budgeting of these specific operations. Here, we will not discuss the ratio between the budget allotted to the event and that allotted to the activation programme. One example will suffice: Crompton (1993) and Kiely (1993) proposed a 1:1 ratio, i.e. $1 budgeted for activation for each $1 budgeted for sponsorship; Abratt and Grober (1989) later suggested a 3:1 ratio. Sponsorship activation methods are tailored to objectives. Wilkinson (1993) proposed using methods such as on-site animation, advertising, sales promotion, public relations, employee motivation seminars, samples and invitations to the public. These means are now supplemented by, for example, broadcasting sponsorship, merchandizing, press relations, lotteries and peripheral events.

Our goal here is not to produce an exhaustive list, given that such means are tailored to specific operations. However, the activation process used by Fuji Xerox Australia for the launch of the Olympic sponsorship programme is a concrete example (Table 1.13). Fuji Xerox sent a customized letter to all of its business partners indicating that on 5 September 1995 Fuji Xerox Australia was hosting an Olympic event in Melbourne's business park. The media were also informed through a press release. During this event, a ceremony was organized to commemorate the lighting of the Olympic flame while a video incorporating successful moments of Australian athletes at previous Olympic Games was presented on a big screen in the background. After Fuji Xerox introduced its new products, it invited its guests to proceed to a cocktail reception. Olympic athletes were present to deliver symbolic 'Olympic Prizes' to certain guests, thereby boosting the atmosphere of the event. Additionally, any guest who acquired Fuji Xerox products during the following weeks earned chances to win a trip to the 1996 Atlanta Olympic Games. The guests had the opportunity to interview and take photographs of celebrities at the event. During the months following the event, several advertisements on television and in the press showcased the commitment of Fuji Xerox as an Olympic Games sponsor.

Table 1.13 Objectives, means and targets of the sponsorship activation platform used by Fuji Xerox for the Atlanta Olympic Games

Objectives	Means	Targets
To reinforce and build trade	Creating a peripheral event	Current customers
To develop a feeling of gratitude	Direct marketing	Prospective customers
To promote a positive company image	Press relations	Journalists
To increase sales and market shares	Video presentation	Sporting associations
	Private sales	Australian public interested in
	Sales promotion	the Olympic Games
	Public relations	
	Advertising	

Thus, Fuji Xerox used a set of means contributing to the development of their brand in order to reach their aforementioned sponsorship objectives. This combination of development and activation was in connection with the following objectives: to reinforce and build trade, to develop a feeling of gratitude, to give a positive image of the company and to increase the sales and the market shares. It is interesting to point out that the OG sponsorship collaboration of this company exemplifies the relationship marketing trends of the twenty-first century.

THIRD STAGE: ACTIVATING THE SPONSOR'S BRAND IN ORDER TO CREATE THE RIGHT EXPERIENCE WITH IT

Three prevailing trends are evident in the evolution of sponsorship into the twenty-first century. First, sponsorship operations are utilized to promote ('activate') the sponsor's brand in a manner that generates the best possible operational result. Second, company sponsors increasingly engage in relationship marketing. The third trend reflects the information technology influence on the relationship between sporting organizations, i.e. rights owners of the event, and the media.

From promotion to sponsor's brand activation

As previously mentioned, sponsors have been investing more and more in the development of their sponsorship operations. At the turn of the twenty-first century, the notion of brand promotion was gradually replaced by the notion of brand activation. According to Coca-Cola's sponsorship manager,

> activation consists in making the brand more active than passive. When a brand is posted on a panel around a stadium, it is passive. When consumers can touch it (e.g. a soft-drink bottle or can, a hat, a T-shirt with a photo of sport team on it, etc.), then it is active. The same applies when consumers can play the sponsor's games in a demonstration game prior to purchasing the game. Each brand is activated in different ways that are most beneficial to the sponsor.

A brand brings a real benefit to the consumer when it is activated in a manner that associates it with an experience with the consumer. Thus, activation is a marketing strategy that aims at bringing an experience with the sponsor's brand in the context of the event to a targeted audience.

To activate a brand, it is essential to use the appropriate means in a well-suited environment. Activation is part of experiential marketing, which dissociates from traditional marketing centred on concrete product characteristics and the benefits these bring to buyers. It goes beyond it by offering an additional experience where customers feel, think, act and relate to the brand. The brand provides an identity, but it primarily provides an experience. Coca-Cola was one of the first companies to rationalize what is referred to as 'experiential sponsorship'. Accordingly, for Coca-Cola, sport offers a unique platform to allow consumers an experience with a brand associated with the concept of fun and entertainment (i.e. physical and mental refreshment). From an overall perspective, their objectives of sponsorship are:

- to build a relationship with young people by associating the brand with their axis of interests and happiness;
- to create an unforgettable moment, i.e. a unique experience in connection with the brand;
- to ensure Coca-Cola is perceived as a brand enhancing everyday life;
- to ensure Coca-Cola is perceived as a dynamic leader;
- to ensure Coca-Cola is perceived as a national sponsor at the local level and as a global sponsor at the international level.

Marketing executives hone the sporting environment in an effort to ensure the optimal experience with the brand. Prior to the 1998 FIFA World Cup, Coca-Cola strategists determined the types of experience it hoped to achieve with the fans/customers of the brand (see Table 1.14).

Once experiential features are defined, it is essential to use appropriate means to trigger the envisioned experience. In this context, the means are used to deliver the envisioned

Table 1.14 Comparison of the type of sensory activation with the means of activation

Experiential features	Characteristics
Delivering a diverse sensational experience	Physical sensations (i.e. touch, taste, kinaesthesia and vision) ensuing from holding, opening and drinking a fresh can of Coke
	Physical sensations related to the experience of a football match (i.e. touch, kinaesthetic, visual and auditory)
Feeling	Refreshment of oneself, to quench thirst, fun, enjoyment, excitement and thrill
	To generate a feeling of gratitude towards the brand
Thinking	Coke is different, superior and extraordinary
	Coke is the drink people seek when they socialize, and watch football and other sports
Reporting	To share this exciting and unique experience with friends and fans
Acting	To express oneself, take part in the event and to drink Coke

experience which enable the activation platform to be developed. Experiential marketing relates to the characteristics of the sponsored event, thus it is essential to make a judicious relational choice. Additionally, the sponsor must collaborate with the organizer to hone the experience. The activation platform used by Coca-Cola during the FIFA World Cup made use of various means.

Slogans
'Always Coca-Cola' was replaced by 'Enjoy' for the Anglo-Saxon market and 'Vivez l'instant' ['Live for the moment'] for the French-speaking market, thereby focusing on the main benefit the brand brings to consumers. During the 1998 Atlanta Football World Cup, Coca-Cola used more assertive slogans such as 'Live Football, Feel Football, Drink Coca-Cola'.

Packaging campaigns
Packaging conveys a sensory stimulation: sight and touch. During those World Cup games, Coca-Cola developed progressive slogans and images on its 'collector's edition' cans. This promotion of phrases and images stimulated the associative connectivity of sight with the tangible effects of touching through their association with football. This was determined to be the most effective means to support the bond between Coke and football; thus it stimulated both product purchases and participation in the event.

Media advertising
Coca-Cola carried out a worldwide campaign in which fans were the focus of the brand promotion. The advertising showed rejoicing fans. The topic of the first ad campaign was 'share the passion and celebrate'. According to the Coca-Cola sponsorship manager, 'the mere act of perceiving the emotion of spectators can at times provide stronger emotions than by watching a football match'. Other ads, such as posters, expressed sadness with fans crying. The purpose was to express the interconnectivity between Coca-Cola and all the World Cup fans. The ad campaign prompted supporters to act, express themselves and engage in the event with tailored messages linked to the aforementioned slogans, such as 'If there was a World Cup for fans, would you qualify?' and 'Shake the World'.

Interval opportunities at the venues or special events
At the celebration site and during special events designed for brand promotion, everything was done to associate positive sensations with the event and football. The intention was to create a cocoon around the sport so people no longer came to watch the event merely for the sake of the sport, but for the atmosphere and social interactions around it.

Thus, in partnership with the French Football Federation, Coca-Cola created peripheral events which allowed children to take part in the opening ceremonies of the World Cup matches, as well as a skills contest through which 564 girls and boys were selected to become ball fetchers, and where 1024 youths were selected to become the flag bearers of the 32 qualifying countries. In any case, these are memorable events or 'winning moments' which reinforce the link between youth, Coca-Cola and football.

Promotion
Promotional operations were carried out on a case-by-case basis through mass marketing.

The intent was not only to grab market shares, but also reinforce the association with the brand and the feeling of goodwill towards Coca-Cola.

Merchandizing
Coca-Cola has extensive experience in this field because merchandizing is traditionally an integral part of the activation platform of sporting events.

Games and contests
These strategies enable 'one-on-one' relationships with consumers in a highly emotional environment. Games and contests are an opportunity for fans to win free passes to football matches, including the finals at the 'Stade de France', as well as insignia products of the brand.

Broadcast sponsorship
This form of activation constitutes the base of this type of sponsorship operation, as it makes it possible to capitalize on the emotional participation of supporters and spectators. Thus, Coca-Cola sponsored the broadcasting of the matches on French television channels.

Internet
Coca-Cola's website was primarily informative. Fans could visit Coca-Cola's website with a view to obtaining updated information concerning the event and ventures of the brand (i.e. other events, packaging promotions, etc.). Today, the Internet is widely used for the activation of sponsorships.

In overview, the sponsorship activation platform Coca-Cola used during the 1998 FIFA World Cup demonstrates the will to mobilize a whole set of means to ensure that supporters and consumers experience the envisioned experience with the brand. However, successful activation requires a synergy between the organizer of the event and the sponsor(s). For these stakeholders, it is essential to choose an adequate environment and the appropriate means to ensure that the envisioned experience occurs. Such a desire generates operations of collaboration whose initiatives enter into the framework of systemic marketing; this will be addressed in the following section.

Implementing relationship marketing

The rationalization of partnerships, building activation platforms, the search for a return on investment, and prevention of ambush-marketing strategies led event-driven organizations to build collaborations with key stakeholders, thereby building a unique marketing network of relationship marketing. According to Sheth and Parvatiyar (2000: 9), relationship marketing is the 'ongoing process of engaging in cooperative and collaborative activities and programs with immediate and end-user customers to create or enhance mutual economical value at reduced cost'. Although relationship marketing primarily involves the event organizer, the television partner and the main sponsors, it extends more and more to other stakeholders.

The marketing operation conducted by the Slovenian National Olympic Committee (SNOC) prior to the Sydney Olympic Games testifies to the efficiency of relationship marketing. The SNOC partnered with its main sponsor, SKB Bank, the official representative of Visa in Slovenia, and designed an operation called 'the Visa Card Project'. Visa is a partner of the TOP programme.

Objectives

The main objectives of the SNOC were to promote itself and its Olympic team. As for Visa, the objectives were to promote credit card usage with the launch of its 'Gold Card' in Slovenia. The third partner, SKB Bank, wished to promote the use of Visa cards in an attempt to increase its market share and reinforce its partnership with Visa.

Implementation

The two originators of this project, the SNOC and SKB Bank, contacted Visa with a request to enter into a joint marketing campaign. Upon reaching an agreement with Visa, the partners designed a mass communication campaign with athletes of the Slovenian Olympic team.
　　The SNOC assured:

- the promotion of Visa and SKB Bank during its weekly television programme dubbed 'the Olympic Perspective';
- the radio broadcast on five different radio stations during the 'The Olympic Rings' programme;
- the advertising in newspapers and all SNOC publications.

　　SKB Bank carried out the following operations:

- an advertising campaign in national daily newspapers and travel magazines, and on the radio, amounting to a total of 54 advertisements in national daily newspapers and 352 on radio stations;
- the presentation of the project on the website of the bank;
- a nationwide billboard advertising campaign.

　　Lastly, prior to the Salt Lake City Olympic Games, Visa designed a global advertising campaign tailored to the Slovenian market. The ad campaign was distributed in eight national newspapers and tourist catalogues. Visa also organized a game inviting participants to bet on the results of Slovenian athletes where the first prize was a two-week stay at the Park City Ski Station during the 2002–3 season.
　　In addition, the SNOC organized two events that Visa was actively involved in. The first event was the official introduction of the Slovenian Olympic team. During this ceremony, Visa offered each athlete participating in the Olympic Games a $100 gift card. The ceremony benefited from nationwide television and newspaper coverage where the logos of SKB Bank and Visa were visible in the background in all transmitted images. Additionally, the ceremony took place at another sponsor of the SNOC, Mercator

Shopping Center, which made it possible to utilize another partner in the operation, thereby reducing costs and increasing the marketing impact.

The second event was a reception of the Slovenian Olympic team when it returned from Salt Lake City. SKB Bank organized a reception in honour of the team and offered a 'Gold Card' with a special bonus to all the Slovenian Olympic medallists.

Results

Between January and June 2002, the number of Visa card holders increased by 24 per cent in Slovenia. The number of transactions by this payment mode and the amounts per transaction increased significantly. Furthermore, a study carried out on behalf of SKB Bank showed that the marketing operation had built a strong association between the bank and the Slovenian Olympic team in the minds of Slovenians.

The result of this marketing strategy was evolutionary in the way sponsors carry sponsorship operations. There was a shift from transactional marketing where sponsors competed with one another on the site of the event to relationship marketing where a certain number of constituents collaborate in programmes designed to achieve their respective goals in a more efficient way.

Relationship marketing is based on a progressive relationship building approach that requires mutual trust. The SNOC met with its sponsors on a regular basis by organizing:

- presentations relating the activity of each partner;
- study trips, meetings with sponsors and other NOCs, and visits to Olympic sites;
- seminars dedicated to sport marketing.

These initiatives enable partners to build relationships with each other which in turn stimulate project partnerships that create a competitive advantage in the business world. The most important phase concerns the maintenance and rationalization of these networks. Thus, the SNOC built an Internet marketing platform involving its partners and the actors of the Slovenian sporting world.

The power shift

Initially, the first operations of relationship marketing relied on the leverage of the media to reach an audience. In 1999, Forester Research published a report by Hardie *et al.* about current and future media broadcast trends called 'The Sport Power Shift'.

Currently, the decision whether or not to cover an event or a sport by means of traditional media distributors (e.g. TV broadcasts, newspapers and radio stations) is based on a certain number of criteria, the most important being the public interest in the event. Thus, depending on the audience size and the market placement of a sport, media distributors decide whether or not to buy the rights of transmission from the rights owner. In this context, fans have free or paying access to sport media content, which can be controlled by the distributor and/or the rights owner under specific conditions. This profit-driven economic model has the following effects:

- Most sports do not have access to powerful media outlets.
- Companies secure the broadcast of the events through broadcasting sponsorships.
- Fans have a controlled experience.

This model is currently challenged due to newly emerging information technologies. Indeed, it is now possible to create a link between the event, the sporting organization and the fans with an Internet platform. The advent of high-speed broadband allows for the transfer of vast quantities of information. In the near future, it will be possible to broadcast videos online, thereby enabling the rights owner of the event to occupy strategic positioning through an Internet platform (see Figure 1.8).

CONCLUSION: AN OPERATIONAL DEFINITION OF SPONSORSHIP

In the past 30 years, sponsorship has evolved both at the operational and strategic levels. Focusing on the essential principles on which sponsorship is built, we suggest the following definition:

> Sponsorship is a communication strategy integrated within the set of strategies used by an organization in pursuit of commercial and/or corporate objectives, exploiting the rights to associate an organization, a brand, a product, with another organization, an event or a celebrity, involving a commercial transaction between the parties.
>
> (Ferrand and Torrigiani 2005: 98)

Figure 1.8 In the future, the rightful owner of the event will occupy a strategic positioning via an Internet platform

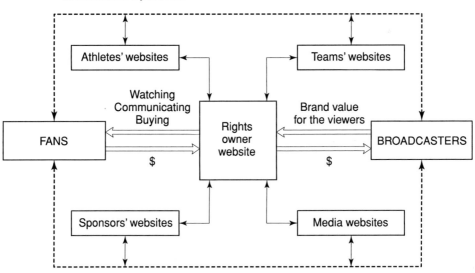

Source: Adapted from Hardie *et al.* (1999)

This definition underlines the most important principles of sponsorship. Thus, the marketing strategy incorporates the components of the marketing mix, and is an integral part of the operational policies of an organization, on an equal par with human resources, finance, R&D and production. As such, sponsorship is anchored in the marketing strategy, whereby it must be consistent with:

• the principle of vertical integration to ensure coherence between the various strategies;
• the interaction with the various strategies and activation.

Indeed, sponsorship operations must work in conjunction with marketing strategies when it comes to stimulating the sales force and the distribution network, while conceiving a new service (e.g. sending sporting results to mobile telephones) or supporting a promotion. Sponsorship operations also create a synergy with the overall strategy by stimulating, for example, the partnership with the institutional network in a country, thereby contributing to the internationalization of the company.

As outlined previously in this chapter, there are two types of sponsorship objectives: commercial communication and corporate communication, as summarized in Table 1.15.

The direct association between an organization, a brand or a product with another organization, event or celebrity is the nucleus of sponsorship. The dynamics of this interaction occurs within the event-driven system we analysed in the introduction. We insist on the fact that it is the event itself, through its high emotional effect on people, which fuels the system. Thereby, a sporting event is a powerful social act associated with a specific image or 'brand equity', generating collectively shared emotions, and whose outcome is uncertain.

The sponsorship exchange process occurs through a legal commercial transaction that may consist of monetary issues, service provisions, products, exposure of a brand or logo within the event, promotions, etc. The following chapters discuss the management principles of the sponsorship exchange process.

Table 1.15 The commercial and corporate objectives of sponsorship

Commercial communication	Corporate communication
To prove the reliability of products and services	To legitimize the social role of the company
To develop brand awareness	To develop relationships with the local community
To manage the image and to enhance perceived quality	To promote the entrepreneurial culture, to reinforce internal cohesion and to motivate company personnel
To generate a feeling of gratitude and a favourable attitude	
To emulate successful companies	To improve recruitment of highly qualified personnel
To create or reinforce relationships (business-to-consumer and business-to-business)	
To increase sales	

2
Legal approach to sporting events

Note: This chapter is aimed at stakeholders involved in the event system who are not specialized legal practitioners. For this reason it is written in an easily accessible form and language.

The economic and social developments of sporting events require the implementation of marketing and communication strategies. As mentioned in the introduction, sponsorship is incorporated within various systems (e.g. event-driven, sporting, geographical and social) which are based on relationships between stakeholders (e.g. sporting organizations, media, companies, local authorities, etc.) Legal analysis of sports sponsorship generally focuses on contractual and legislative elements. However, this analysis does not make it possible to define or strengthen the legal bonds existing between various stakeholders involved in an event.

In this chapter, the concept of the sporting event is analysed from a legal perspective in order to identify the various stakeholders who are likely to own a series of rights in connection with the event. An examination is made of the foundation for these rights, their relationships with the properties, and the protection mechanisms. An international approach is used for focusing on the key legal elements worth considering, regardless of where the event takes place.

Definition of a sporting event

From a socio-economic perspective, an organized activity is regarded as an event only when it has a social impact. From a legal perspective, however, the social impact is not an essential factor for determining the existence of an event. The existence of a sporting 'event' can be defined as when one or more people engage in a sports activity, and when each activity can be identified and differentiated. The participation of a promoter, organizer or broadcaster is essential for individualizing and differentiating the event. The legal dimension is very important in the context and presence of a sporting event.

The sporting event should always be legally protected before it actually creates a social impact – that is, even before the event takes place. It is imperative to integrate legal protection into the design of an event. Once the event has begun, the event organizer can rely on conflict resolution, litigation or arbitration procedures only if the legal protection has been provided for prior to the event.

Furthermore, legal protection of an event is crucial, considering the efforts and significant investments in order to develop it. The event organizer must ensure that unauthorized third parties will neither infringe upon, nor benefit from the event. Additionally, legal protection is an essential element for developing a marketing strategy.

Three elements are necessary to define an event from a legal point of view:

- *Identification:* an event must have an identity (e.g. The Olympic Games, The _____ World Championship, The National _____, etc.). Various legal means exist for the purpose of identifying an event.
- *Differentiation:* An event must also differentiate itself, i.e., it must be unique. The event may share similarities with other events, yet it must have something unique to differentiate itself from other events.
- *Organization:* An event must be organized. Indeed, it is impossible to identify or differentiate an event without someone organizing the event. There is no such thing as a spontaneous event.

Legal protection of an event is necessary because considerable investment is essential for its organization and development of any marketing action. It should be ensured, therefore, that third parties cannot benefit unduly from the event. This protection must always be carried out in the initial concept/stages and integrated into the design. We cannot use procedures for the resolution of conflicts and litigations only when the organization of the event starts.

It is essential to establish the identity of an event and ascertain how it differentiates from other events in order to define it. An analysis of these two elements will determine whether other events are similar or distinct. Many contributing elements serve to define, and thus differentiate, a sporting event. The most significant, from a legal perspective, will be examined.

Identification

First, and foremost, an event must have an identity. In sports, it is the name of the event that typically constitutes the main element of identification (e.g. The Roland Garros Tournament, The China Cup, etc.). Beside the name attributed to an event, there are additional elements contributing to this individuation, such as a:

- sign;
- font;
- image;
- figure;
- symbol;
- graph or graphics;
- colour;
- logo;
- slogan.

Thus, various elements are used to identify an event. However, the only elements that can be legally protected are ones that are legally valid in one or more countries. For example, certain categories of signs are prohibited in certain countries yet authorized in other countries. Likewise, the use of a person's image as an identifying mark is acceptable in certain countries but not in others.

From a legal standpoint, the previously mentioned elements fall within the notion of a trademark. A trademark is a word, symbol or phrase, used to identify a particular manufacturer's or seller's products and distinguish them from the products of another. The trademark is the property of a person or a corporate body. Thus, when conceiving the organization of a sporting event, it is paramount to develop all suitable means that contribute to the identification of the event, especially the following:

- the name of the event;
- the graphics of the name;
- the logo;
- the specific colour(s) used in the name and on the logo of the event;
- the three-dimensional form of the logo and emblem.

The name of an event must be determined with great caution, since there is a series of general limitations applicable to any product or service, and another series of limitations applying exclusively to sport.

The general limitations relate notably to the name. The name of an event cannot be identical, or similar, to a name that has already been used for another event.[1] If it is, the owner of the prior event can legally oppose the use of the name for the new event.

There are also additional limitations or prohibitions specific to the sporting genre regarding the determination of the event name. Some European, African and South American countries have drawn up sport-oriented legal texts which outline the use of the 'official competition' denomination for the exclusive use of sport federations and authorities recognized by law or by the state. In France, Spain and Portugal, for example, it is forbidden to organize a sporting event whose name and purpose consists of organizing a national or regional championship outside the framework of a recognized sport federation.

By contrast, the determination of the name of a sporting event is subject only to general limitations in countries that intervene to a lesser degree in sports.

Differentiation

Differentiation is the second fundamental element contributing to the definition of the 'sporting event' concept. It should be clear that the name is the first element that serves to differentiate an event. Indeed, the name of the event and the previously mentioned elements of identification allow the event to be identified, yet it also differentiates it within the framework of the legal definition of the trademark. Furthermore, the description and rules of the event serve as an additional means to differentiate it.

Differentiation is primarily achieved by the specific elements of identification differentiating the event trademark. Therefore, it is important to specify and protect the elements of the trademark(s) that serve to differentiate the products and services of the event. This act of differentiating is especially important, considering that different products and services can bear the same mark, even the same name.

It is advisable to protect the description of the sporting event, given that its description also helps to differentiate the event. In the sporting field, the organization's systematic description of the event constitutes the essential factor in the differentiation of the 'product/ service/event'.

Note that only a detailed and accurate description of the event will ensure legal protection when registering the trademark. Furthermore, this meticulous description helps secure relations between contracting parties in negotiations (e.g. during the drafting of a television contract, etc.). Elements contributing to the description of a sporting event, which must appear in any event-related contract, are examined in the subsequent sections.

Sport and sporting activities

The description must include the elements of the sport and each sporting activity constituting the event. Two questions should be considered.

- Does the event comprise one or several sports?
- Does the event consist of only one sporting discipline or several sporting disciplines? (For example, the Football World Cup relates to outdoor football only, i.e. it excludes indoor football, which has its own world competition, although it is governed by the same federation – namely FIFA; in contrast, a multitude of disciplines such as swimming, diving, water polo and synchronized swimming are staged during the World Swimming Championship.)

Type and nature of the sports activity

Competitive:

- Is it an official or unofficial competition?
- Is it a championship, tournament, race, games, etc?
- Are all competitors competing against one another? Are there qualification rounds? How many rounds are there?
- What are the intervals and duration of the event?

Non-competitive:

- Is the event staged to exhibit the sport?
- Is the event staged to highlight a performance (e.g. the ascent of Mount Everest)?

Characteristics and modes of participation

- Individuals or teams?
- Men or women only, or mixed?
- What is the age category?
- Clubs or national representatives?

- Is the participation based on preliminary sports results, pre-classification rounds, experience or monetary contributions?

Significance and effects of the sports results

- _____ Champion
- Qualified for _____
- _____ Medalist
- No repercussion in the sporting hierarchy.

Location of the event

- Where does the event occur (e.g. continent, country, region, city)? Is the event taking place in a facility (e.g. stadium, gymnasium, cycle-racing track, etc.) or elsewhere (e.g. road, beach, mountain, etc.)?
- Does the sporting location require special provisions?
- On which type of surface is the event going to take place?

Dates, schedules and duration of the event

- On the ___ (day/s) of _____ (month and year) between ___ (AM/PM) and ___ (AM/PM) for a minimum of ___ hours daily, during a minimum period of ___ days and a maximum period of ___ days.
- Is it a regular or an occasional event? Can the dates and schedule of the event be modified to accommodate participants?
- Is the event interfering with a sporting season? Can the dates and schedule of the event be altered to accommodate participants?
- Is the exact duration of the event known or not?

The legal structure of the organizing entity

Although the legal structure of the organizing entity is discussed further on, some essential aspects that serve to differentiate the organizing entity are introduced here. There are various legal entities, such as:

- public organizations (e.g. multinational corporations, state-owned business enterprises, etc.);
- private, not-for-profit organization, governed by associative law (e.g. IOC, international and national sports federations, professional and non-professional leagues and clubs, foundations);
- privately owned companies (e.g. limited liability companies).

Governing rules

It is also essential to differentiate the event by establishing any rules it will be governed by to ensure solid legal protection. Some events are not necessarily governed by any rules.

Non-competitive sporting events, for instance, generally do not have rules governing the event (e.g. the North Pole crossing does not observe specific rules). However, most events, especially competitive events, are subject to rules.

The set of rules governing a given sport is the primary contributing factor of differentiation for an event. For example, football differentiates from futsal (indoor football) and basketball through its rules of the game. Modifying the rules of the game can change the structure and organization of the event. Therefore, it is essential that the rules of the game governing a given event be precisely defined in all contracts pertaining to that event.

It is not necessary to reference rules of public law in contracts, as these rules are binding to all parties equally. However, if the contracting parties wish to incorporate other rules of law (e.g. if the event is organized in several countries, if foreign athletes participate in the event, etc.), these rules must appear in the contract. Hence, it is only necessary to specify the rules of private law and those imposed by relevant sport governing bodies that are to be applied during the event. Consequently, certain rules are essential given that they serve to define, thus differentiate, sporting events. The following rules should be incorporated into various contracts.

1. The rules of the game, or technical rules, must be incorporated in all marketing-oriented contracts.
2. The competition rules, i.e. the rules governing the system and mode of participation in the competition, must also be incorporated in all marketing-oriented contracts
3. The rules for publicity concerning the sporting event have a significant impact on advertising licence agreements and sponsorship contracts. These rules establish the scope of the advertising and promotions applicable in the framework of the event and should always be included in a contract.
4. The applicable rules to audiovisual transmissions, i.e. the set of rules establishing the technical criteria and means of transmission, have a crucial bearing on television broadcasting contracts.
5. The rules relating to the organization and course of the event must be incorporated in marketing contracts. For instance, the IOC and most international sports federations establish a set of rules which the event organizer must comply with (e.g. equipment characteristics, available infrastructure for athletes, spectators, sponsors, authorities and the press, means of transport available, the marketing system for tickets sales, the mode for selling or transferring rights, etc.).
6. The disciplinary rules governing the prevention of violence and control of doping have an insignificant impact on marketing contracts. However, any modification of these rules can affect the definition and characteristics of the sporting event. Thus, it may be wise to incorporate them in this type of contract.

Subsidiary factors

There are additional factors, albeit not essential to the definition of the event, which confer an additional value to, and thus differentiate, the event itself:

* Does the event have media coverage (e.g. television, radio, newspaper, etc.)?
* Is the event open to the public?

- Is the event publicized?
- Is the event sponsored?

Organization of the event

The organization of the event is the third fundamental element contributing to the definition of the 'sporting event' concept. From a strictly legal standpoint, any sport can be organized, promoted and developed by any type of entity, public or private, associative or commercial, and regardless of whether or not it has traditionally been in charge of governing a sport. Organization can be achieved by:

- a person or a group of individuals;
- a corporate body or several corporate bodies.

Any person can concede, promote, develop and arrange the broadcast of a sporting event for a social or commercial purpose, either alone or in collaboration with others, in the capacity of 'individual contractor'.

Likewise, entities with a legal stature can also organize sporting events. Legal entities refer to:

- public organizations (e.g. state, regional, municipal authorities);
- non-profit organizations (e.g. associations, foundations, sports federations, sports leagues, sports clubs, the IOC, etc.);
- for-profit organizations (e.g. corporations).

Sport itself cannot be legally owned and, as such, cannot be legally protected. However, a sporting event can be owned and protected by law. Given that sporting events can be organized by anyone, the governing bodies of sports must use legal means for ensuring solid legal protection of their events and activities.

One common perception of sports is that competitive sports seek to unify individuals with a view to determining a winner. This tendency to the unification of the structures and rules of sports has led to the creation of independent vertically organized entities whose origin is legal in the Olympic movement:

> The Olympic Movement groups together all those who agree to be guided by the Olympic Charter, and who recognize the authority of the International Olympic Committee (IOC). This includes the International Federations (IF) of sports on the program of the Olympic Games, the National Olympic Committees (NOCs), the Organizing Committees of the Olympic Games (OCOGs), athletes, judges and referees, associations and clubs, as well as all the organizations and institutions recognized by the IOC.[2]

Hence, sports federations have traditionally held the rights of a significant number of sporting events, but this is not true of all sporting events. For instance, some sporting events in football, cycling and tennis are organized by independent organizers, and not by sports federations. Not surprisingly, these entities generally remain in charge of organizing and managing various sporting events. Even though many authorities and national legislations support the traditional hierarchy of the sport, nothing can prevent individuals or entities from lawfully organizing sporting events.

Although international and national sporting federations do not have any property rights on their respective sport, the structure of international federations often cultivates a monopoly over their given sports. World championships are only organized by sporting federations. Monopolies, however, cannot be legally enforced. While many countries are increasing their efforts to restrict monopolistic control of sports, there are certain limitations for organizing sporting events that exist, which are legally binding. For instance:

- It is forbidden to copy, organize and/or develop a sporting event that is already conceived and legally protected by another entity.
- The traditional sporting structure, i.e. the sports federation hierarchy, is protected by law in some countries, thereby allowing the monopoly of these federations with regard to the organizing of sporting events.

The stakeholders of the event

There are various stakeholders in the framework of a sporting event. The number of stakeholders engaging in the event will depend on the sporting, social and economic impact. Stakeholders have particular interests for partaking in an event. The various relationships each stakeholder establishes with the event can be analysed through the following characteristics of links to the event:

- ownership;
- participation;
- contractual;
- legal link relating to the contract.

Thus, within the framework of an event it is possible to have one or more rights owners, one or more participants and one or more parties who have established a contractual framework with the organizer. In this respect, it should be recalled that in certain cases the legislation of each country can fix a series of rights to the benefit of parties not directly involved in the event.

We do not claim to give an exhaustive view of all the parties concerned. We will present the most important and will specify their rights. This is the only means of defining with exactitude the possibilities relating to sponsorship, and with the licences, such as television contracts.

Rights owner

From a legal point of view, it is advisable to provide an answer to the following question: who is the event rights owner and what does this ownership imply?

We underlined previously that the organizing entity is an essential body for the design and the development of sporting events. This entity may be a group of persons or governing bodies which can be of a public or private nature. In all cases, and whatever the adopted form, its presence is essential.

The concept of the event organizer can relate to a very different legal status. In the sporting field, it is not easy to lay down single and absolute rules to establish who the organizer is and under which legal status the organizer operates.

On several occasions we have already stated that the concept of a sporting event was not unique and that it did not answer a uniform reality. The ascent of Everest by an expedition can lead to an event, just like the UEFA Champions League. From a legal and organizational point of view, there are few common points between these two events. A specific event (e.g. a football match) cannot be confused with a group of single events which, when linked together, constitute a complete event of a distinct nature (e.g. a national league is composed of several meetings and the league itself, constituting a complete event in which each meeting is also an event). Thus, the term 'sport' gathers various competitive and non-competitive practices of a distinct nature, with very different models of organization, participation and competition. This is why it is difficult to adopt a single legal position that allows us to specify which is the organizer of a sporting event.

It is easy in some cases to associate an event with an organizer. Nevertheless, it is difficult in the majority of cases. This situation is due to the fact that there are perhaps several organizers, and each one of them can hold and put forward a series of rights related to the event. In order to tackle this question with maximum clarity, we believe that it is useful to propose the following typology:

- single event versus group/set of events;
- rights owner versus manager;
- one rights owner versus rights co-owners.

Single event versus a series of events

Sporting events can be defined as a single event or a series of events, which are more or less independent of one another. It is easier to identify the event organizer with a single event. Where the sporting event consists of a series of events (e.g. a league championship), information must be sought for identifying the event organizer in order to distinguish the rights owner of the event from the event manager. Sporting events can be classified as follows:

- independent event;
- authorized or integrated event;
- complex event.

Independent event

Independent events are characterized by the fact that the contest typically takes place over a relatively short period of time, i.e. a few hours, one day, several days or several weeks in one or more locations. The event can incorporate one or more sports and develop through one or more events or competitions. The overall intention of the event is independent and differentiated from other events; therefore, each sporting outcome has no relevance beyond the event. The following sporting events are examples of independent events:

- the Olympic Games;
- the Intercontinental Cup;
- the America's Cup;
- an exhibition tennis tournament.

Most importantly, an independent event has only one organizer, thus only one rights owner. This single ownership provides the owner with the autonomy to develop the event as deemed appropriate.

Authorized or integrated event

In this model of organization, there is a single owner per authorized event. The right to organize and manage the event, however, is limited by the technical and disciplinary standards of a third party. Thus, the rights holder of each respective event must comply with the rules enacted by this third party, which is generally an international federation. Legal privileges granted to the rights holder of an event can be limited by the entity that sanctions it. Consequently, a rights owner whose event is authorized by and integrated into a larger entity may or may not enjoy full freedom for negotiating marketing, sponsorship, television broadcasting and other types of contracts. The rights owner of this type of event, however, most often has the freedom to choose from a broad array of opportunities. The limitations generally imposed usually pertain to the rules of the game.

This type of event organization model is based on the association of several independently sanctioned events, all of which are organized under the authority of a given sports' governing body, with an additional, primary event. The result of each individual sporting event is significant and meaningful for each single competition. Additionally, the result of every event is tallied, which has an effect on the overall outcome of the primary event. The sanctioned events generally occur in various locations over a period of one year, or a sporting season.

Independent and autonomous sporting events, which are voluntarily located within a lawful framework and the control of another organization, also fit into this category. For example, the organizers of the Tour de France, Giro d'Italia and Vuelta a Espana subjected their respective event to the rules and technical and disciplinary standards of the International Cycling Union (UCI). The following sporting events are characterized as sanctioned events:

- cycling trials (e.g. Buthiers Seine & Marne (France), Knokke – Heist (Belgium), Graz (Austria) and Lorca (Spain)), which are then integrated into the UCI World Cup;
- tennis tournaments, e.g. the NASDAQ-100 Open (USA), the Monte Carlo Open (Monaco), the Telecom Italia Masters Roma (Italy) and the Tennis Masters Hamburg (Germany) integrated into the ATP Masters Series.

These events are typically characterized by the presence of several rights holders, each with the attribute of a single owner. They do not have the complete authority for organizing and managing the event due to the fact that they are integrated into the dynamics of a broader sporting event, whose owner has prerogatives on each singular event.

The rights owner of any event, from a legal perspective, is free to decide whether to subject the event to the rules and disciplinary standards imposed by a third party, such as an international federation. Therefore, the rights owner of the event must evaluate if the benefit of integrating with another competition is greater than the limits imposed by the third party.

The legal structure used in this model of organization is founded on the desire to seek authorization and integration with another party. More specifically, the organizer of an event owns the rights related to it, but voluntarily decides to be integrated with a larger entity to benefit from its technical and organizational advantages, or makes a request to be recognized by an organization with a better marketing position. Event organizers who incorporate their event in the official calendar of a third party do so as a way to gain a competitive advantage in the market. The competitive advantage may be to secure the participation of famous athletes in their event, or to prevent these athletes from participating in unauthorized events.[3]

Complex event

A complex event category is characterized by several events that occur simultaneously in various locations, each with distinct owners and organizers (co-owners). These rights owners or organizers are essentially given autonomy within the development of their respective event; however, each event does not exist in an independent manner. All games are integrated within the framework of a broader event. The sports result of each single event is only significant insofar as it is reflected in its overall ranking in the primary event.

Whereas the focal point of a sanctioned event is the outcome of each single event, the focal point of a comprehensive event is the result of all the particular events combined, i.e. the league championship outcome. The outcome of every single event constituting a comprehensive event would not have the same significance if it were not integrated in a championship. The following events are examples of comprehensive events:

- Moto GP World Championship;
- World Rally Championship;
- national football leagues championships;
- UEFA Champions League;
- NBA, MLB, NFL and NHL.

Complex events involve individual event owners who each manage their own event and accept subordination to another owner or entity in charge of the overall event. As a result, the rights yielded to each owner may vary significantly according to individual situations.

Rights owner versus event manager

The second aspect to be taken into account when defining the entity responsible for organizing an event relates to making a differentiation between the owner and the organizer if a distinction needs to be made. Indeed, any event that is owned by one or more entities may choose to outsource the organization of the event to a third party, i.e. to an event manager. Hence, it is essential to distinguish whether the event manager is also the rights owner of the event. In short, a given entity can be the organizer of an event in two distinct ways:

- rights owner of the event;
- delegated manager of the event.

The IOC, for instance, is the rights owner of the Olympic Games. Yet, pursuant to the Olympic Charter, the sporting and technical organization of the Olympic Games is entrusted to the Organizing Committee of the Olympic Games (OCOG). The OCOG is formed by a number of stakeholders, including city host officials and public authorities, NOC, sponsors, national federations, leagues and clubs. Likewise, FIFA is the exclusive rights owner of the Football World Cup. They routinely delegate the organization of the World Cup to a national football federation, which is integrated in the steering committee of a particular World Cup edition.

When the event is organized by the rights owner, the latter enjoys all the rights and privileges derived from the applicable judicial system. However, the rights and privileges of a delegated organizer of the event (the 'event manager') are limited to those that are stipulated in the contractual agreement between the two entities or in the constitution enacted by the rights owner of the event.

From a legal standpoint, it is crucial not to confuse the delegated organizer of the event with the rights owner of the event or with another entity holding the capacity to manage certain rights or aspects of the event, such as a co owner or licensee. The company that manages the rights of sponsorship or publicity of an event is not necessarily the organizer. It may possess only one contractual relationship pertaining to certain rights associated with the event. A delegation of powers can confer a third party with the capacity for negotiating some or all of the rights and privileges relating to an event. The extent of the assignment depends on the prerogative of the rights owner of the event.

Single versus co-ownership rights

The analysis aimed at determining if ownership rights of an event are singular or plural constitutes the third aspect concerning the statute of the organizer. Individual events are typically singly owned, unless the owner decides otherwise. If the event is co-organized or there is a delegation of powers to a third party, the rights of each organizer are defined according to their mode of collaboration. In the case of authorized and complex events, it is more difficult to identify the rights owner, as there are often several rights holders and organizers. In these two cases, it is not possible to speak about a single owner, nor even a single organizer. There is a plurality of rights owners as well as multiple organizers.

According to popular German jurisprudence, the organizer is the one person or entity assuming the economic risk and as such, the rights owner. This theory can be useful in certain situations of conflicts of interest, but nevertheless we think that it is not applicable to all sporting events, nor can it solve all the problems arising in this field.

In a football league championship, under the terms of this German jurisprudence, the clubs are rights owners of the individual matches of the event, since they assume the economic risk of the competition, thereby strictly limiting the role of the federation or league to organizing the primary event competition. However, the situation is different in other leagues. For example, in the football leagues in the United States, Qatar and the United Arab Emirates, the league or federation contracts players and assigns them to a team. It is thus difficult to establish a generic theory that is valid and applicable in all situations.

A series of questions arise from a logical analysis of this theory. If a club organizing a sporting event is the single rights owner of that event, does the club own the rights concerning the referee? Can it choose the referee? Can it negotiate publicity on the refereeing equipment?

We don't think so because in practice it is not like this, and many rights related to the event remain the property of the league or the federation.

In addition, imagine that a football club decides, in an isolated and autonomous way, to sell the broadcast rights of its home matches. Within the framework of German jurisprudence, it would own the rights to do this because it assumes the economic risk for its home matches. In this scenario, the football club would be able to yield the broadcasting rights of its team, but not those of the opposing team because it is not responsible for the yearly budget of the opposing team.

What are the rights of a football club when it plays at another team's venue? Is the host club the single rights holder for posting publicity in its stadium, for setting up cafeterias, for selling broadcast rights of the match, etc.? It is not possible to answer these questions under the German jurisprudence theory because there are various rights holders in every event who each take an economic risk. Therefore, each situation must be analysed individually. Although the German theory can be useful in situations involving conflicts of interests, it is neither applicable to all types of sporting events nor applicable for identifying the rights owner and the rights holders.

We consider that one must speak about a multiplicity of rights because there is a multiplicity of events. Who can be the rights owners and their associated prerogatives within the framework of these events?

1. the organizer/rights owner of the single event (i.e. tournaments, matches or tests);
2. the organizer/rights owner of the global event in which single events are integrated, or for which they receive an agreement (i.e. championship or total competition);
3. participants (i.e. clubs, athletes, referees, judges, spectators, etc.) who, it should not be forgotten, hold individual rights;
4. the facility or infrastructure owner where the competition takes place. This is less problematic when it is a public place (e.g. road, beach, sea, etc.). If this is a private place, its owner will hold rights on everything that can be organized in that place. Thus, if the facility owner has concluded a contract with a catering company to manage the stadium refreshment bars, the organizer of a meeting being held there will not have the right to contract a company of their choice to manage these bars, except of course, if this were specified in the contract. He or she will also not have the right to withdraw advertising in the stadium, if the facility owner has allocated the advertising exclusively to a company for a given period.

Ultimately, the assumption of competition economic risk responsibility does not grant all the event rights because they depend on a certain number of factors and circumstances. In addition, we consider that there is a multiplicity of properties which involves a multiplicity of rights.

Consequently, it is not always easy to provide an answer to the question concerning the property owner of the rights. In fact, this problem has been solved in very different ways from one country to another, from one sport to another, and from one period to another. Consequently, there cannot be, and does not have to exist, a generic and single theory on this question.

To say that there is a multiplicity of owners means that there can exist various parties who are likely to hold different rights on the event. One must consider various elements for determining the rights of each rights holder, which include the following:

1. *History and origin of the event.* The distribution of rights differs based on the type of event. For example, a comprehensive event created by combining a set of events that existed prior to the creation of the event (e.g. the UEFA Champions League, the World Rally Championship) has a different distribution of rights from an event created by combining various independent single events for the specific purpose of the said comprehensive event (e.g. the Formula 1, NBA Championships or the Volleyball World Cup).
2. *The capacity of each stakeholder to generate revenues generally classifies the priority of the rights distribution.* If clubs, for instance, can generate more revenue individually than jointly with the league, they will push for individual selling of their respective rights. If the league can generate more revenue for them, clubs will push for the joint selling of their individual rights.
3. *The political and social influence of each organization.* The political and social influence of clubs and interested companies operating within a professional league varies from country to country and from one sport to another. In Spain, football clubs enjoy a much greater stronghold within the professional football league than basketball clubs do in their own professional league. Consequently, Spanish professional football broadcast rights are distributed through individual selling, whereas the broadcasting rights to Spanish professional basketball are distributed through joint selling. The selling of broadcast rights is not only a matter of law, but is also based on the strength of influence and the market positioning.
4. *Legal framework of respective countries.* French, Italian and Spanish legislations forbid closed competitions, i.e. franchised leagues, unlike the United States where they are permitted. The various legal differences concerning the organization of these events affect the ownership of the rights. Furthermore, the situation differs according to individual national legislation and/or sporting regulations (is the right to participate in a sporting competition based on sports results, qualifications, etc., or is participation subjected to acceptance by the event organizer based on the European or American model of competition?).
5. *Tax regulations.* The rights owner of a club hosting an event must always ensure that the legal arrangement regarding the stadium where an event takes place is not detrimental to its individual ownership rights. For instance, French legislation mandates that a host club is the owner of the broadcast rights. This minimizes several difficulties because the legislation grants the rights in this case. However, the granting of rights to the host team is still problematic when the host team plays home matches in the stadium of a third party, as the host team is arguably unlikely to enjoy the complete benefit of the broadcast rights. Therefore, additional provisions may be necessary to ensure complete ownership of the rights.

6. *Antitrust and competition laws.* If the entity owning the comprehensive event exerts an abusive and monopolistic position, the owners of the single events can launch an antitrust action. Furthermore, the individual selling of rights to sporting competitions, especially with the exclusive transfer of broadcast rights, can conflict with antitrust and competition laws. In Europe and the United States, leagues and international federations have aggressively fought against the individual selling of broadcast rights.

In summary, given the plurality of rights holders and different types of sporting events, the rights of each interested party are subject to negotiations. In the event of a conflict of interests, the issue can be brought to the ruling court in an effort to consider all circumstances and to prevent abusive monopolistic practices.

Participation modes

Participants constitute the second group of subjects who must be accounted for in the organization of sporting events. The relationship between the participants and the event organizer is legally established through various facets of the participation modes. The factor of participation must be carefully considered because of its related legal characteristics.

Analysis

It was mentioned earlier that for an event to exist from a legal point of view, it needs an organizer for conceiving a name for the event, defining its format of competition, establishing the location where it will take place, etc., and engaging in measures legally protecting the identity and various aspects of the event. The existence of an event without participants is legally possible. For example, the 2008 Beijing Olympic Games already exists as an event, yet the actual organization of the event has yet to be developed. Additionally, broadcasting, merchandizing and sponsorship rights have been secured and marketing strategies have begun, yet no participant has been involved.

Nevertheless, although the event can have a legal existence in the absence of participants and, from a legal standpoint, the presence of participants does not have any significance on the development, organization and legal protection of an event, the justification and essential element for the existence of the event is the participation of athletes.

Participation modes are defined by the relationship existing between an individual or entity and the event. For example, the following individuals and entities are considered as participants to an event:

- athletes as individuals;
- sporting entities as a group (i.e. clubs, federations, sporting goods companies, etc.);
- sport technicians in a broad sense (i.e. coaches, trainers, doctors, physiotherapists, delegates, etc.);
- judges and referees;
- event spectators.

Any subject participating in an event holds and enjoys a series of rights and privileges. The organizer of the event, i.e. the rights owner or event manager, must take into account the individual rights of participants.

Participants do not yield their individual rights to the event organizer by merely taking part in the event. The acceptance of an athlete or club to participate in a sporting event does not automatically involve the transfer of image rights. The image, name, logo and trademark of participants are their property. Consequently, the organizer must obtain the authorization of participants to use the image, name, logo or trademark of any given participant on event-related merchandise. Securing this authorization is important for developing the event, as the image and/or trademark of the participants can be utilized to raise necessary revenues for staging the event.

Based on the assumption that participation in an event is voluntary, it can be said that athletes, clubs and spectators willingly engage in the event. This is a legally relevant fact, as the significance of the legal bond between the participants and the event is based on the principle of voluntary participation. There are two ways by which an organizer and a participant can be tied to an event:

- affiliation;
- contractual.

Ways for an event organizer and a participant to be tied

Participation in sporting events via the affiliation system is typical of traditional sporting structures such as sporting federations, clubs, and the Olympic movement, which are based on the associative model. Under the affiliation system, an athlete is registered with a sporting entity, e.g. a club, which is affiliated to a national federation that is affiliated to an international federation.

The system of subordination is achieved by the intermediation of the participation guidelines. The organizer of the event establishes the conditions of participation by applying various requirements for participation such as entrance fees, publicity agreements, affiliation, etc. These requirements, along with their respective rights and responsibilities, are specified in the technical conditions of the event.

The regulations adopted by the event organizer establish the rights and obligations of each participant. When an athlete, club, trainer or referee voluntarily engages in an event, he or she implicitly accepts the rules, rights and duties implemented by the event organizer. For example, an international federation organizes a competition (e.g. a world championship) where participating athletes are not authorized to wear publicity on their jersey, as stipulated by the bylaws of the international federation. Consequently, participating athletes (by choosing to affiliate with the said federation), are not in a position to plead that they have an individual right to publicize the company of their choice. Thus, these athletes must abide by the competition rules dictated by the event organizer or entity authorizing the event.

However, this general rule of affiliation has characteristics, with some limitations, that require an explanation of how participants are subordinated to the rules of an event. To grasp the peculiarities and limits of these rules, an explanation of how participants are subordinated to the rules of an event is necessary. In short, there are four case scenarios:

1. An athlete, referee, coach or club takes part in a sporting event as the result of the system of voluntary affiliation and without a document of subordination other than a

sporting licence, or a document of affiliation of a club to a national federation. This does not generally contain a reference to any necessary subordination to the standards of the federation nor anything requiring the transfer of individual rights, such as the right to the image, name, trademark, logo, etc. Consequently, the organizer could make a request to a club or federation asking permission to amend the individual rights of participants, but it cannot request the transfer of individual rights.

2. An athlete (in a broad sense), coach, referee or club subscribing to an event is accepting the standards established by the organizer via an adhesion contract, i.e., an explicit document agreeing to subordination. This form of participation is typical when the organizer envisions the transfer of the individual rights of participants. Adhesion contracts, in spite of the voluntary act of tender, are typically imbalanced, which necessitates the need for the event organizer to act in good faith. Regardless, the organizer has the ability to restrict certain individual rights or require a temporary transfer of these rights if it appears essential to the proper execution of the event, but only when it is not individually abusive.

3. An athlete, coach, referee or club who signs a service contract with the organizer enabling participation in an event is bound to the rules of the event. For example, the participants of the Intercontinental Cup enter into a contractual relationship with the event organizer. The organizer thus incorporates all the conditions deemed necessary for the purpose of the event in the contract. In this type of contract, it is essential to incorporate every conceivable clause, particularly when the transfer of broadcast rights and/or image rights with a view to promoting the event is possible, because only provisions provided for in the contract can be legally upheld or enforced. Service contracts are typically more balanced, given that they result from negotiations between the participant and the event organizer.

4. Spectators participate in the event and enter into a contractual relationship with the event organizer via their purchase of an entry ticket, yet they do not yield any individual rights to the organizer in the process. The purchase of an entry ticket falls within the domain of public spectacle regulations, thereby subjecting entry ticket owners to the standards, rights and duties of that regulation. The only requirement of the spectator is compliance with the said regulations of public ordinance while attending the event. Furthermore, the organizer cannot exploit the image of a spectator in promoting an event, unless the promoter enters into a separate commercial relationship with the spectator. For instance, say Zinedine Zidane attended a tennis tournament and the event organizer wanted to use the image of this famous football player to promote the event in order to publicize that the event is a high-level competition that is enjoyed by famous personalities. Without a separate commercial agreement between the organizer and Zinedine Zidane, using his image (or that of any spectator) is illegal.

We have three levels of engagement between the participant and the organizer here:

- participation by the simple fact of voluntary engagement;
- participation by means of the signing of a document of explicit subordination to the organizer (which could be regarded as a contract of adhesion);
- participation by means of a contract.

In each situation, the legal position between the participant and the organizer will be different. We stressed the fact that the event organizer can set conditions by means of regulation, and provide some rights and duties on the participants. This capacity is not absolute and has some limit:

1. if the relation is indirect (i.e. when there is no direct legal relation between the participant and the organizer);
2. where there is no possibility of creating a situation of rights abuse.

Indirect relation

Suppose a football player voluntarily participates with club X in a national league championship and knowingly accepts the rules governing this event. During the season, this club decides to engage in an international competition, which is governed by a different set of rules. The athlete has a legal relationship with the club (he committed to play with this team), including a bond with the national federation (by means of a sporting licence), but does not have any bond with the organization which governs the international competition. Indeed, it is the national federation or the club which signed a tender to take part in the competition. Must the athlete comply with the rules of the international federation, when no legal relationship exists between them, not even an associative bond? Although this athlete does not have any legal obligation to the international federation, the club and/or federation, for which he voluntarily participates, is legally bound to the international federation. The football player is subjected to an indirect normative subordination based on the principle of voluntary participation.

To avoid indirect normative subordination issues, the event organizer should arrange for an explicit voluntary subordination, i.e. a contract. Explicit voluntary subordination relates to the consent of each participant in the sporting event to the rules governing the event in a very precise, clear, manner. Increasingly, event organizers (e.g. of the Olympic Games or World Championships) are requesting that participants sign a contract by which they explicitly accept the rules and standards governing the event. After signing this document one moves from a lawful subordination to a contractual subordination. Actually, when the athlete signs this document, he or she concludes an adhesion contract, and is thus committed to respecting the rights and duties deriving from the contract, whose contents refer to the rules. Moreover, this document of adhesion will be explicit and comprise extended clauses, strengthening the legal safety and guarantees between the parties.

The possibility of creating a situation of individual rights abuse

The capacity of the event organizer to impose a series of rights and obligations upon participants has limitations when the participation is indirect and results in an infringement of individual rights. Although labour law forbids infringement of the rights of others, it is difficult to determine, based solely on the reading of a contract, whether the individual rights of the participants are actually being abused. Indeed, perceptions of what constitutes rights infringement vary according to the dominant political culture and the geographical context during a particular period.

For example, the recording and broadcasting of images of a sporting event in the daily news is neither abusive nor prejudicial to the individual rights of the participants. However, as the previous example demonstrated, publishing images of celebrities, attending the event in a private capacity for commercial, and/or advertising purposes, would be.

There is an infinite variety of case scenarios, which may infringe the individual rights of the participants between the two examples just given. Ultimately, it is up to the courts to determine whether the event organizer is abusing its position or not. The following list contains the principal aspects to consider when determining whether there is a rights abuse.

- Does the event organizer have a monopoly or quasi-monopoly on organizing this type of event?
- Does the event organizer occupy a dominant position?
- Does the event organizer receive any provision of services in exchange for a participant taking part in the event?
- Is the transfer of rights balanced?
- Is the process for the transfer of rights clear and transparent?
- Is it a full or partial transfer of rights?
- Are the rights being transferred to the event organizer going to be marketed?

Circumstances of individual's rights cession

In this domain we must indicate that in terms of cession of participants' individual rights to the organizer (mainly the image, the name, the logo, the trademark, etc.), there are four types of situations:

1. When participation occurs by means of a freely negotiated contract, e.g. a service contract, parties can proceed to any type of transfer and establish unlimited clauses defining their rights and duties, provided they comply with the legal regulation(s) in force.
2. When participation occurs by means of an adhesion contract, i.e. a contractual agreement whereby the participant is compelled to accept the rules imposed by the event organizer, the transfer of the rights of the participant must be limited and achieved solely to ensure the proper execution of the event. Adhesion contracts can explicitly transfer certain individual rights provided that the transfer of rights is legally justifiable.
3. Participation without an adhesion contract or an acceptance of the standards occurs generally by the signature of the sporting licence or the affiliation of the club. When participation occurs without any contract, i.e. by means of a licence, the event organizer cannot use the individual rights of the participant, since the mere signing of a licence does not grant the privilege to transfer individual rights (i.e. image, trademark, logo, etc.).
4. When participation occurs by means of the purchase of an entry ticket for the event, the spectator does not yield any individual rights. Consequently, the event organizer cannot use nor restrict the individual rights of spectators beyond what is necessary for the maintenance of law and order, and the respect of others (e.g. prohibition of wearing of clothes with racist or xenophobic image or slogans).

If we apply this analysis to a given event, we can identify three types of situations.

By means of a contract

A participant can concede any individual right to the organizer in a contract, thereby allowing the latter to market these rights before, during and after the event. It is also possible to reach an agreement whereby athletes must use particular apparel or equipment. Indeed, it is acceptable that a major sponsor bargains for participants to use its material and/or equipment, if such a scenario is freely negotiated and agreed upon by both parties. Furthermore, the organizer can also license the individual rights of the participants to sponsors, if the contract between the organizer and the participant grants this right.

By means of an adhesion contract

In an adhesion contract, the organizer can secure the transfer of certain rights in the rules it establishes for the event. For example, it is reasonable to assume that the organizer will retain the broadcast rights to an event after they officially expire (such as the Olympic Charter for the Olympic Games provides for). Likewise, the marketing rights for the stadium will also remain the property of the stadium owner (e.g. the publicity contract between UEFA and the League Champions). However, it would be abusive to compel all participants to wear the same branded apparel and/or equipment, or require them to use a particular brand, even if it is the brand of a company sponsoring the event. Given the nature of adhesion contracts, the only benefit a participant receives in exchange for yielding its individual rights is the right to participate in the event. The organizer can use the images of the athletes participating in the event for advertising and/or commercial purposes, but he or she cannot concede them to a third party or sponsor to exploit.

If there is no adhesion contract

When participation in an event is granted through a licence, the licence bearer (i.e. athlete, referee or club) retains all its individual rights. Therefore, the event organizer can distribute images of the event for informational purposes only. However, the event organizer can prohibit publicity on participating athletes by imposing certain standards. Likewise, the event organizer (e.g. UEFA) can impose broadcast standards for the distribution of events for which an affiliated club (e.g. Manchester United) is the rights owner. The event organizer cannot appropriate the broadcast rights of the participant, nor can he or she use or transfer the images of the participants to a third party for the purpose of promoting the event.

Contractual bond

The relationship to an event can be formalized through the drafting and signing of a contract between the event organizer and a party interested in the event. This work focuses mostly on the following types of contracts:

- management/organization (presented previously);
- advertising;
- sponsorship;

- TV contract (for the cession of audiovisual rights);
- licensing and merchandising.

Each of the different contract types will be examined in Chapter 4. For now, suffice it to mention that the drafting and negotiating of a contract should be addressed meticulously because it is the cornerstone of the relationship between the event organizer and an interested party. The rights and duties of each party are derived from the terms of the contract, which is binding. Therefore, it is imperative that the range of the rights and duties of each one is precisely defined.

National legislations generally allow contractual freedom and do not set legal obligations with the drafting of contracts. Therefore, the negotiated terms of the contract constitute the only acceptable reference in a court of law.

Legal link relating to the contract

There is a common misperception that sporting event stakeholders are restricted to athletes, federations, sponsors, etc. However, the legislation of some countries may secure a series of rights for the benefit of other stakeholders who are not closely involved in the event. Although not directly involved in the event, other people can be regarded as 'stakeholders' of the event, given the rights they hold in connection with it. For instance, the proprietor of a house or building next to the sporting facility holds a number of irrefragable rights binding the event organizer to ensure, for example, that the environment of the former is safe and peaceful. Encroachment of these rights can cause an event to be cancelled if, for example, that particular proprietor complained about the noise pollution caused by the event.

As a tangible demonstration of a social phenomenon called 'sport', the event must consider the sporting rules governing the concerned sporting activity. The purpose of these standards can be to protect and to promote sport. But they can be enacted from the restrictive point of view, to control and protect the thirds parties' rights.

Sporting events occur within a social environment, and laws have been enacted with the purpose of protecting and promoting public interest. A brief, non-exhaustive overview of important public interest laws relevant to sporting events is addressed in the following section.

Media: rights to information

Freedom of information, a major element of democracy, is the right of access to information for all people. The legislations of many countries assert that public information, including sporting events, must be available to all people. The right of access to information relates to all types of media, such as television, radio and the press, all of which play an essential role in the distribution of information.

The systems protecting or guaranteeing the right to information vary from one country to another. Thus, it is always important to know the legislation of the country where an event takes place. Nevertheless, a broad outline of the guarantees and protection mechanisms of the right of access to information in relation to sporting events can be given.

- The right to publish news essentially depends on the ability to gather information, which is dependent on media access. Hence, the media have a right of access to the facility where the sporting event takes place. This right is neither absolute nor unlimited. A variety of factors can either facilitate or hinder the access of the media to the event (e.g. the environment of the event, facility capacity, technical means, etc.) The event organizer can grant the media free or restricted access by providing different types of accreditations. If media access is prohibited or impossible, the organizer of the event may need to provide the media with information about and/or images of the event.
- Media access to sporting facilities is the subject of an intense debate between polarized groups of advocates. Some advocates claim that by prohibiting media access to a sporting facility and selecting a limited number of images, equivalent to the maximum allotment for sports information (e.g. three minutes), the organizer of a sporting event is actually facilitating the distribution of images and information to the public. However, by law, it would clearly be unacceptable to omit distributing the important goals or facts about a sporting event: the event organizer must submit images and/or information arousing public interest. Other people advocate for the full broadcast of sporting events, arguing that it is the role of the media to select key images and construct information about the event.
- Television broadcasting is subjected to variables such as space and duration. The event organizer can assign the media to any location within the sporting facility, provided that the location offers a reasonable view of the event. Therefore, no legal provision exists regarding the location where a broadcaster must be positioned. Although there is no provision with regard to the duration for which a broadcaster is granted access to an event, restricting a broadcaster's access could be construed as an infringement of the right of media access.
- The media have the right to disseminate information (images included). This right to information is nevertheless subjected to certain material and temporal limits common to all countries.

There are common limitations in all countries on the right to information:

- The information gathered, including images, can only be used for informative purposes. For example, a photographer can sell their picture of a football player to a newspaper for the purpose of inserting it in the sports section; by contrast, the photographer cannot sell their picture to a company for commercial and/or advertising purposes. Likewise, the event broadcaster cannot sell images of the event or participants to a company for commercial and/or advertising purposes.
- The use of gathered information is subject to a limited duration. A television network can take an unlimited number of images of the event, but it cannot invoke its media access right for disseminating the entire event; broadcasting rights must be obtained. According to most jurisprudence, television networks without broadcasting rights can reasonably broadcast information on a sporting event no longer than three minutes. However, this maximum duration criterion must be examined on a case-by-case basis (e.g. three minutes of highlights of a day's events in the Champions League is hardly comparable to three minutes of highlights of a 100 meter sprint).

Consumers and users

From a legal and administrative point of view, a sporting event is a public show. Consequently, an organizer of an event maintains certain benefits and limitations within a given territory. There are specific measures governing public events. These measures have a direct effect on spectators and the media.

Spectators

In most countries, the event organizer must guarantee the safety of spectators by ensuring that police, doctors and paramedics are part of a safety management plan. In addition, there are standards prohibiting access restriction to an event based on discrimination (e.g. sex, age, religion, social status, etc.). However, the access to a sporting event can be restricted based on:

- the capacity of the sporting facility;
- the maintenance of law and order (e.g. prohibited items);
- the payment of an entry fee, etc.

Access to sporting events can, however, be prohibited to certain categories of people specified by law. In addition, it is necessary, to guarantee the safety of spectators and all the people attending the event and for this reason the police force has the right to intervene in any sporting event.

Distant audience

The national legislations of many countries impose a series of rules concerning the television broadcasts which are aimed at protecting media consumers, as well as the organizers of events (e.g. the Television Without Frontier directive[4] (TWF) imposes a series of directives aimed at regulating television broadcast activities across Europe, including advertising). Some of these EU directives have a direct effect on sporting events.

1. The advertisement of tobacco and alcohol is prohibited inside sporting facilities, as well as during the television broadcast of sporting events.
2. The broadcast of commercials during the sporting event is prohibited. However, the broadcast of advertisements during intermissions and breaks is authorized. Bumper breaks are authorized only when the sporting action is stopped.
3. There is an obligation to transmit the sporting event in its entirety. When a sporting event is publicized as a specific programme, the entire event must be transmitted – unless the length of the event exceeds the allotted airtime. According to the TWF directive, viewers are entitled to the complete transmission of the event, without interruptions. There is no such obligation, however, if the transmission of the event is incorporated into a larger programme. Some sports programmes broadcast several sporting events simultaneously and are allowed to stop the transmission of an event for the purpose of inserting advertisements. In this case, the sport event announcer must announce the advertisement insertion beforehand.

4. In certain countries, the sporting event must be broadcast on free-to-air television. France, Spain and Portugal, for example, consider that certain sporting events are of public interest and these events must be accessible to all on free-to-air television. As required by the TWF directive, each country must produce a major events list – that is, a list of events a country deems worth broadcasting on public television. The major events list of most countries generally includes the Olympic Games and the football World Cup, yet the remainder of the list varies from country to country. It is interesting to point out that the Spanish parliament passed a law to the effect that each day of the football Champions League is of public interest. Therefore, a segment of play of each day of the Champions League must be transmitted on public television (irrespective of which football match). Event organizers must be aware that, in some countries, viewers have a legal right to watch certain sporting events live on public television.

Secondary stakeholders and protected commodities

We underlined previously that a sporting event must be regarded as a public spectacle. There is a wide spectrum of people implied or indirectly interested in the unfolding of this spectacle. This list can be very long, from the neighbour who can plead concern for public safety or harmful noise nuisance (e.g. many jurisprudences exist which have restricted the ringing of church bells during the night because they disturbed the sleep of neighbours, and these can be similarly applied to a stage spectacle or event where the singing or noise of spectators disturbs the nearby community). This also concerns the owner of the grounds where a rally test or mountain bike race takes place.

The list of people and public domain property indirectly affected by an event can be substantial. In the context of sports event management, the following standards should be taken into account:

1. *Environmental protection standards.* These concern location and time; sporting events must be organized at approved sites and/or at certain hours. For instance, it is prohibited to organize a sporting event in a protected natural/wildlife area without special authorization. Thus, the organizer of the Spanish cycling tour *La Vuelta* cannot organize stages through certain mountain passes because they are declared protected natural areas.
2. *Public space standards.* Sporting events cannot be organized on roads, streets, public places and beaches unless authorized by the appropriate administrative body.
3. *Standards of public safety, maintenance of law and order, and public health.* Sporting events must comply with the public regulations of safety and policies in place for public events. In certain cities, for example, sporting events cannot be organized late in the evening.
4. *Health standards.* Countries must ensure the health protection of their population. Depending on the legislation of the country where the sporting event takes place, or the standards of the sports body authorizing the event, maintaining health standards can be incumbent on the organizer. For example, the event manager must facilitate access to the sporting facility for authorized regulators, such as accredited anti-doping agency personnel. In the current legal and political context, it is increasingly difficult to justify an absence of doping control during a sporting event or to refuse doping control on the basis that the event is private.

Conclusion

In this chapter, the sporting event has been defined from a legal point of view. Various stakeholders interested in the event have been identified, along with their rights and the protection mechanisms of these rights. In summary, operational sponsorship must address the following tasks.

1. From a legal point of view, the fundamental elements required for defining a sporting event are identification, differentiation and organization.
2. Identification is the naming of the event. Registering trademarks and industrial designs pertaining to the event are included in the identification because they signify the name of the event.
3. Differentiation is a derivative of identification. The definition, description and regulations of an event serve to differentiate it.
4. The description of a sporting event must include the characteristics of the sport; the type of participants; the location, date and duration of the event; the significance of the results at the sporting level; the organizer, etc.
5. The set of rules (e.g. the rules of the game, the rules of publicity, etc.) governing the event must be an integral part of the definition of the event.
6. The organizer has the right to implement legal procedures to protect the sporting event from appropriation by third parties.
7. Sport in general, including sport activities, is not property that can be owned. Anyone can freely participate in and/or organize any type of sporting event. A sporting event, however, can be legally owned, even prior to its full development.
8. The sporting event is the key element of legal protection, not the sport. Sport is the medium; the event is the product or service.
9. The event organizer must orchestrate all available legal mechanisms for ensuring the most comprehensive protection of the event nationally and internationally.
10. The rights and duties derived from the event are based on distinctive modes of participation (i.e. ownership, contractual, peremptory rights, etc.) in the event.
11. The owner of the event can yield its management rights to a third party, so the latter can organize the event on its behalf. The scope of this privilege must be precisely defined in a contract.
12. There are various types of events based on ownership:

    * Independent event: a single event with one owner who has extended rights.
    * Integrated and authorized event: a series of singly owned and authorized events incorporate into a larger event that is governed by a distinct entity. Each single event, or series of single events, is an independent event, but owners must coordinate with the overall event and negotiate with one another. There is a diversity of possible case scenarios according to the situation.
    * Complex event: the overall event has one owner with a number of rights owners for each event. The series of individual events constitutes the overall event; the individual events are dependent on each other for the overall event to exist. The owner of the overall event cannot exert pressure on the constituents and must orchestrate their individual rights.

13. In general, sporting events are owned by a number of parties with individual and collective rights, which must be considered and arranged to achieve the desired outcome.
14. The rights of the event's owner are neither absolute nor unlimited. A number of stake-holders hold a series of rights (e.g. consumer protection) in connection with the event.
15. The system of participation of the event determines the extent of the event owner's rights in relation to the individual rights of the participants.

3
Strategic and operational sponsorship implementation

The sponsorship strategy and implementation must be defined in connection with the desired impact on the targeted group. Meenaghan (2001), in his article devoted to explaining the effects of sponsorship, noted that relatively little is known about the operational methods of sponsorship. Until recently, research was primarily focused on evaluating the impact of such variables as brand awareness, image and perceived acceptance. However, it is important to understand the fundamentals of this strategy of persuasive communication in order to go beyond the traditional trial-and-error empirical approach.

The first part of this chapter focuses on an explanatory model of sponsorship based on the interaction between cognitive and emotional processes. This model serves as a basis for explaining the sponsorship strategies used by potential sponsors and by the sponsored entity. Next, the discussion progresses to the design and implementation of a sponsorship programme. Additionally, the strategy for developing a plan to ensure the satisfaction and loyalty of sponsor partners through quality service is examined. Lastly, this chapter examines the process of evaluating the impact of the sponsorship operation.

Sponsorship and persuasive communication

Cornwell *et al.* (2005) highlight that literature has yet to find a theoretical framework for gauging the effectiveness of sponsorship in a marketing context, and that very little has been done to improve our understanding of sponsorship-linked marketing communications to people. To achieve this understanding, the framework of persuasive communication is utilized to examine the interaction between cognitive and emotional processes more closely.

The processes of persuasive communication

Various models of persuasive communication originate from work at Yale, particularly that of Hovland *et al.* (1945) who proposed analysing the persuasion mechanism based on the interaction of the following factors: the source of the message, the message itself, the channel and the person who receives the message. Independent factors influencing persuasion act not only directly on people's tendencies to accept the conclusions of messages, but also indirectly through their impact on two unintentional prior processes: attention and comprehension. The role of cognitive processes in persuasion was subsequently established as the product of six information-processing steps. In his work on the influence of the media and advertising on behaviour, Kapferer (1988) developed an experimental model where persuasion is understood as 'the modification of attitude and its types of behaviour by exposure to a message'. This concept of attitude constitutes the role of persuasion in sponsorship. The model put in place by Kapferer slightly differs from that of the Yale school, especially in the processes pertaining to the selective exposure to a message, to the allocation of attention required to perceive the message, and the way opinions are being actively modified by it.

As a strategy of persuasive communication, sponsorship is likely to influence a number of variables in the cognitive process:

1. *Exposure to the message.* Although individuals are exposed to a vast number of messages on a daily basis, only a small number are likely to be influential because individuals are either not searching for information or evade it. Sponsorship has a competitive advantage over media advertising as it is anchored in peoples' centre of interest. Thus, targeted people willingly expose themselves to the messages of associated sponsors.
2. *Decoding.* This phase relates to the way in which a targeted person understands the message. Decoding is achieved when the assimilation of a compatible association of the sponsor with the event is made. This process will be examined in detail later in this section.
3. *Process of acceptance or rejection.* The effectiveness of a sponsorship project depends on the compatibility of the association between the sponsor and the sponsored entity (i.e. the 'fit') and the message communicated from this association. The emotions derived from the event are catalysts for the process of acceptance or rejection of the message and association presented.
4. *Attitude modification.* Sponsorship is likely to modify three attitude components with respect to the sponsor: cognitive, emotional and behavioural. For example, Ford, as the sponsor of the UEFA Champions League, may appear in the eyes of the supporters as European and important (i.e. cognitive component) and perceived as a pleasurable brand (i.e. emotional component), which may be influential in the decision to make a purchase (i.e. behavioural component).
5. *Sustainability of attitude changes.* It is essential to reinforce the attitude changes through repeated sponsorship operations. For instance, Mercedes is the official automobile supplier of the ATP Masters Series. It allows this company to be associated with nine premier events organized throughout the year, in Indian Wells, Miami, Monte-Carlo, Rome, Hamburg, Canada, Cincinnati, Madrid and Paris, thereby reinforcing the sustainability of attitude changes.
6. *Change in purchasing behaviour.* The primary concern pertains to the link between an attitude change towards a sponsor and subsequent purchasing behaviour, i.e. purchase or repurchase. The model of Ajzen and Fishbein (1980) suggests that behaviour is strongly influenced by one's attitude and intentions. In the context of sponsorship, it is difficult to validate this assumption given that sponsorship is incorporated within the marketing strategy of an enterprise. Nevertheless, studies by McCarville *et al.* (1998)

and Pracejus and Olsen (2004) substantiate the claim that sponsorship influences purchasing behaviour when it is supported by a number of marketing moves.

Sponsorship interconnects with the psychological process of persuasive communication. Therefore, when the association, or the 'fit', is well managed, sponsorship has an influence on attitude and consequently on purchasing behaviour. However, the model remains cognitive orientated, to the extent that altering the emotional component of attitude relies on information processing, i.e. the comprehension of the message. Sport events supply experiences and that emotion constitutes its essence: sponsorship strategy is based on emotion. Research projects by Speed and Thompson (2000), Becker-Olsen and Simmons (2002) and Ruth and Simonin (2003) have revealed a number of affective outcomes related to sponsorship such as preference and linking. Furthermore, Derbaix et al. (1994) examined the transfer of emotion between the event and the sponsor without an activation of the cognitive processes, thereby suggesting that cognitive processes may be subordinated to emotions.

In analysing the impact of sponsorship as a method of persuasive communication, focus is made on the interaction between cognitive and emotional processes based on the theoretical frameworks of Zajonc and Markus (1982) and Holbrook and Hirschman (1982). Accordingly, sponsored events provide the public with an experience based on sensations, emotions and symbols likely to generate behavioural acquisitions. According to Dussard (1983: 45), 'behavioural acquisition can be defined as the set of changes, due to experiences, influencing the response pattern of a consumer to various stimuli'.

Dynamics model for sponsorship tied to the interaction of cognitive, emotional and behavioural processes

The model presented in Figure 3.1 is based on the dynamic model of emotional response described by Cohen and Areni (1991). It incorporates the three components of attitude towards the sponsor, namely: cognitive, emotional and conative (i.e. behavioural).

The factors influencing attitude ensue from the emotional and cognitive processes derived from the event, by means of which it is possible to influence behaviour.

This model is organized into three phases distinguished by the type of cognitive activity that is likely to be associated with the emotional and the behavioural response. It should be noted that this process can be interrupted prematurely, thus affecting the impact of a sponsorship. The previously mentioned cognitive processes arise from a positive emotional experience. When the association of a sponsor appears legitimate, the sponsor is perceived positively for contributing to the event. In this context, a favourable attitude with respect to a brand does not require cognitive antecedents.

Attitudes predict behavioural trends better than any one behaviour making up that trend. The process can be summarized as follows: a person's interest in the event leads him or her to watch it and have fun; the person identifies the sponsor, then accepts or rejects the association of the sponsor with the event, thereby positively or negatively reinforcing or transferring the association. If positive reinforcement occurs, brand awareness can influence an individual's preference for the sponsor's brand and lead him or her to purchase its brand. This process is similar to the emotional conditioning described by Ganassali and Didelon (1996), Derbaix et al. (1994) and Speed and Thompson (2000).

Figure 3.1 Sports sponsorship effects on components governing attitude towards sponsors

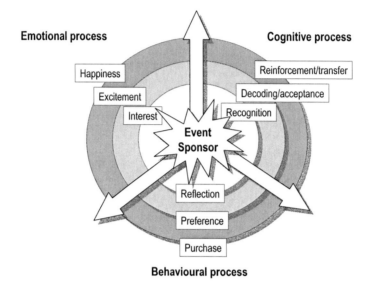

The impact of sponsorship on the cognitive and emotional components of the attitude towards the sponsor is then likely to alter attitude behaviour via the following causal chain: the scope of brands from which to purchase, to a preference for a given brand, followed by a purchase or repurchase of the brand. In any case, it is essential to associate sponsorship with other marketing strategies in order to instigate such behavioural effects.

The interface between the event and the sponsor

The associations between the event and the sponsor occur through mental functions. As shown in Figure 3.2, associations ensue from three features unique to the sports sponsorship platform: (1) characteristics of the event; (2) the fit between the event and the sponsor; (3) characteristics of the sponsor.

Ferrand and Pagès (1996) focused on the interface between the Perrier brand and the Lyon's Tennis Grand Prix, and identified three corresponding associations.

1. characteristics of the event: stylish and commercially oriented;
2. characteristics of Perrier: natural;
3. common characteristics: entertaining, dynamic and successful.

The sustaining partnership between Perrier and the ATP Lyon's Tennis Grand is likely to reinforce existing associations and trigger new associations with the Perrier brand. Figure 3.3 illustrates three processes resulting from this partnership.

1. transfer of certain associations of the event towards the sponsor;
2. transfer of certain associations of the sponsor towards the event;
3. reinforcement of common associations shared by the event and the sponsor.

Figure 3.2 The interactions between the event and the sponsor

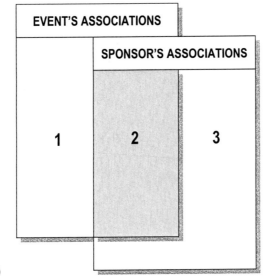

Source: Ferrand (1995)

Figure 3.3 Sponsorship reinforcement and transfer model

Source: Ferrand (1995)

The work of Howard and Sheth (1969) establishes that there is a secondary learning principle supplementing the conditioning principle, i.e. the contiguity principle. This contiguity principle suggests that feelings, symbols/imagery, emotions and fun, as well as other hedonistic or symbolic components blending into the experience, tend to work to reinforce one another.

Processes generated by the activation of a sponsor's brand

The model shown in Figure 3.3 reveals how complex it is to influence people's attitude towards a sponsor through the association of the latter with an event. In order to activate their brand with specific operations, the Olympic Games sponsors, whose respective brands cannot appear on competitor's sites, essentially bought the exclusive rights to exploit their association with the OG. Sponsors tend to invest more in activating their brand via media sponsorship than they do for securing rights with the owner of the event (ratios vary up to 5:1). Additionally, sponsors are also controlling the processes more effectively.

To illustrate the media sponsorship process, let us look at how Continental, official sponsor of the 2006 FIFA World Cup, utilizes this type of sponsorship process. One of Continental's ads begins by zooming in on a crowded football stadium embedded in a Continental tyre. A human goalkeeper remains calm while watching a robot coming out of the pitch. The robot adjusts its lenses while readying itself to shoot the ball into the top corner, but then the goalkeeper easily stops the speeding ball with his glove. When the goalkeeper releases his grip on the ball, his glove leaves a tyre mark imprinted on the surface of the ball. Clearly, Continental's purpose is to reactivate emotions experienced during a football match by reinforcing associations related to Continental tyres' performance, reliability and safety. The ad is merely one component of the sponsorship activation plan, as Continental also organizes lotteries, tournaments, direct marketing, etc. Such marketing operations are essential to obtain a return on investment.

An operational model based on the interaction of dimensions relating to brand equity

The interface model in Figure 3.2 shows the role of emotions in the creation of mental associations between a sporting event and its sponsor. The interface model, however, is just one element of a complex system where the brand equity of multiple sponsorship partners is engaged in various interactions. This section introduces a system for managing brand equity and the dynamics of experiential processes implemented in the field of sponsorship.

The system of brand equity

Chapter 1 illustrates how sponsorship operations aim at generating a particular experience with the brand. Brand equity is created in the minds of consumers, within a given market, in response to competition, and has an effect on consumers' responses. Keller (1993: 8) defines customer-based brand equity as 'the differential effect of brand knowledge on consumer response to the marketing of the brand'.

To demonstrate how the brand equity of the sponsor and that of the sponsored entity are managed, the following model has been developed (Ferrand and Torrigiani 2005). The system of brand equity includes six aspects: stakeholders, foundations, legal protection, brand knowledge, brand experience and relationship value. These dimensions must be linked together in order to constitute a durable and stable unit. They form a ladder (Figure 3.4) where brand foundations and its stakeholders constitute the two sides, which are

Figure 3.4 The brand equity ladder

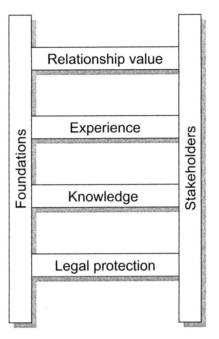

Source: Adapted from Ferrand and Torrigiani (2005)

strongly bounded by four bars (i.e. legal protection, brand knowledge, brand experience and relationship value).

Stakeholders

A brand is primarily an entity with a relationship with interested parties, i.e. with any person or entity exposed to the brand. Earlier, various stakeholders of the event-driven, sporting, and territorial systems were introduced. In line with Freeman's (1984) definition, they are specific people or organizations who have a stake in the brand. They could be current and prospective customers, the sponsor's personnel and suppliers, political authorities, etc. The social and political impact that the brand derives from stakeholders is a key aspect of brand equity. The impact will depend on the number and characteristics of the stakeholders, as well as the influence and nature of their relationships with the brand. Since one of the priorities of sponsorship is to merge interested parties, relationship marketing strategies facilitating collaborative programmes are recommended.

Foundations

The foundations of a brand are related to its history, vision and identity. The sponsorship strategy induces various interactions between the brands of a sponsor and that of a sponsored entity.

History

Each brand possesses its own tangible and intangible assets. At the corporate level, history corresponds to the experience and reputation that the brand acquired over time. Abimbola *et al.* (1999) point out that these characteristics also relate to the origins of the brand and the evolution of its communication. In short, a brand must be consistent with its history, no matter how short it is. Thus, it is imperative to know that the history of a brand considering sponsorship can be aligned, insofar as there is a fit at this level, with the history of a well-known entity such as the America's Cup.

Vision

According to Chappelet (2004), vision refers to shared values and an implicit ideal, which is difficult to achieve per se. It is thus important to examine which values should be associated with the brand. According to Rokeach (1973), value is a strong conviction that a specific mode of behaviour or purpose of existence is individually or socially preferable to another behaviour or purpose of existence. These values are promoted through commercial and corporate sponsorship.

Identity

The process of creating and giving strength to the identity of the brand, as well as the mental concept of the logo and the physical emblem, is what defines identity. While brand image refers to the actual perception of the brand, brand identity refers to 'how strategists want the brand to be perceived' (Aaker 1996). Brand identity emits a message and elicits a response from consumers through sponsorship operations, particularly validity and acceptance of the image.

Legal protection

We stressed this important aspect in Chapter 2. It is imprudent to invest in the development of a brand without protecting it because brands with strong brand equity are frequently imitated. Therefore, legal action must be taken to prevent competitors from using the name, colours, design and theme of a brand. Essentially, each brand is owned by an entity that must engage legal trademark procedures to protect its brand. Sponsorship incorporates legal protection as an integral part of the marketing approach.

Brand awareness

The objective of brand awareness and brand image communication operations is to leave people with a memory of the brand. In developing brand awareness, it is important to design communication messages that reflect the brand's unique value for specific audiences. These two concepts were developed in Chapter 1.

Experience

Experience refers to all the interactions that the stakeholders have with the brand. These interactions occur via the particular interface stakeholders have with the brand (e.g.

communication, personnel, service, equipment, etc.). The experience brings forth two essential psychological conditions of satisfaction and perceived quality (Oliver 1997). Satisfaction depends on both cognitive and emotional components tied to the experience with the brand, whereby the emotional impact of sponsorship can influence satisfaction with the brand. Additionally, the perceived quality can be influenced by sponsorships that strategize to associate a brand with the performance and services of an event.

Value relationship

The brand is at the heart of all transactions occurring between stakeholders. The relationship between stakeholders relies on the emotional component of attitude, i.e. on satisfaction or dissatisfaction of the relationship with the brand. The relationship with the brand can be characterized by its content (i.e. the related benefits; functional, emotional, socio-cultural and psychological), duration (i.e. length of the relationship) and intensity (i.e. frequency and commitment to the brand). The duration and intensity enable the loyalty level of the interested parties towards the brand to be evaluated.

Analysis of fit in brand equity

The analysis of fit for the brand equity of the sponsor and that of the sponsored entity is made up of aspects which can be qualitatively evaluated, i.e. image, perceived quality, interested parties, etc., and aspects which can be quantitatively evaluated, i.e. brand awareness, loyalty, etc. The qualitative analysis identifies common and distinctive features of each entity with a view to forecasting the possible outcome of a sponsorship operation. The analysis of fit is summarized in Figure 3.5.

The first phase of the analysis of fit consists of evaluating the common and distinctive aspects of the brand equity of each partner. The second phase aims at finding ways to reduce possible mismatches between the current brand equity of the potential sponsor and the desired brand equity. The implementation of the second phase can occur through reinforcement (e.g. brand awareness), creation or repositioning (e.g. value relationship) of the brand. Thereafter, it is essential to evaluate the coverage and the credibility of the association between the two partners. The analysis of fit can be carried out using Tables 3.1 and 3.2.

A sponsor can increase the proportion of targeted customers who know about the existence and availability of its products or services by associating its brand with a well-known event, or by associating its brand with an event that is highly valued by the targeted audience.

Acceptance and perceived sincerity

Speed and Thompson (2000) developed a method for analysing the various aspects resulting from the interaction between the sponsored entity and the sponsor. Two aspects are especially useful for the diagnosis: the strength of the association between the event and the sponsor, and the perceived sincerity of the sponsor's intentions.

The strength of the association between the sponsor and event can be assessed through interviews with people interested in the event or by asking them to respond to a

Figure 3.5 Analysis of fit in the interaction between the brand equity of the sponsored entity and that of the sponsor

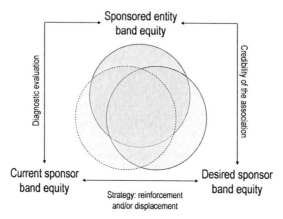

Source: Ferrand and Pagès (2004)

Table 3.1 Qualitative analysis of fit of brand equity

Aspects	Specific to sponsored entity	Common to both entities	Specific to sponsor	Eventual and desirable effects for the sponsor
Values	*(Table to be completed when carrying out analysis of fit)*			
Mission				
Image				
Perceived quality				
Value relationship				
Stakeholders				

Table 3.2 Quantitative analysis of fit of brand equity

	Sponsored entity	Potential sponsor	Eventual and desirable effects for the sponsor
Brand awareness	*(Table to be completed when carrying out analysis of fit)*		
Attitude			
Satisfaction			
Loyalty			

questionnaire similar to the one below on a scale from 1 (completely disagree) to 5 (completely agree).

1. The sponsor and the event associate well together.
2. The company sponsor and the event share the same expressed values.
3. It is logical why the company sponsored the event.

The perceived sincerity of the sponsor is evaluated in the same manner through the following statements:

- The primary reason the sponsor is involved is because the sponsor believes the event deserves to be supported.
- There is appreciation for this sponsor because of its support for the event.

Strategic and operational sponsorship management

Strategic marketing is embedded in the strategy of an organization, thereby enabling the organization to analyse market trends as well as current or potential market segments, based on its resources and competences, with a view to developing a growth strategy. Operational marketing is

> a proactive approach, with a short and mid-term perspective, whose aim is to acquire existing markets. It is an integral part of the traditional mainstream business approach focused on operating revenues that is based on tactical means derived from product, distribution, pricing, and communication policies.
>
> (Lambin 2002: 22)

In Figure 3.6, sponsorship is located at a crossroads between strategic and operational marketing strategies. The perceived value of a sponsorship offer depends on how well it contributes to the success of its own marketing strategy. In a competitive context, where

Figure 3.6 Relationship of sponsorship to strategic and operational marketing

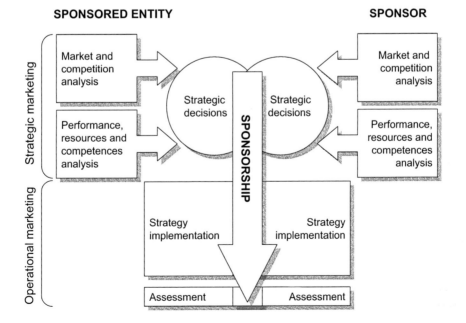

Table 3.3 Possible objectives of the sponsor and the sponsored entity according to their position

Status	Objectives of the sporting organization	Objectives of the company
Current sponsor	Build loyalty Show the ROI Improve the ROI and perceived quality of the service	Confirm the relevance of the sponsorship offer Optimize the ROI
Prospective sponsor ('prospect')	Show the relevance of the offer Customize the offer Deliver quality service	Evaluate the relevance of the offer Incorporate the sponsorship move into the organizational strategy Negotiation

sponsorship competes with other marketing approaches seeking to achieve the same goal, it is essential to optimize the cost/benefit ratio. From the perspective of the sporting organization, the perceived value relates to financial contributions, including products and service provisions of the sponsor, and the coherence between the association with the event and the mission of the sponsor. In discussing the strategic and operational management, it is necessary to use the perspectives of both the sporting organization[1] and the company sponsor.

Traditionally, sporting organizations initiate a sponsorship offer.[2] This same procedure of initiation occurs in the renewing of a sponsorship contract. Therefore, the strategic and operational marketing of the sporting organization and its relationship with a potential sponsor is examined. Table 3.3 shows an example of possible objectives of a company and those of a sporting organization according to their status (positioning).

Method and means for strategic decision-making

The objective of gathering and analysing relevant information in order to make a strategic decision can be achieved by ascertaining a company's strengths, weaknesses, opportunities and threats (SWOT analysis). In the context of sponsorship, a SWOT analysis involves monitoring the internal and external sponsorship environment.

External analysis

The external environment analysis focuses on the environment in which the sporting organization and company sponsor operate. According to Aaker (2001), it is important to:

- analyse the segmentation, expectations, unsatisfied needs, etc. of consumers and customers;
- analyse the strategies, performance, objectives, strengths and weaknesses of direct and indirect competitors;
- conduct a market research (i.e. size, dynamics, entry barriers, key factors of success, etc.);
- analyse the overall environment (i.e. political and legislative context, socio-cultural trends, technological developments, etc.).

The external environment analysis identifies the opportunities and threats tied to changes. Accordingly, it is necessary to identify the elements causing change in an effort to speculate about the future.

Market analysis

Market analysis aims at finding the characteristics, dynamics and attractiveness of the sponsorship market since they greatly influence the operations of companies and their sponsorship strategy. It is important to look at the national and international context by focusing on the dynamics of the sectors in which the two entities operate. The market for sponsorship needs to be analysed, in addition to the market in which competitors operate.

Consumer analysis

Marketing is directed towards consumers. Therefore, it is crucial to identify prospective customers. In the sponsorship context, it is important to analyse the expectations and decision-making process of the targeted customers and organizations, as well as their expectations that have not been met.

Competitor analysis

Competitor analysis is an assessment of the strengths and weaknesses of current and potential competitors in the market. The aim is to identify direct and indirect competitors, as well as new entrants and products. It also consists in analysing the negotiating advantages of the main stakeholders.

Once competitors have been identified, it is imperative to outline their objectives, strategies, positioning, brand equity, weaknesses and competitive advantages.

Environment analysis

Environment analysis is an assessment of the economic, legislative, cultural and techno-logical environment of a particular market.

Economic factors
Companies are very sensitive to business conditions, which can influence them to reduce their communication expenditures. In general, a sustained growth positively affects sponsorship investments. It is important to know the evolution of any sectors in which the sporting organization and its potential sponsors operate.

Socio-cultural factors
Both sport and company operations intermingle with socio-cultural trends which influence consumer behaviour and expenditure. Socio-cultural trends indicate a system of values, key ideas and common attitudes originating in the collective psychology. These trends have a social impact and penetration rate that can be measured at any given moment in various social groups. The analysis of emerging trends is indicative of people's current interests and preoccupations.

Legal factors

The legal framework refers to the laws, decrees and regulations in the countries where the sporting organization or the company sponsor operate. A careful analysis of any change at the legislative level should be examined with a view to determine how it can affect the sponsorship operation.

Technological factors

Technology continually changes as companies develop new products and processes that can be put to use on the market. Marketing technology is a way to benefit from research by striving to answer the following question: how will research integrate or disturb the market? The objective of marketing technology is to promote a technology by showing the added benefit it offers. Technology is a resource for an organization (e.g. Internet and video games) that provides an avenue that further develops products aimed at satisfying consumers' expectations. Therefore, it is important to keep abreast of technological innovation, research and patent filings relating to the operations of company sponsors.

Analysis of internal resources and competences

Internal analysis is an assessment of the resources and competences of the sporting organization that aims at identifying its strengths and weaknesses.

Trade and mission

Trade is a specific proficiency requiring expertise in a particular sector, which creates value by coordinating physical, human and organizational resources. As trade evolves, so must sponsorship.

The mission of an organization indicates the purposes of its business. It must be clear and known to all. For example, the mission of the IOC is in the Olympic charter.[3] It states

> The goal of the Olympic Movement is to contribute to building a peaceful and better world by educating youth through sport practiced without discrimination of any kind and in accordance with the Olympic spirit which requires mutual comprehension, friendship, solidarity, and fair play.

Resource management

Resource management is formalizing the strategy, planning the sponsorship operation, setting the modes for data gathering and processing, establishing the systems of control and rewards, and setting informal policies within the organization and with its environment. A systematic, rational approach is more effective than an intuitive approach.

Physical resources

Physical resources primarily relate to the location, facilities, installations and equipment of the organization, as well as technologies for which it possesses expertise. Physical resources are essential in the framework of sporting event sponsorship.

Financial resources

The stockholder's equity and accessibility of financing are important aspects for a sporting organization. The amount of available funds determines the strength of its financial position to engage in sponsorship activities requiring liquid assets.

Brand equity

Given that the brand equity of an organization is at the heart of the sponsorship system, it is essential to have a precise analysis of it to make reliable decisions based on facts. Pertinent information about the various aspects of brand equity is shown in Figure 3.4.

Strategic choices

The previous methods and tools facilitate the collection of important information required to carry out a strategic analysis. The next step is to summarize the information with the purpose of answering the following questions:

1. What overall corporate strategy would it be desirable to implement?
2. Which sustainable competitive advantage(s) would it be preferable to develop?
3. How should the organization be positioned?
4. How should the sponsorship offer be packaged?
5. To which type of potential sponsor (prospects) should the focus be directed?

Selecting an overall corporate strategy

There are two general types of strategies: cost leadership and differentiation. In the context of sponsorship, the cost leadership strategy seeks a competitive advantage by presenting a low-cost offer made available to a very large customer base, thereby yielding small profit margins by producing large offer volumes. This strategy is both risky and difficult to implement. Differentiation strategy should be implemented into the framework of sponsorship. It involves creating an offer that is perceived as unique. The concept is to avoid price-cutting while increasing the perceived value in order to obtain a higher profit margin. This can be achieved by focusing on certain expectations and attributes highly valued by the sponsor. There are several ways to differentiate specific offers.

Differentiation by aspects of the offer
The sponsorship offer must incorporate a certain number of tangible and intangible features of the sporting organization's brand equity in order to satisfy the expectations of the sponsor. The delivery of these components is done before, during and after the sponsorship operation.

Differentiation by intangible aspects of the offer. The intangible components of the offer pertain to the following aspects of brand equity: foundations, brand awareness, brand experience, value relationships and brand positioning.

Differentiation by tangible aspects of the offer. There are a number of tangible elements, including:

1. the main physical aspects of the offer, which include billboards, logos, advertising spaces, hospitality, etc.;
2. products directly or indirectly related to the sponsored entity, subsequently licensed products, and merchandizing licence agreements;
3. service provision regarding consulting and impact studies;
4. media partners and the broadcast of the event;
5. communication and promotion plan of the event.

However, it is occasionally difficult to differentiate these aspects because successful sponsorship programmes are often emulated. Therefore, incorporating latent expectations of sponsors into an offer is an effective way to differentiate. Likewise, it is possible to make a differentiation by focusing on various aspects of quality such as reliability, customer service and the ability to respond in the event of an incident, thus effectively satisfying the expectations of the sponsor.

Differentiation by service and personnel quality. The personnel of an organization constitute a pivotal asset of an offer. Indeed, the personnel ensure that the aspects of perceived quality are well managed. To achieve this type of differentiation, the organization must recruit and adequately train its personnel in the standards shown in Table 3.4

Differentiation by physical resources. In the context of a sporting event, physical resources relate to the site, sporting facilities and equipment, as well as the structure, design, location, access, etc. Physical resource management facilitates communication by creating or avoiding contacts. It contributes to triggering desirable emotions (e.g. joy, thrill, etc.) or undesirable emotions (e.g. frustration, wrath, etc.) Likewise, customers expect the environment to be clean and enjoyable. As such, music, colours and scent help generate the desired experience. Although creating a unique atmosphere conducive to positive emotions is expensive, it is essential to create such an environment given the expectations of the sponsors.

Differentiation by the stakeholders and their alliances. This dimension is noted given the important role it performs in a sponsorship operation. The characteristics of the stakeholders influence the social impact of the operation, namely the number and categories of

Table 3.4 Aspects influencing the perceived quality of services in relation to the abilities and competences of the personnel liaisons with sponsors

Aspects of the perceived quality of services	Abilities and competences of the liaison personnel
Tangible aspects	Competence for actualizing expectations
Reliability	Consistency and compliance of the service provision
Responsiveness	Consideration of customers' problems
Reassurance	Credibility, trustworthiness
Empathy	Ability to listen to and communicate with customers with courtesy

people directly involved (e.g. athletes, spectators, officials, etc.) and indirectly involved (TV viewers, listeners, readers, Internet users, etc.) in the operations involving the media, sponsors, local authorities, etc.

This type of differentiation constitutes one component of the service provision. Indeed, it is important to conceive and facilitate alliances between various stakeholders. Partnerships result in the implementation of specific programmes such as educational programmes, the Winter Olympics for Youth, the Olympics, and the cultural Olympiad developed by the organizing committee of the 2006 Turin Olympic Games in collaboration with its partners and the IOC, etc.

Differentiation through risk reduction. Any transaction involves a risk due to the possible inability of one party to honour the terms of the contract as a result of a lack of financial resources, expertise or ethical commercial practices. Some sporting organizations and marketing agencies specializing in marketing rights have got into considerable difficulties by deceiving the public. Europeans still remember the bankruptcy of the former marketing giant ISL which for decades was the leader in the world of football. Because of an adventurous mismanagement, this company went into liquidation on May 2001, with damages of more than 3 billion euros and owing more than 450 million euros to creditors. This collapse badly affected FIFA, and its president announced that he was shocked to discover that the company had withheld around 75 million euros from a TV contract with TV Globo.

Reducing the risk perceived by the sponsor is an essential component contributing to the differentiation of a sponsorship offer. This can be achieved by establishing guarantees regarding the level of expertise, strong financial stability, political stability, etc., of the organization. Although potential sponsors conduct an in-house risk analysis when they receive a sponsorship proposal, insuring the risk with specialized brokers is helpful for reassuring potential sponsors.

Creating sustainable competitive advantages

The purpose of differentiating an offer is to gain a sustainable competitive advantage over competitors. The source of the advantage can be something the sporting organization achieves that is distinctive and difficult to duplicate, or something that correlates with the core competencies of the organization.

Competitive advantages are tied to the resources and competences of the organization in conjunction with the strengths and weaknesses of direct and indirect competitors. The primary aspects that contribute to creating sustainable competitive advantages are presented in Table 3.5.

Positioning

According to Ries and Trout (1981), positioning relates to how, in the minds of prospective customers, the brand (or product) is represented in comparison with the brand (or product) of competitors. For example, AC Milan fans believe that the football club exhibits strong sporting values, such as professional expertise, passion, creativity, sense of belonging, loyalty and generosity. These same values are associated with company values such as

Table 3.5 Aspects contributing to competitive advantages

Variables	Dimensions
Offer	Tangible and intangible aspects (including brand equity)
	Quality service and personnel
	Physical resources
	Stakeholders and alliances
	Perceived risk
	Responsiveness
	Empathy
	Trustworthiness
	Reliability
Price	Comparison with competitors
	Flexibility based on duration and loyalty
Communication	Strategy of communication
Sales and distribution network	Accessibility
	Availability
	Responsiveness
	Customization
	Expertise

effectiveness, organization, power and discipline. The brand positioning of the AC Milan football club includes six dimensions: passion, unity, internationality, sporting entertainment, planning and style. Thus, the positioning of the club must answer three key questions.

Who is targeted?
It is important to determine the characteristics and consumption habits of the targeted people. Thus, AC Milan targets any passionate football fan eager for a highly talented, well-managed, large international club.

What sector is targeted?
It is important to specify the sector encompassed by the offer. Here, AC Milan positions itself amongst the world's premier football clubs.

Why is the offer to be preferred over alternatives?
The positioning must also incorporate why the offer is preferable to that of competitors. In the case of the AC Milan club, emphasizing their success in the course of the past 100 years with memorable games won in Italy and elsewhere around the world, their legendary players, passion and style can provide excellent positioning.

Structure of the sponsorship offer

The structure of the sponsorship offer reflects the will to provide differentiated services, which provide for the satisfaction of the expectations and financial resources of sponsors. There are three inclusive criteria used for defining the various categories of sponsorship.

Level of association with the event

The highest level of association occurs when the event bears the name of the sponsor, which is referred to as the 'naming right sponsor'. This type of sponsorship involves a major strategic decision because the sponsor is perceived as the owner of the event. If there are additional sponsors involved in the event, their communications will be carried out under the umbrella of the title sponsor's brand (e.g. Siemens and National Citer are partners of the Gaz de France Tennis Open[4]).

Association can be achieved through an individual element within an event. Sponsors here are often referred to as official suppliers for a product category, prize, day or peripheral event. For instance, Tag Heuer is the official timekeeper of the Indy Car Series, an American automobile championship; Wanadoo sponsors the Wanadoo Challenge for young football players aged 13 to 15 years, which takes place at half-times during league matches of the French football championship. However, association can also occur where the involvement of the sponsor is communicated only through billboards, public relations, etc.

Exclusiveness

Exclusiveness relates to one or more product categories. For example, the TOP partners of the Olympic Games benefit from exclusive marketing rights and opportunities within their respective product category. According to the IOC, 'they may exercise these rights on a worldwide basis and they may develop marketing programs with the various members of the Olympic Movement – the IOC, the NOCs, and the Organizing Committees'.[5]

Level of exposure 'on and off camera'

The level of exposure is tied to the number and nature of the platform displaying the sponsor in the context of the event (e.g. billboards, logo on jerseys, media advertising). Sponsors receive a level of exposure reflecting their level of involvement in the event. Consequently, it is essential to assess the impact of every platform.

Hierarchical organization of sponsors

By combining the three previous criteria, sponsors can be organized into a hierarchy (see Figure 3.7). Establishing a compromise between the sponsor's financial resources and the perceived quality of the sponsorship offer is essential. A typical mistake involves utilizing several sponsors to increase both revenues and the exchange of products and services. Subsequently, sponsors end up dissatisfied with the quality of the service provided.

As shown in Table 3.6, it is recommended that both the number of sponsor categories and the number of sponsors per category be limited to three because it is difficult to propose a quality offer beyond that.

Table 3.6 Example of how to structure various categories of sponsors

Type of sponsor	Numbers	Level of association	Level of exclusiveness	Level of exposure (%)
Primary level	2	Simple	Product category	25
Secondary level	3	Subset		10
Official suppliers	4			5

Figure 3.7 Structuring aspects of the sponsorship offer

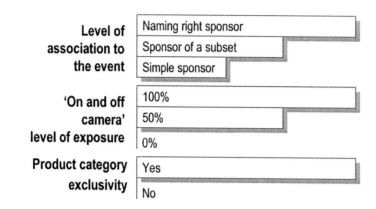

Choosing potential sponsors

It is useful to make a complete list of potential sponsors to contact when contemplating sponsorship. Appraising the list should be based on discriminating criteria showing the relevance of the proposal both at the strategic and operational levels. Therefore, a thorough examination must be conducted concerning each potential company sponsor, using the following five criteria, which constitute the foundation of the analysis of fit.

- Is there a fit between the brand equity of the potential sponsor and that of the sponsored entity?
- Is there a fit between the positioning of the sponsored entity and the identity com-municated by the potential sponsor?
- Is the association between the brand of the sponsor and that of the sponsored entity accepted by the stakeholders?
- Is the target of the communication and marketing strategy of the potential sponsor coherent with the sponsored entity in the eyes of the stakeholders?
- Is there a fit between the communication and marketing objectives of the potential sponsor and the opportunities offered by the sponsorship operation?

Utilizing these criteria helps to reduce the number of potential sponsors. Potential sponsors not fulfilling all the criteria should be eliminated from consideration. The next step consists of validating each criterion to determine the attractiveness of potential sponsors versus entry barriers. This is discussed in the following section.

Operational sponsorship strategy

The operational sponsorship strategy is narrow in focus and deals with day-to-day oper-ational activities. This focus typically consists of two phases. The first phase initiates the design of the offer and is finalized with the acceptance (i.e. the signing of the contract). The second phase is the administration of a quality service provision in an endeavour to build sponsor loyalty.

From the offer development to the contract acceptance

The purpose of the first phase is to develop a quality sponsorship offer enticing the potential sponsor to commit by signing a contract. For existing sponsors, the purpose is to promote their continued loyalty. Furthermore, it is important to combine the marketing and legal actions together. The recommended structure of the first phase is presented in the following sections.

Analysis and design of the products and service offer

Products and services have a value for the customer insofar as they have the capacity to satisfy expectations in a way that surpasses competition alone. The following list outlines the various aspects that serve as a guideline for the design of a customized offer that will satisfy the expectations of prospective sponsors:

- the quality of the basic convergence (i.e. the five criteria in the previous section);
- the brand equity of the sponsored entity;
- physical attributes;
- characteristics of people managing the sponsorship operation;
- licensed products and other licences;
- the communication platform;
- activation opportunities;
- opportunities for implementing relationship marketing;
- product sales;
- service provisions relating to market research and consultations.

Design analysis of the sponsorship offer

It is necessary to analyse current contract proposals if they exist. It is an important step which will allow one to precisely tailor the characteristics of the offer. This process will help to differentiate it from the competitors and to improve the fit with sponsors' expectations.

One will be able to answer the following three questions.

- How many offers should be proposed?
- What are the components making up the offers?
- What are the components differentiating the offers?

Analysing the perceived quality of current offers

A quality product or service embodies characteristics meeting the implicit or explicit expectations of consumers. Consequently, quality is a notion based on specific or common expectations that are based on perception. Thus, the perceived quality has more impact than some 'objectives measures' of the best quality.

Parasuraman *et al.* (1988) developed a model for analysing a sponsor's perception regarding the quality of a service provision managed by a sporting organization. Their model, which is based on the analysis of the gaps between the customers' perceived quality and the management abilities of an organization, reveals how an organization could improve the quality of its service provision.

Gap between sponsor's expectations and perception of expectations by an organization. Sporting organizations often misconceive the expectations of the sponsors. To get an accurate understanding of sponsors' expectations, an organization can research websites, journal and newspaper articles, as well as holding debriefings with sponsors. Then, classifying their known expectations on a 1 to 5 scale, where 1 = not important, and 5 = very important, will reveal which components are perceived as important to the sponsor.

Gap between an organization's perception of the sponsors' expectations and quality standards implemented by the organization. Once the sponsors' expectations have been analysed, it is advisable to assign them quality standards. To formalize these standards, it is necessary to establish procedures and criteria of performance. For example, an organization may find it advantageous to arrange a monthly meeting with each sponsor to review the progress of the sponsorship operation.

Gap between quality standards and service provided. Sponsors expect a quality service provision that meets their expectations. It is important to provide this provision, but more importantly, to be able to fulfil it. Therefore, the sporting organization must ensure it has the ability and the financial resources to recruit and train human resources, maintain its equipment and establish an information system for controlling the sponsorship process.

Gap between service provision and external communication. External communication (i.e. files, proposals, presentations, press conferences, etc.) is a key indication of the capacity to deliver the sponsorship offer and satisfy a certain number of expectations. External communication influences both the expectations of the sponsors and their decision to sponsor an organization. However, it can also become a source of frustration for the sponsor if the service provided does not correspond to the service agreed to.

Gap between service provision and expectations of the sponsor. Often referred to as the 'consumer gap', this difference assesses the satisfaction of the sponsor in relation to its expectations. This is the core indication around which all quality processes are built. Table 3.7 provides the organization with a strategy based on the result analysis of the sponsors' perceived quality regarding the service provided by them and those of competitors.

At the operational level, resources and competences must be mobilized to respond quickly if needed. Additionally, offers may need to be redrawn to better coincide with sponsors' expectations about content and fee. At the strategic level, the organization must determine whether to invest, maintain the status quo or give up the sponsor by taking into account the resources and competences previously mentioned in conjunction with the importance of the sponsor and the position of competitors.

Designing and structuring the sponsorship offer

The difficulty in designing a sponsorship offer comes from the complexity of structuring and defining various packages to satisfy the general expectations of sponsors (e.g. exposure, hospitality, etc.) while also customizing each offer according to the particular expectations of each sponsor. To accomplish this dual task, the conception and structure of a sponsorship offer can be formulated utilizing a basic list of components compiled within the framework of a sporting event:

Table 3.7 Strategies to be implemented following the quality analysis

Case	Perceived quality of the service by the sponsors	Perceived quality of the services of the competitors	Strategy to be implemented
1	Good	Bad	Maintain the current situation and monitor the moves of your competitors
2	Good	Good	Maintain the current level of quality and improve upon the differentiation of your offer
3	Bad	Good	Improve failing components immediately, or give up this sponsor if you do not have the resources and competences required
4	Bad	Bad	Immediately invest on failing components if the sponsor is important for you, provided you have the resources and competences required, or else give up this sponsor

1. *Common components.* These relate to intangible components (i.e. history, values, image, positioning, etc.) and tangible components (i.e. target and impact of the communication) of the offer.
2. *Customizable components.* These relate to tangible elements of the offer corresponding to the five categories appearing in Table 3.8.

Validating the prospect list

Once the list of potential sponsors is drafted based on the perceived fit, the next step is to get further information about each one to validate the selection and narrow down the list of prospects. The Internet greatly facilitates this research, since many companies post their sponsorship policies and expectations. The compilation of this information becomes especially useful to evaluate the attractiveness and competitiveness of a sponsorship offer.

The attractiveness of a company can be established or evaluated based on the following criteria:

- financial resources;
- compatibility with the mission of the sporting organization;
- the brand equity of the company.

The competitiveness of an offer depends on:

- the capacity to satisfy the expectations of the potential sponsor via means that surpass that of competitors;
- the duration of the sponsorship contract;
- the perceived quality of other sponsorship offers.

The combination of the two dimensions assigns companies to one of the three categories presented in Figure 3.8.

Table 3.8 Characteristics of the customizable components of a sponsorship offer per category

Categories	Components
Sponsorship category	Level of association: title sponsor or official supplier Exclusiveness Level of exposure
Facilities and equipment	Billboards, tag jerseys, placards, advertisements, trailers, directory maps, hoardings Characteristics of sporting area: press room, architectural design Location Access, accreditations, tickets, etc. Parking Hospitality venue: • capacity (number of seats) • size, volume • equipment of various spaces • air-conditioning, electrical, etc. Video, sound system Exposure, samples, etc.
Personnel in liaison with the sponsor	Number Expertise Appearance
Communication and marketing strategy	Customized offer of services associated with the various targets Plan of communication with media and additional means
Management of relationships between stakeholders	Characteristics of the stakeholders Relationship marketing programmes (e.g. peripheral events, partnership marketing, cross-promotions, etc.)

Customizing the offer

Once the list of prospective company sponsors is validated, the next step is to present a sponsorship proposal tailored to each prospective company by using available information to define synergies between the respective marketing strategy and the sponsorship offer. It is imperative that the proposal includes an activation platform where it is possible to include additional stakeholders in this strategy. Relationship marketing augments relationships between stakeholders (e.g. media, partners, etc.). Thus, the sporting organization ought to incorporate partnership opportunities in the customized package it offers to sponsors that will intensify the impact of the proposed activation strategy.

Increasing perceived value through negotiations and amendments

Negotiations with a potential sponsor are always delicate as the sponsor has a significant bargaining advantage given the number of alternatives it can choose from to achieve its marketing goals. Hence, it is wise to design a flexible sponsorship offer in which amendments to the offer remain possible in order to accommodate the strategy of each prospective customer, thus increasing the perceived quality of the offer while making it

Figure 3.8 Matrix of potential sponsors' attractiveness versus offering competitiveness

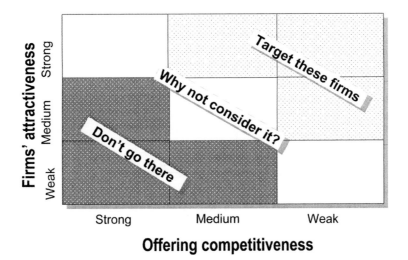

more attractive than other marketing alternatives. Successful negotiations require the following measures:

- knowing company resources and competences, and those of competitors;
- having a thorough knowledge of a prospective customer before negotiating;
- listening to expectations, comments and desires of the prospective customer;
- negotiating on the quality of the offer first rather than the fee;
- retaining a few service offers in reserve as opposed to immediately offering all service provisions envisioned;
- proposing activation programmes that publicize the sponsor in the course of the sponsorship operation;
- negotiating the fee and exchange of service only after the proposal enthrals the prospective customer.

During negotiations, it is prudent to guarantee that the product category offered to the sponsor is offered exclusively to them. The organization must ensure that each product category does not encroach on a category allotted to another sponsor. Consequently, the organization should market only the rights it can deliver from a legal and technical standpoint.

Formalizing the agreement

A contract is a document formalizing an agreement between two parties that becomes legally binding upon the 'signing' of it. Chapter 4 is devoted to an in-depth examination of the various aspects of contractual agreements.

Establishing the price for sponsorship offers

The most frequent mistake made by sporting organizations is establishing the price of an offer according to its budgeting needs. For example, a sporting organization needs €40,000 to balance its budget. As a result, it seeks two main sponsors who could each contribute €20,000, or four sponsors who could contribute €10,000 each, etc.

It is necessary to perform a complex deliberation that takes into consideration the following three components in an effort to establish the price of a sponsorship offer:

- the organization itself, i.e. its strategy, objectives, positioning, market influence and costs associated to servicing sponsors;
- the potential sponsors, i.e. reference prices, price sensitivity, perceived value, price vs. quality, etc.;
- the environment and competition, i.e. economic situation, price in the sector and pricing policies of competitors.

Furthermore, trade negotiations have dynamics of their own, and this influences and modifies the content and price of sponsorship offers.

Environment and competition

The external analysis gave an outlook on the socio-economic context in which the sponsorship operation takes place. The sporting organization must now decide on the price of its offers in view of the competitive environment. What is the price of competitors' offers? Have they modified their price recently? What is the perceived value of their offer?

It is important to note that sponsors have answers to these questions, as dozens of sponsorship proposals routinely accumulate for their perusal. Therefore, constant knowledge of the sponsorship pricing policies of competitors is imperative. For this purpose, reading professional newspapers (e.g. *Advertising Age*, *IEG Sponsorship*) is very useful. Monitoring the pricing situation will help to determine the price range in the market, which allows one to know whether the price is competitive or whether additional manoeuvres are required to make it competitive. Depending on a given market, it is possible to make the price strategy lower, equal to or higher than that of the competitors.

Pricing lower than competitors
This strategy of market penetration could be used insofar as pricing lower than competitors is compatible with one's analysis of internal costs, with the positioning of the sponsorship offer, and with the expectations of the company sponsors (i.e. price/quality).

Pricing at the average market price
This is the dominant pricing trend when the sponsorship market cannot tolerate a price higher than competition, and when the cost structure to deliver a service prevents the organization from setting its price under a certain threshold.

Pricing higher than competitors
If a sporting organization has a top-notch position, it can set the price of its sponsorship

offer higher than competitors do, insofar as sponsors consider the offer has a distinctive advantage that adds value, which in the eye of the sponsors justifies a higher price. However, this pricing strategy is seldom used.

In any case, it is necessary to emphasize the difficulty a company experiences in comparing the price of sponsorship offers, given that these offers are generally specific, differentiated and tied to a particular sponsorship activation platform. Typically, sponsorship offers are exclusively designed and differentiated in association with a particular sponsorship activation platform. This makes it especially difficult for a company to compare prices between multiple offers.

Potential company sponsors

The experimental sponsorship pricing methods seen in the 1980s are no longer used. Companies have better knowledge of the sponsorship market and its pitfalls. Many companies now have a sponsorship department with managers who know what the reference prices are. Based on the impact of the events for which they hold rights to, only a few sporting organizations are in a position of power to negotiate sponsorship agreements.

The perceived value is regarded as the main factor influencing purchasing decisions. Insight into the sponsor's perception of the offer and the influence it has on its decision is achieved through an analysis of the relationships between price, quality and value. Ultimately, the sponsorship manager has to ensure that the sponsorship operation brings a benefit to the company. Thus, the manager makes a decision by balancing the company's expectations in relation to the perceived characteristics and benefits of the offer.

The sponsorship manager's perception of price values occurs via comparison of the supply price with the internal reference price,[6] the price of competitors' offers, and alternative marketing options. In this process, the decision to enter into a sponsorship operation is likely when the perceived value of the quality of the sponsorship offer is high with a relatively low price.

In this context, a key factor in securing a contract is customizing a sponsorship offer according to the expectations of company sponsors. Likewise, it is essential to manage the relationships between perceived quality and price. Therefore, finding a balance between price, perceived quality, and cost optimizes the perceived value.

The sporting organization

The internal analysis process is twofold. First, the cost relating to the design and delivery of the service provision in relation to the desired margin rate needs to be analysed. The second phase relates to the strategy of the organization and its positioning.

Estimating the cost and the profit margin

In establishing the price of a sponsorship offer, it is imperative to ensure that it will cover the overall costs of the service provision. Fixed and variable costs are the two types of costs that must be accounted for. When it is not possible or desirable to carry out a detailed financial analysis, one can calculate the cost of the service provision by estimating the combined total of the following:

- administrative and personnel costs;
- costs of the services delivered to the sponsor;
- costs of the marketing operation.

It is advisable to then calculate the potential profit margin and modify, if needed, certain parameters influencing the cost of the service provision when the profit margin appears to be too low, in an effort to increase the profit margin.

Rationalizing the price of the tangible elements of the offer
In spite of its complexity, there are elements of the offer for which price can be estimated.[7] For example:

- number of seats in the stadium;
- public relations;
- meals, cocktails;
- personnel employed;
- promotion of the sponsor through media partners;
- promotional events.

Calculating and communicating the price of these services to the potential sponsor serves to validate the price of an offer.

Attractiveness and price positioning of the sporting organization
A top-notch position generally increases the sponsor's reference price. However, the attractiveness of a proposal depends on the perceived quality and competitiveness of the offer in the market. Companies have learned how to evaluate the relevance of an offer in relation to their expectations. Hence, the sporting organization needs to balance its positioning against the perceived quality/price ratio.

A comprehensive move towards price establishment

As mentioned earlier, establishing a desirable price entails a delicate compromise and deliberation between the four dimensions presented in Figure 3.9. Merely affixing a price to a proposal is not sufficient. It is necessary to justify that price against market competition. Moreover, the sporting organization must be consistent throughout its marketing activities and resist the temptation to reduce prices when its goals are not achieved.

Conceiving and implementing the communication plan of the marketing operation

The marketing operation of sponsorship must be supported by a twofold plan of communication consisting of the design of the supporting communication means necessary for the commercial operation, and the media coverage of the commercial prospecting phase. This second phase is often neglected by a sporting organization due to their desire to operate in a low-profile manner if the anticipated results are not attained. It is a miscalculation to do this, since the communication plan is essential to support the marketing operation.

Figure 3.9 Three aspects relating to establishing the prices of a sponsorship offer

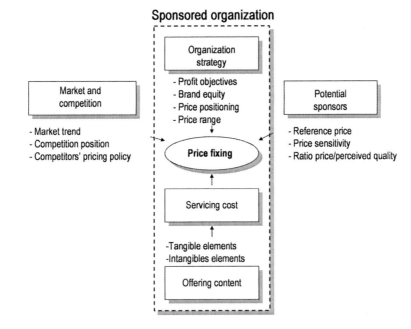

Source: Ferrand and Nardi (2005)

Means supporting the communication and marketing operations

Marketing operations require the use of supporting communication means (e.g. files, commercial proposals, PowerPoint presentations, videos, photographs, business cards, etc.), which must be created in accordance with the 'corporate design'. This signature of the organization must be visible in all forms of correspondence and documents, thus creating a system of visual identity. The development of this system serves as a means to establishing its territory, and reinforces positioning of the organization, which contributes to the enhancement of perceived quality.

A system of visual identity comprises one or more logos (which can also include a soundtrack) and a graphic charter, i.e. the book of standards. The graphic charter establishes the parameter defining coherent graphic components that portray the identity of the organization. For example, the graphic charter gives precise directives regarding the typography, colours, and page-setting parameters that must be strictly adhered to and incorporated into all correspondence and documents.

The design and realization of a system of visual identity is typically achieved in collaboration with specialists. The organization must brief the agency (or the independent professional) about the market and the identity it seeks to communicate, as well as those of competitors. Establishing the system of visual identity is relatively inexpensive given its duration of exploitation.

The various printed documents incorporating the system of visual identity of the company serve to provide information about the company, products, services and contact information. Despite the increasing usage of electronic devices for sharing information, people still prefer to have printed documents in their hands. Such documents must be informative, attractive, legible and practical.

For designing files and commercial proposals, it is most efficient and practical to use a PowerPoint document, which can easily incorporate photographs, video clips, tables and graphs. PowerPoint presentations can also be displayed using a laptop and video projector. This is very useful when it comes to increasing the perceived quality of the offer during negotiations because this document format allows for rapid changes when integrating or modifying elements required for adapting to the desires of a prospective customer. This document can also be printed, or distributed as a PDF file or CD ROM.

A sponsorship file must provide the sponsor with the data essential for evaluating the relevance of an offer. Table 3.9 presents a generic example.

The communication strategy of the sponsorship programme

The communication plan should support the marketing operation by taking into account the target audiences, objectives of the key messages, activities, planning, budget and evaluation.

Definition of the communication targets

There are a number of possible communication targets. If resources are limited, it is imperative to focus on at least the following targets:

- current sponsors and prospective customers;
- journalists;
- mains stakeholders.

Objectives and activities of communication

The objectives of communication activities are diversified (to inform, to entertain, to

Table 3.9 The content of the sponsorship offer in the framework of an event

Outline View	Contents
1st slide	Title of the presentation (name of the event, name of the rights holder, date)
2nd slide	Purpose of the presentation
3rd slide	Outline of the presentation
4th slide	Positioning and communicated identity of the event
5th slide	Index card (calendar, location, potential audience, etc.)
6th slide and following	Presentation of the rights owner of the event
7th slide and following	Presentation of the brand equity of the event and justification for the convergence with the potential sponsor's brand
Following slide	Programme of on-site activities
Following slide	Marketing and communication plan
Following slide	Details of customized proposal
Following slide	Proposed activation plan
Last slide	Contact details

explain, to reassure, etc.). These objectives evolve according to the dynamics of the commercial operation. Table 3.10 presents principal objectives in relation to the media utilized for attaining the objectives.

From a general point of view, the sporting organization can rely on above-the-line advertising and below-the-line advertising.

- Advertising enables the promotion of information, the ability to modify its image, and offers reassurance. The cost of above-the-line advertising is the main barrier for sporting organizations. Therefore, creating a partnership with the media is a logical way to generate such publicity. Consequently, the media partnership must precede any commercial operation with sponsors by considering media coverage which determines the size of the indirect audience, the impact, and thus, the price of the sponsorship offer.
- Press relations allow dissemination of information via the media at a reduced cost. However, managing a relationship with the press can be complicated. The success or failure of a press relations operation depends on various uncontrollable factors such as the quality of the information release, relationships with journalists, the availability of the media, and current news items. Nevertheless, a relationship with the press is essential whatever the subjects and means used (e.g. press kit, press release, news conference, interview, etc.).
- Public relations facilitate trust and relationships between the sporting organization and stakeholders, primarily the sponsors (current and potential), journalists, opinion leaders, public authorities, etc. There are possibilities to develop public relations during a reception at an existing sporting event or a conference, etc.
- Organizing an event within the framework of the marketing operation is a way to bring people together (e.g. creating a situation where individuals are invited to participate and/or meet with athletes and celebrities).
- Engaging in social causes allows the corporation to communicate universal values such as solidarity. For instance, FIFA joined UNICEF[8] in an effort to promote international solidarity for child welfare.
- The Internet is a very useful communication platform in the context of sponsorship. It enables the sporting organization to disseminate information worldwide at very low cost, present sponsors in a favourable way, create an interaction with Internet users, and use an Internet website as a sales channel. In order to activate the sponsorship programme using a web-based strategy, the sporting organization should benchmark its

Table 3.10 Comparison of the communication objectives and the type of media to use

Communication objectives	Media examples
To increase brand awareness	Press relations and press conferences
To publicize opportunities	Advertising campaign with media partners
To promote quality of the service	Organizing an event
To reinforce or modify certain dimensions of the image	Organizing an event
	Public relations with athletes and personalities
	Advertising campaign with media partners
To reassure and increase the gratitude/acceptance	Public relations with athletes and personalities
	Press release or press conference with sponsors

website against the websites of company leaders in this field. The sporting organization should also consult websites of various international federations[9] from a sponsor's perspective.

Communication programming for communication targets

This phase correlates to the operational communication plan. Conceiving a communication programme for each communication target is advisable. It is an important step used for the budgeting and evaluation processes. Table 3.11 presents a hypothetical programme intended for sponsors.

Each operation has a code assigned to it, which is linked to a credential with detailed information such as objective, description of content, precise dates, success indicators and allocated financial and human resources.

The sales process

Again, the sales process is tied to the coherence between the contents and price of the offer on the one hand, and the expectations of the prospective customer on the other. The following aspects are particularly important: selecting the sales force, implementing a sales process in relation to the decision-making process of the prospective customer, and managing the commercial operation.

Who carries out the commercial operation?

The rights holder can decide to carry out the commercial operation in-house or entrust it to an independent agent or agency. The choice for either option should be based on the situation and objectives of the organization (Table 3.12).

The complexity of managing sponsorships has increased due to the significant development of specialized service companies. Currently, the trend is a desire for in-house sponsorship management, as evidenced by the moves of FIFA, FIVB, UCI and UEFA. The growing complexity of sponsorship management can be exemplified with the case of the IOC. As the rights holder of the Olympic Games and Olympic brands, the IOC is responsible for the direction and the general management of the Olympic marketing programme. In an effort to utilize the benefits of both in-house management and outsourced management, the IOC, in June 2005, purchased Meridian Management SA and subsequently

Table 3.11 Example of operational programming for current and potential sponsors

	Sept	Oct	Nov	Dec	Jan	Feb	Mar	Apr	May	June
Printed documents					All year long					
Internet					All year long					
Advertising	A1	A2					A3			
Press relations		PRR1					PRR2			PRR3
Public relations		PR1					PR2			PR3
Peripheral event(s)		E1					E2			E3
Monthly cost in €	8,000	12,000	0	0	0	0	12,000	0	0	8,000

Table 3.12 Advantages and disadvantages of retaining versus outsourcing the management of a sponsorship operation

	In-house	Outsourcing
Advantages	Continuing development of competences	Experience
		Expertise tailored to expectations
	Stronger commitment to the project	Quality service
	Direct contact with companies	Credibility
	Network building	Exclusiveness
	Directly responsible for the application of the contract's terms	Use of an existing network of customers
		Interaction with the customer
		Possibility of securing financial guarantees
		Indirect responsibility for the application of the terms of the contract
Disadvantages	Expertise not always adaptable to expectations	Possibility of a conflict of interest
		Potential conflict concerning the fees
	Adaptation period required	charged for the service provision
	Credibility	Potential for weaker commitment

changed the name to IOC Television & Marketing Services SA, thereby combining the specialized expertise of the said company with the benefits of in-house management.

Managing the sales process in relation to the decision-making process of prospective customers

Regardless of whether the sponsorship management is carried out in-house or is outsourced, the decision-making process of the prospective customer should be taken into account when implementing the commercial operation. Zeyl and Dayan (2003) classified the operations of the sales force according to various phases of the decision-making process (Figure 3.10). The involvement of the sales force, although it is active throughout the duration of the contract, varies quantitatively and qualitatively according to the various phases of the decision-making process.

Directing and managing the marketing operation

The direction and management of the commercial operation must take into account the marketing approach and the management of human and financial resources. To achieve the commercial operation objectives, it is necessary to:

- adopt an appropriate marketing approach for sponsorship and sporting organizations;
- break down the marketing strategy into sales operations for promotional goals, policies and action sequences (tactics);
- build an organizational structure;
- allocate human and financial resources;
- lead and motivate staff;
- control the results;

Figure 3.10 Purchase and sale process model

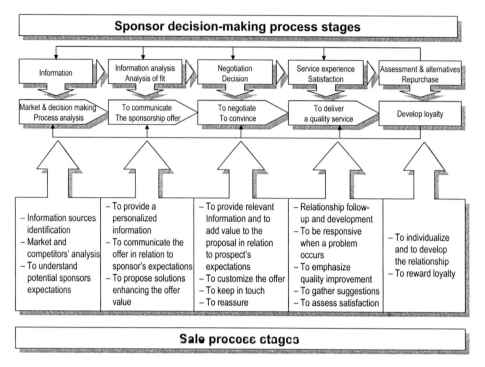

Source: Adapted from Zeyl and Dayan (2003)

- set up an information system;
- do all the above in a dynamic way.

Achieving effective results depends on employing qualified, motivated and communicative people. The sporting organization must lead, organize and manage available human resources via the creation of collaboration between various departments.

Delivering quality service to build sponsor loyalty

Everyone is satisfied and relieved when the sponsorship contract is signed. For the sporting organization, however, it marks the beginning of the second and most important phase of the sponsorship operation, considering the delivery of the service provision which must meet, if not surpass, the sponsor's expectations. In order to satisfy the sponsor and establish loyalty, the organization must set up a system to manage the quality provision.

Quality management foundations

Quality management is a systematic way of ensuring that the entire organization is mobilized for achieving all the activities necessary to develop and implement the sponsorship operation in order to secure the lasting satisfaction of the stakeholders. In the sports sponsorship context, the essential stakeholders are primarily the sponsors, media partners, local authorities and the sporting organization itself. Quality management also ensures that the activities are carried out cost effectively.

Sponsors obviously expect that contractual elements of the sponsorship service provision will be fulfilled (e.g. billboards, posters, VIP seats, etc.). The fulfilment of expectations will not increase the level of satisfaction of the sponsor, since the contractual elements of the service provision are compulsory, whereas failing to achieve the objective will have a very negative effect on the level of satisfaction of the sponsor. There are proportional expectations (accessibility, competence and responsiveness of the personnel, empathy, etc.), however, that positively influence the level of satisfaction of the sponsor, i.e. the better the performance of the service provision, the higher the sponsor's level of satisfaction. Sponsors also have latent expectations, which are unexpressed because the sponsor is unaware of them, or of their utility. These latent expectations, which can positively influence the sponsor's satisfaction, could be exploited through an activation programme built in collaboration with other primary sponsors and/or local authorities in an effort to increase the satisfaction level.

Implementing a management process for quality

The sporting organization must be acutely aware that managing the quality of the service delivered to sponsors depends directly on the organization and execution of various processes designed to ensure quality services. For example, in managing 50 VIP seats promised to a sponsor in a contract, marketers must cooperate with logistics, security, etc. Therefore, it is crucial to implement procedures to manage each process, i.e. each series of interactive tasks contributing to the delivery of the service provision.

Process management is the result of a unified effort to identify, share, clarify and improve practices, which generally creates value for sponsors and stakeholders. Sponsorship implementation must be looked upon as a network of processes that are formalized into procedures. Consequently, the sporting organization must identify which processes contribute to providing the promised service. In the framework of an event-driven sponsorship operation, the operational processes are actually organized in four detailed phases (see Figure 3.11).

It is necessary to have process supports to implement the operational processes being identified and described that contribute to the effective execution of the operational processes. In the case of an event-driven sponsorship operation, it acts to direct information, control legal aspects, and manage the infrastructure and resources, as well as the event-driven experiment.

The last phase consists of organizing the series of processes by establishing management procedures to determine priorities, objectives and communication methods, as well as to manage information and monitoring performances. Thus, the delivery of quality service to sponsors depends on implementing and coordinating these types of processes.

Review

Quality management identifies the most important processes in the delivery of a customized service that satisfies each of the sponsor's various expectations. There are five steps to follow in defining the quality procedure of each process:

Figure 3.11 Operational processes relating to the event-driven sponsorship operation

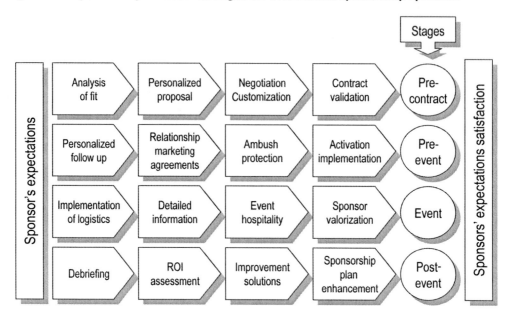

- identification and organization of the prioritization of sponsors' expectations;
- definition of the service offer that enables the satisfaction of expectations;
- identification of the operational processes facilitating the delivery of the service provision;
- identification of additional processes supporting the implementation of operational processes;
- identification of management processes permitting the implementation of a quality provision.

Evaluating the impact of an event-driven sponsorship operation

Evaluating the impact of a sponsorship operation is a major element in the management of service quality because it provides the organization with data justifying the sponsor's return on investment, such as during contract negotiations and/or when the organization is seeking new partnership opportunities. Nevertheless, evaluating the full impact is difficult to achieve since the effect of a sponsorship operation can hardly be isolated; sponsorship is integrated into the various strategies of the company. Therefore, measuring all the effects of sponsorship alone is impossible.

The direct and indirect approaches to evaluating sponsorship

There are two methodological approaches to evaluating a sponsorship operation: the direct approach and the indirect approach. The direct approach consists of measuring the impact of a sponsorship operation based on sales, which is the ultimate objective of communications integrated into a marketing strategy. This approach is based on the assumption that one can isolate the impact of a sponsorship operation by incorporating the sales activation strategy, which is theoretically possible to do when the effect is immediate and when no other major marketing operation overlapping with the sponsorship operation exists. Crompton (2004) provides the example of DeWalt Industrial Tool NASCAR Winston Cup Team sponsorship which led to a 30 per cent sales increase during the promotion period. Cars with theirs drivers were displayed at major retailers.

The indirect approach, however, is used in the majority of situations. This second approach serves to evaluate the effect of a sponsorship operation via intermediate variables of the persuasive communication process (through brand awareness, image, attitude, etc.). The objectives of sponsorship operations are based on persuasion criterion as summarized in Table 3.13.

Three dimensions of the evaluation

From a methodological perspective, it is advisable to define a three-dimensional evaluation prior to engaging in a sponsorship operation. This evaluation must answer the following three questions.

Who is evaluated?

The initial evaluation should be carried out on the communication target, and it is necessary to be able to reach it. If the organization is using an indirect approach that also seeks an effect on purchase advisors or opinion leaders (e.g. salespeople), then the evaluation must focus on these two indirect targets as well as on the communication target.

What is evaluated?

In addition to the indirect or direct evaluation methods, there is an alternative approach for evaluating the impact of a sponsorship operation. The third approach consists of measuring the quantitative impact of the sponsorship operation on both the direct and indirect public. This approach is based on the assumption of what is perceived by the direct or indirect public in the context of the event. From the sponsor's perspective, it is essential to achieve media exposure given the size of the audience. It is easy to gather essential quantitative information (e.g. TV and radio reach, newspaper articles) for evaluating the media impact of an event-driven sponsorship operation. Measuring the impact of an

Table 3.13 Indirect effects of sponsorship based on persuasion criteria

Activity	Intermediate variables	Behavioural variables
Sponsorship	Brand awareness	Purchasing intention
	Image	Trial
	Perceived quality	Purchase or repurchase
	Attitude	

event-driven sponsorship operation focuses on the two primary media approaches: television and in the press.

When to evaluate?

It is possible to evaluate the impact by taking measurements before, during and after a sponsorship operation. The most basic measurement protocol consists of an evaluation before and after the sponsorship operation. However, it becomes more complex when the evaluation after an operation is also considered the pre-operation evaluation, as is the case when a sponsorship is in the position to be renewed. The organization should conduct an evaluation during the operation if it wishes to:

- make adaptations to the activation programme (if time allows);
- probe the direct or indirect public;
- measure the impact in the media;
- measure the perception of the sponsor image during and after the operation (e.g. has the sponsor's image changed?).

These decisions concern all the stakeholders of a sponsorship operation. Therefore, they must be addressed and decided prior to the launch of the sponsorship operation.

The measurement of the audience and impact in the media

The measurement of the audience of a sports event is an important indicator of its impact. The audience is defined by the number of people who had the opportunity to see or hear about the event in the media during a given period. When an *ad hoc* study is carried out, it is important to collect data concerning people's centres of interest and consumption habits, since sponsors use these pieces of information to better target their sponsorship operations and leverage their brand.

Indicators of sponsor visibility

Due to cognitive limitations imposed on our memory capabilities, sponsors seek to get the best possible visibility with the direct and indirect public. The current trend is to reduce the number of sponsors to give them increased exposure (e.g. the UEFA Champions League has only four main sponsors). The visibility of a sponsor, i.e. the logo and name, must be evaluated in each media sector.

Indicators of sponsor visibility on television

In the context of an aggressive sponsorship campaign, where the sponsor seeks to have a strong impact in the event, the injection method is used during the television programme to remind viewers about the sponsor's association with the event. The viewers cannot escape the sponsor's advertising due to saturation. Data relating to the Formula 1 Championship show that the best visibility a sponsor gets on television results from a combination of visibilities on drivers, on-site billboards and on-screen injections of the sponsor's logo. This piece of information is used for distributing revenues between the various stakeholders, i.e. between broadcasters, the rights owners of the event, F1 teams and drivers, etc.

Indicators of sponsor visibility in the media

By subscribing to a specialist magazine, one can collect all the newspaper clippings needed to build a portfolio from which to calculate indicators such as the cumulative audience, the editorial surface area devoted to the event, and the chronology of published articles. The newspaper-clippings-based indicator is referred to as the advertising equivalent value, whereby the media characteristics, number of quotations, duration, surface area, etc., are rated. That value is compared with the tariff of each media advertisement in order to calculate its overall advertising equivalent.

The impact of each sponsor is accounted for by measuring the duration of the exposure of the sponsor (e.g. the size and visibility allotted to the sponsor). The overall duration of the exposure is then referred to an equivalent advertising value. For example, between 1998 and 2000, Schweppes was the official soft-drink sponsor of the West McLaren Mercedes Formula 1 team. The value of that contract was estimated at £1 million per season. The objective of the sponsorship operation carried out by Schweppes was to enhance the brand through an image transfer with Formula 1, the West McLaren Mercedes' team, and drivers, specifically, David Coulthard and Mika Hakkinen. The Schweppes brand appeared on the helmet of the drivers, on the sleeves of the team's outfit and on printed documents released by the team. Afterward, a study was conducted in five major European markets, i.e. France, Spain, Italy, Germany and the UK, whereby the duration of exposure of the Schweppes brand was measured during a six-day period on all television channels covering an F1 Grand Prix. The total value in advertising equivalent was estimated at £1.9 million. By extrapolating these results over the entire season on all markets covered by Schweppes, it was estimated that the equivalent advertising cost would have been £5.36 million, which is twice the total amount of sponsorship investment per season (contract and activation costs). The intention here is not to comment on these results, but to point out that calculating the advertising equivalent is open to criticism. Indeed, it is difficult to compare the duration of the visibility of a logo with a commercial advertising spot.

It is advisable to complete this gathering of press information. The collection of data is generally conducted by using a company specializing in such gathering and creation of portfolios for calculating the indicators previously mentioned. It is especially difficult for sponsors to have press media exposure, as journalists seldom quote the names of sponsors. More often, the sponsor's name will only appear in photographs. To optimize impact in the press, sponsors will seek to incorporate their name into:

- the title of the event (e.g. Rogers Cup with the Tennis Masters Series in Canada);
- a team (e.g. Vodafone with Manchester United Football Club);
- a stadium (e.g. the Allianz Arena of the Bayern Munich Football Club);
- a boat (e.g. Alinghi, BMW Oracle in the America's Cup).

Evaluating the impact of sponsorship on the intermediate variables of the persuasion process

This method serves to evaluate the impact of sponsorship on the variables constituting the process of persuasive communication. This method is based on a combination of qualitative (e.g. interview assessment) and quantitative (e.g. questionnaire data analysis) methods. In addition, it is necessary to follow the evolution of these variables through surveys. This form of evaluation is expensive and it is difficult to isolate all the effects of a sponsorship operation.

Evaluating the impact on brand awareness

Brand awareness is an unstable indicator because it typically peaks during the sponsorship operation and falls abruptly afterwards. It is possible to analyse the brand awareness levels recorded with various targets. With regard to sponsorship studies, the indicators of brand awareness are similar to those used in advertising.

Each indicator bears a specific meaning that contributes to the evaluation of the sponsorship operation's impact. The first brand to be quoted spontaneously by targeted people often indicates the pre-eminent sponsor in a given event. There is indeed a correlation between the first quoted brand and the main sponsor of an event. Beyond the first quotation, it is significant to look at the overall spontaneous memory results, as the overall score provides an insight as to how the sponsor's brand is anchored in the minds of targeted people.

Brand awareness is the ability either to recall or recognize a brand within a category. Unprompted brand awareness – the ability to recall a brand – is a recall measurement of how well the association between the sponsor and the sponsored event has been memorized. The previous example of the Schweppes sponsorship of the West McLaren Mercedes Formula 1 team was used in a study by Ipsos-RSL. The data of that study reveal that three companies sponsoring the F1 team stand out, where the first two are actually main sponsors whose name is incorporated into the name of the event, Mercedes (38 per cent) and West (27 per cent); Bridgestone (18 per cent) comes in third place. Schweppes was tied in fourth place with Mobil, obtaining a score of 10 per cent on the brand awareness test. In addition, a results analysis comparing people who associated Schweppes with F1 with those who did not make this association reveals that unprompted brand awareness was significantly higher with the group of people making the association with F1. From an operational point of view, this information proves favourable for the brand positioning of Schweppes.

Prompted brand awareness measures the recognition – knowledge of the brand in memory – of the sponsors from a list, thus revealing the impact of the sponsor in the minds of people following its sponsorship operation. Recall results indicate either the level of recollection of the sponsor's brand in the minds of targeted people or the level of confusion thereof. If there is confusion, the sponsor can use the results to evaluate the reason for it in an effort to adjust its next sponsorship operation. There is a close correlation between unprompted and prompted brand awareness.

In addition, studies on brand awareness show that people interested in an event associate sponsors with the event that are not directly associated with it. The 'pseudo sponsor' phenomenon can be explained by assuming that people systematically associate famous brands with sponsorship or because of ambush marketing. A study following the 1994 Lillehammer Olympic Games showed that most Americans (i.e. between 52 per cent and 66 per cent) believed that American Express (AMEX) was the official sponsor of the OG. In fact, Visa was the official sponsor in the credit card category. These results can be attributed to the ambush-marketing strategy AMEX implemented for the advertising campaign it launched in the context of the OG via a campaign based on the slogan: 'If you are travelling to Norway this winter, you will need a passport, but you won't need a visa!'

Evaluating the impact of the image and perceived quality

Image is the set of characteristics, beliefs, ideas and impressions a person holds and associates with a brand. In the previous example, Schweppes can be perceived as stylish, interesting, cool, refreshing, etc. Certain image characteristics also correspond to perceived quality (e.g. refreshing).

The results analysis of the example given show that respondents who knew about the sponsorship operation carried out by Schweppes have a strong image impression regarding the following dimensions of Schweppes beverages: refreshing soft drink (+33 per cent), teenagers' drink (+13 per cent), good to drink (+10 per cent), quality soft drink (+9 per cent) and to mix with alcohol (+16 per cent).

Several methods exist to grasp the significance of the image content, all of which can be classified into two categories. The first category refers to surveys based on a scale of values. The second category refers to surveys based on the notion of latent variables. These methods are presented in the case study in Chapter 5.

Evaluating the impact on the attitude towards the sponsor

Again, one of the objectives of sponsorship is to enhance or maintain a favourable attitude towards the sponsor, which can be evaluated through a scale ranging from 'I appreciate the sponsor' to 'I do not appreciate the sponsor'. The objective of the sponsor is to achieve a transfer of the favourable attitude towards the sponsored entity to its brand. The transfer is positively supported by the goodwill towards the sponsor. This friendly disposition towards the sponsor must be evaluated systematically.

The following data relate to the perception and attitude of spectators towards the official sponsors of the 1996 Atlanta Olympic Games:

- spectators that perceive the sponsors are leaders in their field of activity: 83 per cent;
- spectators expressing their preference for the sponsors of the Olympic Games: 55 per cent;
- spectators that feel the sponsorship of the Olympic Games by the company sponsor contributed to improving their opinion towards the sponsor: 45 per cent;
- spectators claiming that the company sponsorship of the Olympic Games will have a positive effect on the purchasing intention of the products of the sponsors: 33 per cent.

(Adapted from IOC 2000)

This shows not only that official sponsors are perceived as leaders in their field, but also that their sponsorship of the games has a positive impact on people's attitude towards both the company sponsors and on purchasing intentions.

From a methodological perspective, two aspects of this attitude must be evaluated: goodwill towards the sponsor and the evolution of the attitude of those targeted. Indeed, the purchasing intention is but one indicator. It is essential to conduct additional marketing operations so that intentions are actualized and become purchases.

Conclusion

In this chapter we developed a method and tools allowing both sporting organizations and companies to manage strategic and operational sponsorship. This method is based on persuasive communication impacting the components of the attitude towards the sponsor (i.e. cognitive, emotional and conative). On this occasion we stressed the importance of the activation programmes which make it possible to achieve the marketing objectives.

In this conclusion, we want to stress the fact that the entire process a potential sponsor would use to analyse the strategic and operational convergence of a sponsorship operation is condensed into a model incorporating five dimensions (see Figure 3.12).

1. *Strategic fit with the company.* A series of strategic and operational criteria must be taken into account to identify the competitive advantages of a sponsorship operation. This diagnosis is compiled from nine aspects as summarized in Table 3.14.

Figure 3.12 Platform for analysing the sponsorship fit operation from the sponsor's perspective

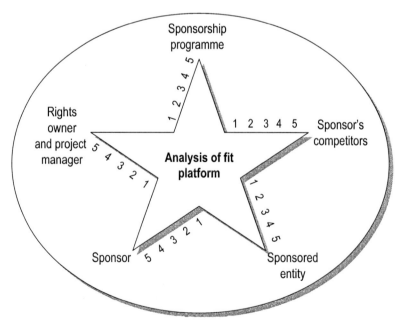

2. *Fit with dimensions of the sponsored entity.* The sponsored entity has certain characteristics that may complement the characteristics of the company sponsor. The following characteristics must be taken into account to determine the fit with the sponsored entity (see Table 3.15).

3. *Fit with the sponsorship programme.* The fit analysis with the sponsorship programme is conducted by taking into account the variables shown in Table 3.16.

4. *Benchmarking with competitors.* The three aspects presented in Table 3.17 must be taken into account for the benchmark analysis with the competitors.

5. *Fit with the rights owner of the event and/or the project manager.* In the framework of an event-driven project, the rights owner of the event is the legal person or company which profits from the operations of an event. However, the rightful owner can call upon the service provision of a third party, or project manager, to control the event in part or its

Table 3.14 Aspects pertaining to the strategic convergence

Aspects	Essential information required
Entity targeted	Do the company's products, services and brand share functional and socio-cultural characteristics with the sponsored entity?
Strategic and marketing objectives	Which strategic and marketing objectives is the sponsorship operation likely to help the company attain?
Communication target and marketing target	Are the company's communication and marketing targets accomplished by the sponsorship operation?
Desired brand positioning	Is the operation coherent with the intended positioning of the brand?
Duration	Will the operation enable the company to achieve its goals within an acceptable term?
In-house acceptance of the sponsorship operation	Is the operation mobilizing company personnel? Is there a fit with the internal culture of the company? (The interest in sponsorship is reinforced when the operation mobilizes the whole company)
Cost	Is the total cost of the operation (including activation cost) compatible with the company's marketing and communication budget?
In-house capabilities to manage the sponsorship programme	Does the company have the competences and resources required to manage a sponsorship programme? (If a company does not have the resources required to handle the entire process, a specialized agency can assume management of the programme. However, this will lead to an increase in the budget required to conduct the operation and perhaps cause issues during the implementation of the programme)
Effects of the interaction between the brand equity of the two partnering entities	What are the possible and desirable effects of the interaction between the dimensions of the brand equity of the sponsored entity and those of the company?
Competitive advantages of the operation	What are the competitive advantages of the sponsorship operation? How is the operation more beneficial than other marketing alternatives (e.g. publicity, public relations, etc.)?

Table 3.15 Dimensions of the sponsored entity contributing to the fit

Dimensions	Information necessary
Concept[a] and characteristic of the operation	Is the concept sufficiently unique and differentiated?
Positioning and communicated identity	Is there a fit between the positioning and communicated identity of the company and the sponsorship operation?
Acceptance and gratitude	Will the stakeholders accept the sponsorship operation? Will the stakeholders be appreciative towards the sponsor?

a The notion of concept relates to the original idea(s) on which the sponsored entity is conceived.

Table 3.16 Dimensions relating to the fit of the sponsorship programme

Dimensions	Information necessary
Structure of the sponsorship programme	Is the company at an appropriate position given the structure of the programme? Does the sponsorship programme ensure a balance between sponsors?
Stakeholders involved in the sponsorship operation	Which media are involved? Are there additional partners? Is the proposed partnership ensuring the desired social impact? Is there a programme of collaboration? Is there any opportunity for relationship marketing?
Data and evaluation process envisioned to monitor the impact of the sponsorship operation	Are the provided data relevant and reliable? Does the process of evaluation envisioned by the sporting organization provide sufficient information to evaluate the return on investment? Does the company have to set up a particular system to evaluate the impact of the operation? Does the company have the resources required to implement the operation?
Communication plan	Is the communication plan ensuring the desired impact? What are the synergies with the communications of the company?
Design of the sponsorship proposal	Does the sponsorship proposal provide the company with relevant information for evaluating the fit? Are the documents clear and easy to read? Is the design of the documents coherent with the communicated identity?
Activation programme	Does the proposed programme of activation correspond to the expectations of the company? Is the activation cost justified?
Nature of the conceded rights	Do the conceded rights enable the company to achieve its goals? Can it exploit the conceded rights?
Protection against ambush marketing	Is the brand registered or trademarked? If so, where? Is the sporting organization taking the appropriate measure to prevent ambush marketing?
Resources and competences of the sporting organization	Is the sporting organization able to deliver the quality service expected by the company? Is the sporting organization responsive, reliable and competent?
Nature of the quality procedures	Are the quality procedures (operational, support, management) tailored to the expectations of the company?
Price and trade negotiations	Does the content of the offer justify the price? Are the expectations of the company taken into account during the negotiations?
Competitive advantages	What are the competitive advantages tied to the sponsorship offer?

Table 3.17 Dimensions of benchmarking aspects of competitors

Aspects	Information required
Capacity to differentiate from competitors	Will this operation enable the company to differentiate from competitors? If yes, how? Will such differentiation become a competitive advantage?
Capacity to maintain the position of the company regarding competitors	In the event of successes, could the company defend its position with respect to competition?
Leverage forces	Do competitors have an advantage over the company (brand equity, financial resources, etc.)?

entirety. Therefore, it is essential to analyse the advantages or disadvantages to the management arrangement of the event as summarized in Table 3.18.

Analysing the processes of the fit and value

The suggested platform used to carry the fit analysis enables the evaluation of the perceived quality of the sponsorship proposal. The potential sponsor must evaluate possible disparity between its expectations and the characteristics of the operation while also considering other alternatives. Companies will define their preferred platform of convergence according to their respective culture, experience, resources, competences, perceived risk, etc. The platform is a means to balance each dimension according to the importance a company attaches to it.

All these dimensions are important and the decision-making could be time consuming and rather complex. In this context it is imperative to keep in mind the main questions and steps referring to strategic and operational processes. Strategic analysis allows both the sponsored party and the sponsor to answer the following five questions:

- What is the overall corporate strategy you wish to implement?
- Which sustainable competitive advantage(s) would you prefer to develop?
- How should the organization be positioned?
- How should the sponsorship offer be packaged?
- To which type of potential sponsor (prospects) should the focus be directed?

The operational sponsorship processes should implement the following steps:

- designing and structuring the sponsorship offer;
- targeting the potential sponsors;
- customizing the offer;
- establishing the price for sponsorship offers;
- conceiving and implementing the communication plan of the marketing operation;
- developing the sales process;
- delivering quality service to build sponsor loyalty;
- evaluating the impact of the sponsorship operation.

Consequently, this chapter has shown how the complexity of this system should be managed by taking into consideration key success factors, resources and competencies.

Table 3.18 Aspects relating to the fit between the rights owner and the project manager

Aspects	Information required
Rights owner	Does the rights owner have the competences and resources to conduct the operation? Does its brand equity constitute a competitive advantage?
Project manager (if applicable)	Does the project manager have the competences and resources to conduct the operation? Does the project managing organization's brand equity constitute a competitive advantage?
Relationship between the rights owner and the project manager (if necessary)	Is the relationship between the rights owner and the project manager a source of conflict? What are the risks?

4

Contracts associated with events

This chapter is an analysis of various sport contracts from a European perspective. The principles of defining a contract must take into account any international legal differences, which can influence business negotiations in significant and unexpected ways. Therefore, it is prudent to contact a specialized legal advisor before beginning any contractual negotiation.

The establishment of a solid legal agreement is one of the key elements for structuring the relationship between the event organizer and its partners. The procedures for developing a contract are determined in accordance with the legal system in which the contract is to be effective. The existence of a contract should not only define the rights and obligations of each partner, but also provide resolutions for conflicts or litigations that may arise during the execution of the contract. There are general procedures for developing contracts. Any contractual agreement should include the following key elements:

- the identity of each party;
- information defining the contractual relationship;
- the rights, obligations, duties and responsibilities of each party;
- governing law and dispute resolution mechanisms.

As previously mentioned in Chapter 2, marketers or managers in charge of the organization of a sporting event must consult a specialized lawyer in this field. It is essential that advice is provided by a specialist who knows the local codes of conduct which must be taken into account and who can evaluate the contractual needs correctly.

Each legal framework lays down its own codes of conduct in the development of contracts. A contract based on common law (e.g. as is the case in the Anglo-Saxon legal system) will differ from one based on codification. Nevertheless, most sporting event contracts worldwide relate to audiovisual rights, publicity, sponsorship and merchandizing licences. Event organizers may also develop additional categories of contracts, particularly in connection with commercial and civil laws when there is no explicit legislation applying to a particular situation.

General characteristics of contractual relationships

Common elements to be considered in contractual relationships are described below.

Location and date of the contract

The designation of the location and dates of the contract's validity are required to be included in any contract. However, the jurisdiction applied to the contract does not necessarily have to be the location where the contract is signed. Contractual parties can decide to be subjected to the jurisdiction of any mutually agreed country. Similarly, the parties can agree upon an effective date that is either before or after the actual signing of the contract.

Representatives

A detailed description of the individuals entering into a contract is required. It should include their full name, a reference to their status (e.g. ID card, passport, visa, etc.), place of residence, and in which capacity they are representing a particular organization or person. A description of the organization being represented is also required, including its name, place of residence, inscription of the commercial register, and any other pertinent data useful for identification.

Purpose and antecedents of the contract

It is important to define the purpose of the contract because it clarifies the will of the parties. The purpose of a contract reveals the nature of the legal relationship between parties and defines the nature of the relationship. If there is a detailed definitions section, it is possible to incorporate the purpose of the contract and the manner in which the objectives will be achieved in that particular section. However, in its absence, the purpose of the contract must appear in the agreement section and it must include a definition and description of the contractual relationship.

Most event-management-oriented contracts are based on rights held by the event organizer or a third party with the legal capacity to negotiate certain rights. Despite the occasional sale of image rights, the majority of event-management-oriented contracts are based on the temporary transfer of rights, not on the actual sale of any rights. The purpose or objectives section of a contract will provide for the full or partial transfer of rights for either using the rights directly, or negotiating rights to another party.

It is advisable, although not imperative, to include a subparagraph explaining the objectives and anticipated results from the execution of the contract. The antecedents of the association of the businesses, including the position of each party (e.g. a reference to the organizer as the rights owner of the broadcast rights to the event), can be included in this subparagraph. Additionally, it is advisable to include a statement expressing the intention of each respective party.

Definitions

The owner of an event is actually the rights owner of a series of rights, which are most often intangible. Therefore, the first challenge in developing a contract is to demarcate this series of rights.

Each sport has a unique model of competition. It is necessary to establish the specific rights relating to individual sporting events, given the differences between competitions. For example, certain activities relate to a one-time and/or a continuous event. Other rights relate to either an official or an unofficial competition, and so forth. It is thus essential to specify the content, form, conditions and characteristics of the event.

Additionally, it is useful to include a definition of key concepts that are introduced in the contract. Not only should legal concepts be defined (e.g. definition of a licence), but technical notions of the legal relationship should also be defined. A lawyer can contribute to the definition of legal concepts, but it is imperative to have input from the technical experts while establishing the definitions of the technical factors. The following elements should be included in the contractual definition of the event.

Name of the competition

All competitions must have a name, which can correspond to a brand. If the name of the event is modified, it can alter the value of the event for the purchase of the rights.

Category and nature of the sporting event

Each sporting event falls within a category (e.g. official or unofficial, international or national, professional or amateur), which must be specified in the contract. In addition, it is relevant to mention the impact of the results of the sporting event.

Number, origin and sporting level of the participants

If 18 teams are designated to participate in an event but only six teams do, there is a failure to provide what was guaranteed in the contract. There is arguably a significant difference between a league made up of 18 teams and one of only eight teams. Likewise, a difference exists between a competition of international top-level athletes and amateur athletes. For this reason, the specific elements must appear in the contract.

System, format and characteristic of the sporting event

It is necessary to define the characteristics of the competition from the point of view of the sporting organization (e.g. is it a league-type competition where teams play against one another? How many rounds are there? How many breaks are there during the event?) and specify the rules of the game by annexing them to the contract.

*Calendar of events, dates and schedules, and duration of the competition
and event*

This includes establishing the dates of the competition, the days of the week when the trials proceed (e.g. weekend, weekdays, the number of consecutive days), the schedules (e.g. time, time margin, time of the most interesting sporting events from the media's point of view) and the duration of the competition (e.g. one hour, two hours, or an established maximum time limit). It is also important to specify whether qualification rounds are included in the event. For instance, spectators and viewers are greatly interested in Formula 1 qualification rounds.

Location and venues

The location (e.g. city, country) and venue where the sporting event takes place must appear in the contract. Public interest in a sporting event can vary according to the location and/or the venue. For example, if the event is held in the open, inclement weather can adversely affect interests, whereas an event held under a covered space is less likely to be affected.

Media partners have increasingly strict requirements with regard to the scheduling, duration, transmission techniques and competition system of sporting events. Given the importance of broadcast rights and audience to an event's budget, it is important to specify the aforementioned elements in the TV rights contract in order to ensure proper media coverage.

Objectives of the contract

It is important to define precisely the object of the contract because it reflects the intention of the parties. A contract starts with a series of preliminary definitions concerning essential elements in a paragraph devoted to the definition of the objectives of the contract. Its purpose will be to describe what each of the parties want to achieve and how they will go about achieving these objectives.

The object of the contract thus leads us to indicate the nature of the established legal relation and on what it is founded.

Within the framework of the organization of an event, the majority of the existing contractual relations are based on rights and not on tangible elements (e.g. right to use, right of occupation, right to have, right to negotiate, etc.). Most such contracts are based on the rights owned by an event organizer, or a third party. These parties have the legal capacity to negotiate the reallocation of these rights.

The majority of the contractual relations are based on the concept of 'transfer of rights' and not on a sale. In certain cases, nevertheless, there can be a sale (e.g. acquisition of rights of images), but this is less common. The cession of rights may be total or partial.

Unforeseen circumstances in the contract

The licensee expects to obtain all that was purchased in the transfer of rights. It is impossible to predict with certainty what will happen during the sporting event – the essence of sport resides in the uncertainty of outcome; however, the event organizer must pledge a number of guarantees. The event organizer obviously cannot prevent unknown factors inherent to certain sporting activities such as accidents or bad weather (e.g. rain or snow).

Sporting-event-related contracts are concluded and signed before the commencement of the event, and thus relate to the future. There is always the possibility that between the signing of the contract and the commencement of the event, a series of unforeseen circumstances can occur, thereby modifying the terms of the contract. Therefore, it is wise to incorporate 'frustration of purpose' clauses specifying possible modifications to certain phases of event management, as well as remedies to be used in the occurrence of unforeseen events. There are two types of modifications to a contract from unexpected circumstances in the conditions relating to the event.

Modifications to core elements of the contract

In order to modify the core elements of a contract, an agreement between the two parties is required. Failure of an agreement can result in one of the following:

- the termination of the contract with a penalty to one party;
- the execution of the contract with a modification to the financial payment;
- the execution of the contract with a penalty to one party.

The following modifications are examples that can be made to the core elements of a contract:

- modification to the date and/or place of the event;
- modification to the nature of the event (e.g. official vs. unofficial, national vs. international);
- modification to the sporting level of the event (e.g. professional vs. amateur);
- modification to the media coverage (e.g. broadcast or no broadcast);
- change of ownership of the event.

Modifications to incidental elements of the contract

Modifications to incidental elements of the contract require the authorization of one party after receipt of a formal notification, which must allow an appropriate time for a response. This type of modification can either lead to a modification of the price or the payment of a penalty, or can bear no consequence at all. The following are examples of modifications to the incidental elements of a contract:

- a number of participants below the figure agreed upon;
- a change of the sporting facility;
- schedule modification (from the broadcaster's perspective, this can be considered a core element modification);
- stadium location modification (within the same city).

Validity period

In any type of contractual agreement, especially with the cession and possession of rights, it is necessary to specify the duration of the contract by establishing the beginning date and the termination date. The validity period of the contract refers to the period when it is acceptable under law to perform any provision written in a contract.

It is possible, for example, to sign a licence agreement and make it effective as of the date of signing, yet specify that the use of distinctive marks and industrial designs by the licensee are to be effective on a different date. In other words, the transfer of image rights may be effective upon the signing of a contract, yet obviously, the recording of images cannot be accomplished before the commencement of the event.

At the termination of a contract, certain derived rights (e.g. copyright and licensing rights) may or may not remain effective depending upon what is provided for. If the use of images, trademarks, logos, etc., is accepted after the termination of the contract, it is still necessary to specify what can be done with them and how long they can be used. For instance, supposing the rights owner of an event omits to specify the termination date in the merchandizing licence agreement with a third party. In the worst case, the licensee could still sell merchandise during the next staging of the event, thereby causing conflict with the new licensee for this subsequent staging of the event.

Although a contract has a fixed validity period, this period can be extended in the following ways:

* *Automatic prolongation:* when a series of relevant conditions is included in the contract and neither party denounces the prolongation of the contract, it can be prolonged automatically.
* *Unilateral prolongation:* a contract can be prolonged unilaterally when either party is able to require it in certain circumstances. However, this type of prolongation cannot bind the other party to the extension of the contract without conditions, and the extension must be conducted in accordance with relevant regulations.

Territorial validity

It is necessary to define the territory to which the contract is applicable. For instance, the rights owner of an event can choose either a country-to-country approach or a value-at-the-end approach when selling exploitation rights. Therefore, it is imperative to include the scope of the territory for which the rights pertain.

The reach of the contract by authorization or cession could extend worldwide or be limited to a given geographical area. In the latter case, it will be necessary to precisely define the area which carries the authorization and/or the cession.

Exclusivity

Account also should be taken of the material scope of the rights and the obligations deriving from the contract. We reiterate the fact that the type of contract to which we refer uses legal instruments relating to the authorization and/or the transfer of rights.

On this assumption, we must emphasize that it is essential to specify whether a particular right is exclusive or non-exclusive.

Exclusivity will be given according to the type of right, product or service, during one period and in a given geographical area. The same applies to the non-exclusive transfer. Thus, at the time of establishing criteria of exclusivity (as is usual for the sporting events), we must announce and define with precision the material, temporal and territorial applicability.

Exclusiveness is primarily determined and given by the:

- type of rights;
- type of product or service;
- duration;
- territory;
- term.

Price

In a contract, one party agrees to confer some benefit upon another in return for a financial payment. The price is a key element of the contract and must be precisely specified in the contract. The cost can be set in cash, in value in kind or in rights. In the two last cases the economic value must be assessed and the relevant criteria must be included.

Establishing the price of a contract

Fixed in cash
Rights can be assigned a predetermined economic value based on specific criteria, such as their ability to generate income.

Variable
Set pursuant to pre-established variable criteria that were provided for in the contract, such as the duration and number of broadcast matches; the overall audience or pay-per-view users; a percentage on the sales benefits or sales turnover of the licensee, etc.

Mixed
Established pursuant to pre-established fixed and variable criteria that were provided for in the contract; TV contracts and merchandizing licence agreements of the Basketball Euro League often use this particular formula.

Miscellaneous price-related elements

In any contract, one must not only consider the total price, but also take into account additional elements. Although not exhaustive, the following elements should be accounted for.

The currency used for determining the price or financial payment

In general, the price is denominated in the currency that is valid for payment in the country of the rights owner of the rights concerned. When several parties originating from various countries with distinct currencies contract with one another, it is advisable to incorporate a clause establishing a given exchange rate. Thus, for example, it could be useful to introduce a clause which, in addition to fixing the price, establishes the conditions of exchange between the currencies in which this price is in force, and in turn, fixes its mode of calculation if the rate of exchange did not reach or exceeded the limits fixed at the moment of the signature of the contract.

Currency evaluation system

It is equally important to take into account currency fluctuations, especially with long-term contracts. Short and long-term movements in the exchange rate during the course of a contract can change instalment amounts significantly. For the purpose of protecting individual interests, it is prudent for parties to agree on a currency valuation system should extraordinary currency fluctuations occur. In this regard, there are two key aspects to incorporate in the contract: (1) the name of the price index, regulator and country (NY Stock Exchange, SEC, etc.), and (2) the date and interval when the price must be calculated.

Terms and payments

A contract must always define how and when each instalment amount is to be paid. For example, party A can agree to pay a given amount in a series of 2, 3 or 20 fixed or variable instalments to party B.

The dates of required payments must also appear in the contract. For example, it can be 20 days after the end of the event or every two weeks until the full payment of the amount is made.

Guarantees of collection

Parties are able to establish additional guarantees in relation to payments and stipulated provision of services. If the payment of the overall amount is pending, it is possible to request a down payment, a personal guarantee or a preferential transfer of rights.

Liquidated damages

In the payment and terms section, one can establish a financial penalty in the event of non-payment on or before the fixed date, i.e. establish a liquidated damages clause. Typically, both parties agree on an appropriate interest rate that factors in a lag payment. In the event of a serious delay in payment, however, the interest rate charged can be a fixed amount, or the party at fault can be charged, for example, a fee equal to the common bank's interest rate plus a rate of X per cent above the base interest rate. It is important to specify in the contract the method for determining the penalty to be assessed for payment defaults.

Taxation

In most countries, monetary transfers are subject to taxation. Advertising, licensing, sponsorship and TV contracts are regarded as services and as such, they are not tax-exempt. In addition to paying the licence or transfer fee, the buyer must pay any applicable taxes. Thus, the following points must be addressed by the interested parties while developing any contract:

- Are the headquarters of the partnering entities in the same country and subject to a service tax in that country (e.g. VAT)?
- Are the partnering entities headquartered in different countries, yet both provide services in the same foreign country?
- Is there any international agreement (e.g. OECD Model Tax Convention on Income and on Capital) that can be used to avoid double taxation?
- What are the applicable legal statutes of activities developed in various countries? In certain countries, for example, the transfer of image rights may be regarded as a provision of service, while in other countries it may be regarded as a transfer of patrimonial rights. Furthermore, in the presence of an international agreement on double taxation, a transfer of image rights may be subjected to royalties tax or it may be tax-exempt.

Hence, two factors must be taken into account:

- Are the figures discussed in the contract based on net or on gross amounts?
- Which of the parties is to pay the tax burden?

When a contract does not provide for various taxation issues, both parties are obliged to pay tax according to the standards of each country.

Administration costs

Financial transactions through an intermediary, such as a bank or financial organization, tend to increase administrative costs. Depending on the number of transactions, these costs can add up to significant administrative expenditures. To avoid unnecessary administrative cost issues, the contract must expressly establish which party will assume the administrative and financial expenses concerning the payments.

Collection and payment

It is commonly believed that sport-related contracts must always follow the arrangement where the event organizer collects money in exchange for yielding rights, whereas a third party pays to acquire and use these rights. Such an arrangement is only valid with large, well-established sporting events where the brand identity of the event has a substantial value, which enables the event itself to generate revenue.

However, when an event or brand does not arouse much interest in the market, such as when it fails to attract a prominent sponsor or sufficient TV advertising revenues, the organizer must supplement the promotion of the event at an added cost. In this scenario, the organizer must buy advertising slots on television and/or spaces in newspapers for promoting the event.

Transfer to third parties

With a transfer of rights contract, it is advisable to determine whether these rights can be sublicensed or not. When there is no explicit authorization to sublicense the rights, third parties cannot use them. Therefore, the terms and wording of the contract must implicitly grant the rights to be sublicensed to third parties.

Using an example of the various audiovisual rights, the buyer of these rights is arguably interested in being allowed to sublicense rights to third parties. The buyer may wish to distribute the event to other countries, use additional transmission techniques, or enhance the audiovisual product. Therefore, it is always important to specify which rights can be sublicensed, as there is an increasing need to protect and limit rights associated in any transfer.

Right of first refusal and option to renew

Typically, sporting event contracts include a 'right of first refusal' clause, whereby one party such as a sponsor, broadcaster or advertiser secures a right to match the terms of a proposed contract with another party. At the conclusion of a contract, the 'right of first refusal' gives the buyer of the rights the option to either repurchase the use of certain rights in preference to others, or withdraw its commitment. Likewise, when a third party makes a proposal to obtain certain rights available at the end of a contract period, the 'right of first refusal' secures the privilege to match the offer during a tender procedure and thus maintains the preferential right to conclude the new contract.

This type of arrangement, i.e. right of first refusal, is not generally welcomed by authorities within the framework of sporting events because they tend to limit free competition. Consequently, their inclusion in a contract must be justified. However, all parties remain bound by the rules governing the free market competition.

Representation rights

Representation rights can be included in a contract that will allow the licensee to intervene directly in the event where licensed rights are violated or damaged. This authorization is given by the original rights owner and can be incorporated in a contract with a view to protecting the licensee against third-party infringement.

For example, suppose a football club sold the broadcast rights for the exclusive transmission of matches played in its stadium and another broadcaster infringes these rights. In theory, the club should act against the violator for using rights not legally obtained. However, the club can authorize its broadcast partner to act on its behalf for settling the encroachment because the broadcast partner is the one who suffers from the infringement.

Confidentiality

Contracts typically contain a confidentiality clause, whereby each party assumes the obligation not to disclose any information regarding contract conditions over a given period and to adopt appropriate measures for ensuring this confidentiality. Failure by a party to comply with the confidentiality clause is subject to a stipulated financial retribution payable to the party in good faith. The primary purpose of this clause is to ensure that sensitive data are not disclosed to competitors.

Breach of contract

Contracts are expected to be carried out in accordance with what has been agreed upon but conditions can change, which can lead to a breach of contract. Failure to fulfil any contractual obligation, i.e. non-performance, by either party, or by both parties, constitutes a breach of contract. As a result, it is necessary to specify which remedies to apply following a breach of contract. A breach of contract can be caused by:

- the rights owner (e.g. to prohibit the access of the media to the sporting facility or to authorize the access of unaccredited competitors to the sporting facility);
- the buyer of the rights (e.g. failure to comply with minimum broadcast obligations);
- both parties (e.g. failure to comply with the non-disclosure of confidential information).

There are three types of consequences resulting from a breach of contract:

- resolution or cancellation of the contract;
- obligation of additional requirements (e.g. upon a delay in payment, a personal guarantee can be requested by the creditor);
- liquidated damages (this consequence can be combined with the two previous consequences in a given breach of contract). A system of calculation for compensation or penalty must be determined during the drafting of the contract and specified in the liquidated damages clause whereby it accounts for both concrete damages and lost opportunities. For example, the system of calculation can be based on criteria such as sales turnover, duration of the breach, degree of seriousness of the non-performance, etc.

Subordination to superior norms

A contract or agreement describes the conditions of the relationship between two parties. Furthermore, each contracting party is legally subjected to the terms of the contract. However, contracts cannot account for every possible development and not all provisions are enforceable. The subordination of the parties to the terms of a contract is neither absolute, nor exclusive. Indeed, the rules enacted by government authorities and sports governing bodies are pre-eminent. Unlike other types of public events, activities developing within the world of sport must take into account the following legal parameters:

- the contract concluded between the parties;
- the sporting rules enacted by the governing entity that organizes and/or authorizes the event (i.e. IOC, sporting federation, league, etc.);
- the public legal provisions in force where the event takes place.

From an event management perspective, the organizer must subordinate to the hierarchy of normative authority (this procedure is typically more common in legal systems governed by a civil code, rather than in Anglo-Saxon legal systems, which are governed by common law). The sporting federation rules and public legislation are utilized to solve contractual issues, such as participation rights, breach of contract, or contract validity. There are two forms of normative subordination:

- subordination to the rules established by sporting organizations;
- subordination to public regulations in force in countries concerned by the development of the sporting event.

Conflict resolution is simplified when there is an explicit statement in the contract that an event is subordinated to a particular sporting entity's governing body (e.g. International Federation or Court of Arbitration for Sport) and/or public law accordingly, whereby both parties agree to be subjected to the said sporting authority's regulations.

Subordination to sporting organization rules

The rules enacted by the federation authorizing the event, or the entity organizing it, which relate to the organization and/or the development of a competition, can have an impact on a contract. Specifying the hierarchy of normative authority is necessary, given that it is important, for example, to know whether the rules governing the event allow publicity within the sporting facilities and the broadcast of the event on television.

Subordination to public regulations of countries concerned

Legal and subordination issues are relatively straightforward and easy to address when parties originate from the same country, and services are provided within that country. Conversely, when parties originate from different countries and activities are carried out in one or more foreign countries where legislation differs, it is more difficult to establish which hierarchy of normative authority the parties must subordinate to. Hence, it is necessary to consult a legal advisor to establish the proper authority.

Court of jurisdiction

A contract shall be governed in accordance with the laws of a particular court of jurisdiction, which must be specified in the contract, when contracting parties originate from various countries or territories. This is vital should the two sides disagree about the interpretation or execution of the contract.

Dispute resolution mechanism

There are various methods for resolving sports-related disputes.

Submission to an ordinary court of law

The ordinary court of law specified in the contract (e.g. the Court of Paris) is the most frequent option. The court of law can be chosen based on the nationality of either one of the contracting parties.

Submission to a court of arbitration

Pursuant to the Convention on the Recognition and Enforcement of Foreign Arbitral Awards[1] (the 'New York' Convention, 1958), the European Convention on International Commercial Arbitration[2] (Geneva, 1961) and the UNCITRAL Model Law on International Commercial Arbitration[3] (Vienna, 1985), the parties wishing to submit a dispute to arbitration must mutually agree to this in writing and outline their arbitration procedures.

Administering arbitration

There are two ways of selecting how to administer arbitration.

- The parties exercise their will by agreeing to specific arbitration procedures rather than merely opting for an undefined agreement of arbitration, which will leave much of the choice of the arbitration procedure to the arbitrator or organization selected to administer the arbitration process.
- An organization itself appoints arbitrators and establishes procedures that require consenting parties to agree to abide by these rulings. This second option is convenient and useful.

Choosing a court of arbitration

When contracting parties mutually agree to submit a dispute to arbitration, they have two options.

- They can submit their dispute to an ordinary court of arbitration (e.g. the Court of Arbitration of Barcelona).
- They can submit their dispute to a specialized court of arbitration designated for a particular field, such as international trade, transport, insurances or sport. It is practical to submit a sports-related dispute to a court of arbitration for sport, since their procedural rules are adapted to the specific needs of the sports world.

In the environment of sport there are several bodies or arbitration courts.

a. With a universal scope (but which will not always be qualified to solve a problem internal to a particular country)

> The Court of Arbitration for Sport (CAS) is an institution independent of any sports organization, which provides services to facilitate the settlement of sports-related disputes through arbitration or mediation by means of procedural rules adapted to the specific needs of the sports world. The CAS is governed by the administrative and financial authority of the International Council of Arbitration for Sport (ICAS). The CAS has nearly 300 arbitrators from 87 countries, chosen for their specialized knowledge of arbitration and sports law.[4]

The court of arbitration for football, which was created on the initiative of FIFA, regroups continental federations, national federations and football player unions. Based on FIFA statutory provisions, most disputes are now referred to the CAS.

The arbitration courts of certain international federations – volleyball, bobsledding, cycling, motoring, motorcycle racing, just to name a few – have an internal disciplinary body for arbitration. However, such bodies do not meet all the requirements established in the New York Convention, and as such may not necessarily be regarded as a valid arbitration body.

b. With a national and regional scope (used for country-specific issues)

- arbitration courts created upon the initiative of various National Olympic Committees (e.g. Spanish NOC, Luxemburg NOC, Belgian NOC, etc.);
- arbitration courts created upon the initiative of national or regional sporting federations or professional leagues (e.g. UEFA Disciplinary Services);
- arbitration courts for sport created upon the initiative of, and under the authority of, public sport authorities (e.g. certain autonomous communities in Spain).

Signatures

As previously mentioned, all contracts must have a signature to become legally binding. Signatures, or initials, are often required on every page of the contract, including any possible appendices.

TV contracts

All the elements presented in the previous section are fully applicable to this type of contract. This section discusses various aspects of TV contracts. Although it is important to remember that the term 'audiovisual' refers to television and radio transmission, the focus of this section is primarily on the aspects of television.

There is an absence of a proper legal definition of TV rights specific to sport. According to one major actor, Zen-Ruffinen, former FIFA Secretary General, speaking in 2002, TV rights should include the right to film, record, transmit, and sell the images and sounds of a sporting event.

TV rights packages

TV rights can be packaged into three primary categories.

Primary exploitation rights
These derive from the live broadcast of the event, which can be transmitted either through terrestrial, satellite or cable methods, as well as 'pay-per-view' (PPV), 'video-on-demand' (VOD), encrypted or free-to-air television, and any new emerging technology, such as digital subscriber lines (DSLs).

- *Pay-TV:* Pay television usually refers to subscription-based television services, usually provided by both analogue and digital cable and satellite, but also increasingly by digital terrestrial methods.
- *VOD:* Video-on-demand systems allow users to select and watch video content over a network of an interactive television system. VOD systems are either 'streamed', in which viewing takes place via video streaming over the Internet (or other network), or 'downloaded', in which the programme is brought in its entirety to a set-top box before viewing starts.
- *PPV:* Pay-per-view is the system where television viewers can purchase a private telecast of an event in their home. The event is shown at the same time to everyone ordering it. Events can be purchased using an on-screen guide, an automated telephone system, or through a live customer service representative. PPV services are similar to subscription-based pay-TV services in that the viewer must pay to have the broadcast decrypted for viewing, but usually only entail a one-time payment per single or time-limited viewing.
- *ADSL:* Asymmetric digital subscriber line is a form of DSL technology, a data communications technology that enables faster data transmission over copper telephone lines than a conventional modem can provide. The distinguishing characteristic of ADSL from DSL is that the volume of data flow is greater in one direction, i.e. it is asymmetric. ADSL can be used to deliver bandwidth-intensive applications like high-speed access to the Internet, streaming audio/video, videoconferencing, online games, application programmes, telephone calls, and other high-bandwidth services.
- *FTA:* Free-to-air is a term used to describe television and radio broadcasts that are not encrypted during transmission and thus may be picked up via any suitable receiver. The term should not be confused with free-to-view (FTV), which is television that is available without subscription, but which is encoded and thus may be restricted geographically. The term usually refers to delivery by satellite television, but in various parts of the world where encrypted digital terrestrial television channels exist, broadcasts on UHF or VHF bands can also be applied to those systems. Although these channels are described as free, the viewer does in fact pay for them. Some are paid directly by payment of a licence fee (as in the case of the BBC) or voluntary donation (in the case of educational broadcasters like PBS), others indirectly by paying for consumer products and services where part of the cost goes towards television advertising and sponsorship.

Secondary exploitation rights
These correspond to the recording of a sporting event with a view to distributing it in full or in part.

Tertiary exploitation rights
These correspond to the right to exploit images of a sporting event through the sale of DVDs or CD-ROMs on the Internet, and/or distribute them to sponsors.

Definition of content

An event organizer must examine the jurisdictional rules governing the transfer of TV rights to analyse the content of a TV contract properly. In general, the subject of a sports-related

TV contract is related to a rights owner of a sporting event authorizing or selling the right to transmit the sporting event to a broadcaster, enabling the latter to exploit the event in parts or in its entirety.

This authorization and/or transfer includes the images as well as the sound. Those could be the subject of an authorization or a transfer of their use. To simplify, we will refer primarily to the images, but in these cases all that is applicable to the images also relates to the sound. The term 'images' will be employed in a generic way, and will include both the images themselves and the sound deriving from or occurring at the time of the event portrayed.

Regarding the content of a TV contract, it is necessary to distinguish two distinct options: the authorization to transmit images and the transfer of broadcast rights.

Authorization to transmit images

In this case, the rights owner of the event explicitly authorizes a third party to transmit images during a given period and under specific conditions. This authorization can include:

- an authorization to record and produce images of the event;
- an authorization to only produce images of the event, not to record them;
- an authorization to merely broadcast images of the event without any right to record or produce images.

Likewise, image broadcast rights and image production rights can be transferred in their entirety or on a limited basis, such as only to one event, to a particular site of the event, or to a limited period and duration (at the end of the competition to interview the winner, or certain participants only, etc.).

Transfer or lease of broadcast rights

In this case, the event organizer may be interested in retaining certain image rights with a view to exploiting additional opportunities with a third party.

In theory and according to circumstances, a TV contract is considered concluded when the images are transmitted. The licensee, however, may be interested in retaining the copyright on images it produced for marketing them and implementing alternative programmes. Suppose, for example, that a company is sponsoring an athlete and wishes to include images of the said athlete in its publicity for a World Championship or the Olympic Games. Do these images belong to the athlete, a club or federation, the organizer of the event, or to the broadcaster who produced these images?

When a broadcaster is authorized to transmit an event, it cannot market any images it produces unless it obtains the expressed consent of the event organizer. The broadcaster's capacity to produce images grants it the intellectual property on images it produces. However, intellectual property does not give a *de facto* right to exploit these images.

The various forms of image transfer

Partial transfer of images

The event organizer, i.e. the rights owner of images, not only grants a third party the right to broadcast the event, but also to market these images in various ways where images still belong to their originator. (This is a compromise between the authorization to broadcast and the full transfer of image ownership.) There are three distinct ways to limit this type of image transfer.

Term limitations
According to the provisions of the contract, the licensee may continue to use and sublicense images for a given time period such as one week, one month, one year, or ten years beyond the event itself for reportages, special programmes, extracts, compiled highlights, etc.

Limitations to certain types of images
The licensee or a third party is restricted to using only certain images pursuant to the terms of the contract. The licensee, for example, may be restricted to marketing only compiled highlights of a game, images of a particular athlete or team, images of the finals, or only images recorded and produced by the broadcasting company which transmitted them, etc.

Usage limitations
The licensee or a third party may only use images for a particular usage or programme. For example, images can be used to produce additional sports programmes, reportages, or summaries of events, etc. Likewise, usage can be limited to certain distribution platforms such as television platforms, PC and console video game platforms, Internet platforms, mobile TV platforms, etc.

Full transfer of images

This type of transfer is also called a 'transfer of copyright ownership'. The purchaser of the rights acquires the full right to broadcast certain events as well as the proprietary rights to all of the images it records and/or transmits for a specified span of time. Depending on the terms of the contract, the buyer can thus sublicense image rights to third parties and engage in as many marketing opportunities as it deems appropriate.

It is important to stress that the ownership of the exclusive use of images is subject to a temporal limit pursuant to national legislation and/or international agreements with regard to intellectual property. Copyright protection generally expires after approximately 50–60 years. The images then fall into the public domain, meaning that they are no longer protected by copyright. Subject to certain exceptions, these images may be freely copied or used in the creation of derivative works without permission, or authorization, of the former copyright owner.

Forms of authorization

There are various forms of authorization with regard to the broadcasting of an event:

- authorization to transmit only the live broadcast of an event;
- authorization to transmit the live broadcast and/or a delayed broadcast of an event;
- authorization to broadcast the event and use certain images in other types of programmes (as previously provided for);
- authorization to broadcast an event in its entirety or in parts.

The authorization regarding the term of the contract can also take various forms:

- one-time authorization (e.g. 2008 Beijing Olympic Games, 2007 IIHF Championship);
- authorization is valid for an uninterrupted sporting event (e.g. UEFA Championship).

In the latter case, the authorization can last one or more seasons. When an authorization or transfer of image rights is valid for several seasons, the term of the contract cannot be overly long. Anti-monopolistic and fair competition rules prohibit excessively long-term contracts, especially when they consist of exclusive agreements.

In short, when a contract for the transfer of image rights merely consists of an authorization to broadcast images of an event, the contract is concluded upon the broadcast of that event irrespective of whether the authorization was granted for a live broadcast or tape-delay broadcast. When a contract consists of a partial transfer of image rights, it is imperative to specify the term of this transfer. If the contract provides for a full transfer of image rights, the term is subject to the copyright legislation in force, whereupon images belong to the public domain upon its expiration.

The systems and methods for transmitting images are constantly evolving. Although this section focuses exclusively on current technologies, the event organizer must take into account newly emerging technology and applications during contract negotiations. There are various telecommunications methods and systems which can be used to send and receive images.

Methods for sending a signal/transmission:

- direct satellite;
- radio waves (UHF and VHF bands);
- cable;
- satellite-to-cable;
- wireless;
- copper wire;
- power line communications systems (hertz transmission).

Systems for receiving a signal:

- open or free (requires open standards equipment);
- closed or encrypted systems (requires proprietary reception equipment);

- black and white, or colour;
- pay-per-view.

Communications systems:

- analogue or digital;
- information and communications technology (e.g. GPS);
- PPV, VOD, FTA;
- Internet, Ethernet, Extranet;
- mobile telephony;
- third generation/UMTS and fourth generation wireless technology (e.g. the WAP protocol, which enables PDAs and mobile phones to access to the Internet);
- ADSL.

Two aspects should be considered with regard to signal processing. In a communications system, a transmitter encodes a message into a signal, which is carried to a receiver by the communications channel. The signal affects transmission quality and accounts for the principal expenditure for broadcasting the images of an event. The ultimate beneficiary of this signal is the broadcaster.

The event organizer must ideally own the signal because a third party, e.g. a direct broadcast provider (DBS) may decide to collect the event organizer's programmes available via satellite and resell them to the viewer. When an event organizer is the rights owner of the signal, additional opportunities can be exploited. For instance, the event organizer can charge the said DBS a fee in exchange for the right to broadcast images of the event at a later date (although there is a risk of cannibalizing[5] the broadcaster that bought the broadcast rights).

Therefore, the contract must define who owns the signal, given that image production and image broadcast ensue from it.

Access to sporting venues and equipment

A clause stipulating that the broadcaster, and any necessary crew members, be granted access to the sporting event facilities must be incorporated into a TV contract. This clause serves to facilitate access for cameras, technicians, and other broadcasting equipment, thereby ensuring optimal conditions for the broadcast of the event.

Nevertheless, certain limitations and/or conditions may be imposed upon the recording of images. For example, the event organizer may choose to prohibit or limit camera access to a team's dressing room. Alternatively, the broadcast company partner may require recording images of a VIP seating area and its people. However, stadiums equipped with closed-access backstage VIP areas may restrict media access to this area. Thus, specific details of any said limitations must be provided for in the contract. Otherwise, the broadcast company partner may assume it has the right to record images anywhere within the sporting facilities to which it has access.

Exclusivity

Exclusiveness constitutes one of the most significant clauses in any contract of authorization or transfer of audiovisual rights of an event. Given the competitive advantages it creates, exclusiveness clauses warrant a higher price. The perceived value received from an offer of exclusivity affects the negotiation of price between parties. The contract must precisely define the scope of the exclusiveness and justify the price paid for it in accordance with both parties.

In the absence of an exclusiveness agreement between the event organizer and the broadcast company partner, the transfer of image rights is regarded as non-exclusive unless the terms of the contract imply otherwise. In case of dispute, the matter can be brought before a court of law or an arbitration panel.

The recourse to exclusiveness is frequent in the sporting environment. The cost of using a satellite communications system for broadcasting a sporting event is significantly high. From the broadcaster's perspective, however, an exclusiveness agreement can offset or recoup the investment made for securing the broadcast rights to a sporting event.

Exclusiveness must be defined in terms of duration, territory, content and modes of communication.

Duration term

There are two comprehensive issues regarding exclusive TV broadcast licence agreements, namely the maximum term of exclusiveness and the right to information.

Maximum term

In Europe, national and international policies support free-market competition. The Commission of the European Communities, in particular, has reservations concerning the duration of exclusive TV broadcast licence agreements. Nevertheless, European Commission competition regulators occasionally allow the granting of exclusive TV broadcast licensees under certain conditions, yet ensure that access to sports rights remains open and non-discriminatory. Unfortunately, there is no standard between countries of the European Community, whereby it would be possible to insist that exclusiveness cannot last, for example, more than three years. Generally, the provisions of the European Commission are taken with a view to supplement the national law of a particular country. Thus, conditions of exclusivity vary from country to country.

The European Court of Justice (ECJ), which is responsible for upholding Competition Law and Policy in the European Union, has traditionally ruled that exclusiveness concerning TV broadcast licence agreements is essential for the proficient execution of sporting competitions and economic requirements. However, the ECJ maintains a restriction on the duration of exclusive TV broadcast licence agreements to, for example, three, four or five years depending on the situation. Currently, ECJ judges tend to determine the duration of exclusiveness by striking a balance with the minimum term required to leverage the investment made for securing an exclusive TV broadcast licence.

Right to information

The broadcast of a sporting event has an impact on the event itself and on the right to information of citizens.

Irrespective of whether there is an entry fee or not, a sporting event is a social activity open to the public, whereby it can be considered of public interest. European Union law and policy consider that the sport and certain events (e.g. Olympic Games, World Championships) are activities of public interest that go beyond the private interest of participants and interested parties.

Citizens of democratic societies have the right to information. This recognizes that citizens have the right to be informed about important developments in society, including information about sport and sporting events. The debate around the right to information relates to determining which sporting events are of public interest. There are only two processes for determining whether a sporting event is of public interest.

Provision contained in a national law
Pursuant to an EC directive, European Union members draw up their respective lists of annual events which the government of each of country regards as of public interest. This list is bundled with a series of conditions for the broadcast of the event (e.g. the event must be broadcast on free-to-air TV so that it is accessible to all).

Terms of a jurisprudential decision
In some European countries, such as the United Kingdom, Spain and Germany, ECJ judges typically consider that citizens have a right to information, including information pertaining to sport and the broadcast of sporting events.

Media access right

The media also have the right to be informed about sporting events, a phenomenon which is referred to as the 'media access right'. The media have the right and obligation to inform the public objectively and sufficiently. The right to publish news essentially depends on the ability to gather information, which is dependent on media access. Hence, the media have a right of access to the facility where the sporting event takes place. This right of access is subject to a licence fee in exchange for the recording of images. When drafting a contract, it is important to specify the number of people being accredited, the accessible areas, technical conditions granted to them, etc.

Although the media access right is undeniable, determining whether this right includes the direct recording of images is often debated when a broadcaster has purchased an exclusive right for the recording of images of the sporting event. Regardless of the arrangement, any exclusive TV rights holder must facilitate access to images it records directly.

Consequently, it is also important to determine which images must be facilitated, e.g. showing of the entire event, extracts and/or compiled highlights. The ECJ and state courts insist on the following two criteria:

- The images to be facilitated must relate to important and relevant moments of the sporting event. Image relevance is established through a mutual agreement between parties interested in the event (i.e. the owner of the event, the rights holder of the TV rights and various media stakeholders in the event). In the absence of a mutual agreement, a judge can determine which images must be facilitated. Due to the broad variety of sporting events, it is impossible to determine a universally accepted system to determine which images must be facilitated. Thus, a case-by-case approach must be utilized.

- The right to information is restricted in terms of duration and space. Unauthorized third parties can use recorded images for informational purposes only, not for a full retransmission of the event. This restriction was initially imposed by several national legislations with a view to setting a maximum time limit to media access right, which was set to a three-minute time limit. However, this limit is not universally suitable for the sport world when one considers that the lengths of some sporting events are mere seconds such as the 100 metre sprint. Thus, the time limit for media access of sporting events must correlate to the length of a given competition.

Another related issue consists of determining whether media access rights grant free access to the direct recording of images, or just facilitate access to recorded images. It is better to negotiate this settlement rather than risk settling the dispute in court. It is feasible that the court determines who is allowed to directly record images, but with such restrictions that limit or hamper the quality of the said images (e.g. only one camera in a single corner of the venue).

With regard to disputes relating to the exploitation of TV rights, neither the European Commission nor the jurisprudence of European Union member states have precisely defined conditions for the broadcasting of sporting events. In fact, common sense and public relations usually takes precedence in contracts relating to exploitation rights. It is important to balance the interest of each party. Thus, the event organizer, when granting a licence for the exclusive right to record and broadcast images, must incorporate a clause in the contract whereby the leasing or transfer of exclusive rights is subject to the applicable right to information regulations in each respective country. Likewise, in the event where an EC directive or national law binds the acquirer of TV exploitation rights to facilitate images of a sporting event to the media, the contract must be written accordingly.

Territory

The contract must stipulate to which territory the exclusive exploitation of TV rights applies, i.e. a particular region or country, or worldwide. Currently, it is not possible to guarantee an exclusive transmission of an event worldwide. This is due to current technical issues regarding the distribution of the moving signal ('overspill'), or to the fact that some individuals may be viewing the event through the Internet platform. In any case, the exclusiveness of the transmission can be guaranteed insofar as no unauthorized broadcaster or TV operator can legally transmit the same event in the same territory.

Communications methods and platforms

The exclusive selling or leasing of commercial broadcasting rights can also be subject to one or more techniques of communication. Thus, it is possible to conceive that the leasing or transfer of broadcast rights includes the live/near-live/delayed coverage, on Pay-TV or free-to-air TV, via cable or satellite, or any combination of the above, of a sporting event, as long as the time, duration, territory and methods of transmissions are specified.

Clearly, the acquirer of the exploitation rights has an interest in securing all the methods and platforms available. Nevertheless, as mentioned earlier, that is subject to its technical and marketing capabilities, as well as to the price it is willing to pay.

When one wishes to guarantee exclusive commercial broadcasting rights, it is prudent to include a clause in the contract whereby future technical developments in new media not anticipated at the current time are taken into account (i.e. the Internet, mobile telecommunications and other future exploitation rights not yet considered). For this purpose, one must specify that the exclusiveness incorporate any prospective methods and platforms developed to record, file, copy, distribute and process images.

Content

The content of a contract for the exploitation of TV rights will vary according to the type of sporting event. Content refers to the various issues, topics and questions which must be addressed to ensure the execution of a contractual agreement.

A TV operator negotiating licence rights may assume that the right to broadcast a sporting event includes the right to broadcast a pre-game interview with a coach. Likewise, another may presume broadcast rights include the right to interview athletes after a competition. Indeed, pre- and post-event moments are tied to an exploitation rights package. To avoid possible disputes and misconceptions, it is imperative that all elements related to any transfer of rights are precisely defined and established in the contract.

When a TV rights contract is concluded on a non-exclusive basis, it is relatively simple to define the scope of rights granted. Conversely, when a TV rights contract is concluded on an exclusive basis, and the scope of exclusiveness is not properly defined, many problems can occur. Thus, the entire scope of exclusiveness of TV exploitation rights must be defined in the contract to avoid possible arbitration.

Based on the legal analysis regarding the selling or leasing of TV exploitation rights, two conclusions can be made concerning the content and opportunities offered through a TV contract.

Essential exploitation content

Every moment, fact or act likely to occur during a sporting event, including peripheral events, must be defined if subject to the lease or transfer of TV rights. For example:

- drawing of matches, tests/trials or groups;
- opening and closing ceremonies;
- the sporting event itself;
- press conferences;
- training sessions;
- presentation of official selections, teams, new players, coaches, new car prototypes, engines, etc.;
- medal or trophy awards;

- other peripheral events organized inside and/or outside the sporting facilities during the course of an event.

In general, the purchaser of the exploitation rights seeks to obtain a comprehensive rights package for the event. Subsequently, the price is proportional to the scope of the rights granted to the purchaser. The value of TV rights is usually in balance with the investment made to secure TV exploitation rights and the cost of service provisions, scope of rights, and exclusiveness offered by the event organizer (rights owner).

Substantive exploitation packages

The leasing or selling of TV exploitation rights is organized into various packages. Sporting events, for instance, consisting of several stages and simultaneous qualifying rounds (e.g. the tournament of the EUFA Champions League), make it impossible for a sole TV operator to broadcast all the matches in their entirety simultaneously on live, free-to-air TV. Consequently, various packages for leasing and/or selling exploitation rights are necessary.

In this case, the event owner, i.e. owner of the broadcast rights, typically offers the live broadcasts of the competition in various packages to both free-TV and pay-TV programme suppliers. As a result, a TV operator can bid on and acquire the TV rights exploitation package it desires or can afford, via an established award procedure.

The direct sale of exploitation rights by the rights owner must occur by an official public invitation to tender. The official announcement for the exploitation rights tendering must always be advertised prior to the start of the procedure. Pursuant to an EC decision,[6] for example, the joint selling of the media rights to the German Bundesliga must be advertised four weeks in advance. The rights owner must ensure that the invitation to submit a bid contains all the relevant information about the content of available rights packages, as well as the terms and conditions that an applicant (TV operator or broadcaster) must satisfy when acquiring the exploitation rights.

Advertising

Advertising is one of the key aspects surrounding the sporting event concerning the leasing/ selling of TV exploitation rights. There are two categories to consider.

- *On-site sponsorship:* static, dynamic and/or sound publicity and advertising inside the facilities where the sporting event takes place.
- *Media sponsorship:* broadcasting publicity and advertising on TV, Internet, mobile platform, etc.

On-site publicity and media sponsorship are to be separated insofar as the rights to each belong to distinct individuals or entities.

The event rights owner (or the sporting facility owner) can determine the sale of publicity spaces within the sporting facilities where the event takes place. Likewise, it can contemplate selling publicity on athletes' garments if the rules of competition allow, or promote the products or services of an associated sponsor through loudspeaker announcements.

TV broadcasts bring an added value to publicity. When an event is broadcast on television, sponsors and advertisers are willing to pay higher prices to have their products, services or logos associated with the event. Furthermore, the value of media publicity varies according to what is in the camera shot background (e.g. signs, billboards, hoardings, etc.). From the perspective of the event rights owner, it is important to know whether the broadcaster holds any rights on this advertising.

It is technically possible to modify broadcast images, whereby it is possible to retransmit altered images to the viewing public. Additionally, TV cameras are increasingly publicizing and highlighting sponsors' logos plastered across the playing surface. In the UK, for example, logos can be seen on hoardings but cannot be introduced specifically by the TV operator. To evade this regulation, sponsors paint their logo on the pitch, at a distorted perspective so that when the camera is at the right angle (usually a wide shot), the logo appears to stand up and appear as if generated on the pitches. Likewise, logo injections, which serve to remind viewers of a sponsor's association with a sporting programme, are more frequent than in the past. Consequently, it is crucial from the perspective of the event rights owner to define the scope and content of the TV exploitation rights granted to a TV operator or broadcaster to prevent ambush marketing and cannibalization. This serves to ensure the enduring satisfaction of associated sponsors and the financial longevity of the event.

It is difficult to satisfy all the needs of the sport and broadcasters in relation to the matter of sponsors, given the legal framework in place and case law. Currently, each of the aforementioned protagonists holds a legitimate claim to portions of the benefits generated through media sponsorships. Indeed, neither the event rights holder nor the TV rights exploiter has the absolute right to appropriate and use images of the sporting event without the express consent of the other partner.

In order to avoid a series of disputes, the interested parties must negotiate and define every aspect of the TV exploitation rights package. Specifically, the contract must establish answers to the following questions:

- Who holds the right to sell publicity spaces within the sporting facilities? Who determines which companies can buy advertising allotments? Are there any royalties required to be paid, and who has to pay them to whom?
- Who holds the right to sell sponsorship and advertising slots during the broadcast of the event? Can the licensee inject advertisements and place bumper breaks[7] during the broadcast of the sporting event?
- Are there any measures in place to prevent ambush marketing?

Sporting events offer a unique marketing platform to access a large audience. When a sporting event is broadcast on television, significant sums of money are generated through sponsorship deals with the TV rights licensee and/or the event rights owner. When the event rights owner is in control of sponsorship deals, it must ensure that the rights of exclusiveness granted to sponsors are not infringed by ambushers. Therefore, the event rights owner and TV operators must guarantee a right of first refusal to sponsors regarding advertising spaces (camera background shot) and advertising slots. Consequently, companies sponsoring the event can select advertising spaces and slots before their competitors do.

For instance, the Olympic Games TOP sponsor companies receive exclusive marketing rights and opportunities within their designated product category. These rights and opportunities are an integral part of the contract they can sign with the various members of the Olympic Movement. Likewise, TOP sponsors are provided with a contract containing a right of first refusal to acquire advertising slots before, during, and after the broadcast of the Olympic Games.

In the case of the EUFA Champions League, the TV operator is in command of negotiating all types of publicity surrounding the EUFA football championship. Therefore, the TV operator has the right to negotiate on-site publicity and advertising, as well as media sponsorships before, during and after the broadcast of football matches.

Technical conditions and qualitative criteria of TV coverage

Television contracts must include the technical conditions and qualitative criteria regarding the coverage of a sporting event. Intellectual property rights concerning images broadcast during a sporting event are for the moving video signal only. Several TV operators can broadcast the same sporting event, yet their coverage of the event is dependent on the moving video signal, which is produced by the sole entity owning the rights to it. Ideally, the event rights owner should be the only one entitled to produce or have produced the moving video signal.

From the perspective of the event organizer, the moving video signal is important, since it has an effect on the quality of image transmission and cost. When TV exploitation rights are merely leased to a broadcaster or TV operator and the responsibility for producing the moving video signal remains in the hands of the event organizer, the latter must define the required technical conditions and qualitative criteria that the TV operator must adhere to while covering the event.

In some cases, however, the event organizer does not own the rights to the moving video signal. This reduces its ability to exploit images of the sporting event and to manage the quality of the coverage of the event. In this case, the event organizer must request a provision in the contract whereby it can maintain a certain control over the quality of the signal.

For purposes of quality management and branding of the event, the organizer/rights owner of the event must have an interest in the moving video signal. The signal is vital for ensuring that the quality of the broadcast of the event is adequate for the marketing strategy and positioning of the sporting event. The quality and selection of images that are broadcast can have a positive or negative influence on the image of an event as well as the satisfaction level of sponsors.

Therefore, TV contracts must define a series of technical conditions with regard to the recording, production, realization, transmission and transformation of images to be broadcast.

Some sports organizations, such as the IOC for the Olympic Games, the IAAF for international athletic tests and the UEFA for the Champions League championship, have produced broadcast guidelines that establish technical conditions for the recording, production, realization, transmission, modification and transformation of images taken during the sporting events which they govern. Technical conditions can include the following:

- the type and number of cameras to be used in each position (e.g. fixed, tracking, etc.);
- the kind of camera mounting devices, platforms or scaffolding needed (e.g. are cranes or jibs needed?);
- the location(s) providing the best coverage and the best lighting (this is a key factor when determining the best angle from which to capture the event);
- characteristics of the moving video signal (i.e. bandwidth, number of pixels and refresh, image resolution, etc.);
- specifications for the realization (e.g. determination of the shots and images to be broadcast, the sequence in which this must be done; priority of must-show moments – e.g. is there an obligation to broadcast the award of medals at the end of an event?).

Broadcast obligations

A contract must explicitly state the obligation that the exploiter has to broadcast the event or specific moments of the event, whichever is stipulated in the contract. In addition, the event rights owner must establish a procedure for unused exploitation packages: a liquidated damages clause must stipulate the compensation for a failure to execute, in a proper manner, any provision of the TV contract.

The purpose of securing a TV contract is not only to generate financial resources for a sporting event, but also to execute the communication strategy encompassing the promotion of the event. Thus, proper execution of a sponsor's TV rights package, as well as advertising agreements negotiated with the media, are crucial considering the tremendous influence it has on the overall strategies.

Therefore, it is prudent for TV contracts to include explicit details on broadcast obligations such as specific broadcast hours (e.g. prime time), the duration of the broadcast, and the types of broadcast media.

Advertising contracts

Advertising contracts contain various categories of legal agreements. These agreements are formed in an attempt to direct the public's perception of a product, service or brand by using the sport and sporting events as a marketing platform.

This section is based on the following EC directive regarding publicity: 'commercial communication' means 'any form of communication designed to promote, directly or indirectly, the goods, services, or image of an undertaking, organization, or person engaged in commercial, industrial or craft activity, or practicing a regulated profession'.[8]

Over the years, a number of discussions have been conducted with the vain purpose of reaching an agreement on what name should be attached to sports-related contracts, such as sponsorship, patronage, charity, publicity, PR, media advertising and advertising contracts. Given that the current legislation has yet to come up with a clear definition of what is a sports-related sponsorship contract, the various types of legal relationships between parties will be analysed rather than allotting a name to any specific contract. It is more important to examine the existing legal agreements of the various types of publicity contracts between sponsors and an event organizer, all of which share the following common elements:

- an entity that wishes to communicate its brand, image, or product to an audience;
- an entity that is interested in associating with the communication strategy of another entity and willing to pay;
- a communication strategy involving one or both parties.

We have already pointed out that in the sporting sector, the communication strategy relates to only one party (i.e. the sponsor). It is generally associated with both (i.e. sponsor and organizer of the event). Thus, both parties may use this type of legal relation.

In the sports context, there are two different types of legal agreements regarding publicity that can be utilized separately or together.

- *Advertising insertion agreement:* An entity enters into an advertising insertion agreement with an advertiser or a media interest to put in place a communications campaign in line with its marketing strategy in an effort to promote its name, product, brand or services.
- *Collaborative agreement of association (sponsorship):* An entity implements a collaborative communications campaign with a view to strengthening its marketing strategy by associating its name, product, brand, or services, to the name, brand, or image of a third party (e.g. the event organizer or its event) via a sponsorship programme.

Subsequently, three types of sports-related publicity contracts can be defined, in general, the first type corresponds to what is called advertising and the two others to sponsorship

- advertising contract;
- sponsorship contract without advertising insertion;
- sponsorship contract with advertising insertion.[9]

Let us analyse each of these separately.

Delimitation of each case

We will consider only the cases relating to independent sporting events. This can also relate to fields which are not associated with sport.

Advertising insertion

Advertising insertion occurs when an entity uses the sport as a marketing platform to communicate its brand, logo, services or product. Although not exhaustive, the following list highlights various forms of such insertion:

- advertising insertion during the commercial breaks of a programme;
- break bumper during the TV broadcast of a sporting event placed between a pause in the programme and its commercial break (and vice versa);
- bumper music during the radio broadcast of the event;
- brand, trademark, logo or message insert in advertising spaces inside and outside the sporting facility (e.g. billboards, signs, virtual ad insert displayed on scoreboards and hoardings);

- use of brand, trademark, logo or message on athletes' apparel and equipment (e.g. shoes, jerseys, bicycles, hockey sticks, helmets, etc.);
- use of brand, trademark, logo or message on or within various materials (e.g. sporting event programmes, entry tickets, official magazine, etc.);
- loudspeaker announcements.

Sponsorship without advertising insertion

Sponsorship without advertising insertion occurs when an entity associates its name, brand, trademark, products or services with a sporting event or athlete to achieve a communications strategy. Here are a few examples:

- use of the name, trademark or logo of the event on the entity's products or services (e.g. on product packaging);
- use of the name, trademark or logo of the sporting entity to develop its products or services in the form of a slogan, such as 'Proud Sponsor of _____';
- use of the image of an athlete for commercial purposes (e.g. in TV ads);
- any combination of the above (e.g. the company uses the event name or sport entity, or the image of a sporting personality, for its advertising campaigns, by associating its brand, logo or image with its products or services), or by mentioning that it is the 'official sponsor' of the event, the sporting entity or a group of athletes (e.g. sponsor of the national selection).

It is very common to view TV commercials in which the products/services of a sponsor are associated with the logo or name of a sporting event/organization.

The constitution, bylaws and sporting regulations of the sponsored entity are key variables that help determine the kind of legal and publicity arrangements it can engage in. Pursuant to the Olympic Charter:

> no form of publicity or propaganda, commercial or otherwise, may appear on persons, on sportswear, accessories or, more generally, on any article of clothing or equipment whatsoever worn or used by the athletes or other participants in the Olympic Games, except for the identification – as defined in paragraph 8 below – of the manufacturer of the article or equipment concerned, provided that such identification shall not be marked conspicuously for advertising purposes.

Thus, any form of advertising or publicity is unauthorized in and above the venues and other competition areas that are considered as part of the Olympic sites.

An entity might sponsor a famous golfer of the Professional Golfers' Association of America (PGA) Tour without imposing any obligation on the said golfer to promote the entity's brand. It may choose instead to use the image and name of this golfer for advertising purposes only. In this case, where there is no advertising insert provision in the sponsorship contract, the said golfer is exempted from wearing the sponsor's brand.

In the preceding scenario, if the golfer were required to wear the sponsor's brand, the agreement would closely resemble a licensing contract. The main difference between a sponsorship contract and a licensing agreement lies in the fact that in a sponsorship operation, the association is achieved exclusively for an advertising purpose; in a licensing agreement, however, the association is achieved as a condition for the sale of products/services.

Sponsorship with advertising insertion

Sponsorship contracts are frequently subject to advertising insertions. When the constitution, bylaws and sporting regulations of the sponsored entity do not contain advertising restrictions, sponsorship with advertising insertion is allowable. This explains why Formula 1 team sponsors, for example, can brand the cars and drivers they sponsor by plastering them with advertisements.

Advertising contract content

In order to define precisely the scope of legal relations concerning the content of a publicity contract, the previously mentioned classification is used again in reference to the two categories of advertising insertion and sponsorship (collaborative agreement of association).

Advertising insertion

The content of an advertising insertion contract must contain the following information:

- placement and location;
- frequency and length;
- technical specifications.

Placement and location

First, it is important to define where to place the advertising insertion as the impact of publicity varies according to the location of the advertising space. During the broadcast of a football match, for instance, advertising billboards (hoardings) and signs placed in the camera background shot close to the action of the game (e.g. next to the pitch) are seen more often than those placed outside of the camera shot away from the action (e.g. on the VIP stand). In order to avoid ad insertion issues with sponsors and advertisers, the contract must include a plan showing the exact available spaces for advertising insertion.

Advertising insertions placed on sporting apparel and equipment should always be specified in the contract as to whether the insertion is to appear during official competitions and/or practice sessions.

Frequency and length

Second, the contract must state the times when publicity is to be presented to viewers during a sports programme (e.g. the last advertising slot available immediately before the start of the broadcast of the event). Furthermore, the length and frequency of TV slots must be clearly defined in the contract. Of course, the type of advertising insertion helps define available opportunities, order of presentation, length and frequency. If an advertiser's

TV slot is 20 seconds long, for example, this is stated in the contract, which defines a precise moment and length, whereas when publicity is placed on an athlete's apparel or on sporting equipment the contract must simply mention that the advertising insertion is to appear at all times, thus defining the duration and frequency.

When an advertisement is placed on a 'removable support', such as a cap belonging to an athlete, the contract must specify when the athlete has the obligation to wear it (e.g. during press conferences and interviews).

Advertisement insertions by loudspeaker must also be defined in the contract by the frequency and length of the advertisement (e.g. three times during the sporting event such as at the beginning, during halftime and at the end, or it can be each time a particular action occurs).

It is often assumed that when an advertisement is placed on billboards inside a stadium the insert is visible at all times during the sporting event. However, emerging technologies are changing the traditional way ads are presented to audiences, such as newly developed digitized billboards allowing animations and rotating advertisements. Electronic billboards currently allow interaction with an audience. Therefore, it is necessary to define the length, frequency and order in which the ads are presented to the audience.

Moreover, billboard ad insertion must be defined according to spectators or viewers – that is, the contract should specify which audience counts when it comes to measuring publicity length and frequency. If the contract stipulates that a sponsor's billboard advertisement is to appear, for instance, for a total of two minutes on television, then the sponsor's billboard advertisement must be synchronized with the camera background shot. Additionally, the length of the said billboard advertisement varies according to the targeted audience, i.e. the ad may be presented more often to spectators than to TV viewers in order to comply with what is stipulated in the contract.

Technical specifications

Lastly, the technical specifications for advertising insertion need to be incorporated in the contract. Technical specifications include the format, colour, dimension and shape of symbols, letters, logos, etc., of the advertisement. The advertisement specs must also be communicated to the producer and the broadcaster of the TV rights.

Sponsorship

While establishing the content of a contract, examination of the obligations of each party, especially those imposed by the entity authorizing the partnership, must be made.

The purpose of a sponsorship contract may be to authorize the use of images, or the name or logo of an athlete, club or sporting event. Whatever the purpose might be, the conditions of advertising insertions are established through negotiations.

Sponsorship contracts often include provisions of services which the company sponsor is interested in. ('Provision of services' is also called 'counter-benefits'.) From a legal and marketing perspective, the following provisions of services are not considered inclusive of advertising insertions. Sponsorship provisions of services typically relate to communication strategies based on public relations. In the context of sport, here are a few examples of sponsorship-related service provisions:

- to provide a sponsor with a number of tickets, free or at a discount, to view the event;
- to grant a sponsor free access to VIP areas during the event;
- to guarantee accommodation for the sponsor in the city where the event takes place;
- to arrange a personal interview between the sponsor and an athlete who partakes in the event;
- to invite the sponsor near the athletes during training sessions;
- to participate in various social or promotional events with the purpose of promoting the products of the company sponsor;
- to arrange photograph and autograph sessions in stores or spaces related to the company sponsor.

Exclusivity

Exclusiveness clauses are not essential to a contract from a legal perspective. However, their relevance and importance are quite common in sponsorship contracts. Sponsorship exclusiveness clauses generally relate to location, term and product category.

The most difficult task with a sponsorship contract is in defining exclusive product categories. The task consists of making a detailed description of each product category, i.e. to specify that which is and is not included in each product category. When the event rights owner is not organizing the event, product categories should be determined in collaboration with the event organizer.

Licensing agreements

Certain companies are interested in remuneration for the right to use the image, logo or name of an athlete, team and/or event. These companies desire to associate a particular product or service they provide with an athlete, team or sporting event. From a legal perspective, this occurs through a licence. A licence is a document or agreement giving permission to do something. According to Lehu (2004: 429), a licence 'details the responsibilities of each party, the conditions and terms of use, as well as the royalties payable to the owner based upon the limitations on use of the license'.

Licensing agreements are similar to broadcasting contracts, albeit they contain differentiating characteristics.

In the competitive sport market, a licensing agreement is not only a way for the event organizer to generate additional economic resources, but it also forms an integral part of the communication strategy whereby the event is promoted. When the company sponsor takes responsibility for the design, creation, marketing and distribution of products for an event, the licensing agreement thus corresponds to a system of general financing as well as a mode of constant communication.

Definition of content

From a legal perspective, licensing agreements are based on an authorization to do something. The purpose of the authorization is to grant a licensee the right to use a name, image or logo. The licence agreement can correspond to the use of an athlete's name and image, or the use of the logo, image and/or name of a sporting event.

There are close similarities between sponsorship and licensing contracts, as previously mentioned. A sponsorship contract may often include a licensing agreement, so it is important to clarify the differences between the two contracts. The following three questions help define what a licence agreement consists of:

- What can be subject to a licence?
- Which products and services can be licensed?
- During which marketing phase can a licence be used?

What can be subject to a licence?

Broadly speaking, a licence may concern:

- the logo of a sporting organization or event;
- the symbol, emblem, logo, name or image of the sporting event or organization;
- the name and image of the sporting venue where an event takes place;
- the name and image of the event mascot.

Which products and services can be licensed?

A licence may be granted for any type of product or service. Any manufacturer or distributor can be interested in associating one of its products or services with a sporting event. There is no legal restriction in this regard. In actuality, restrictions derive from the communications and marketing strategies of the event organizer, who may prefer not to associate the event with certain products or services based on the assumption that they are not compatible with the image and values of the event. For example, an event organizer may prefer not to licence the logo of the sporting event to a cigarette manufacturer or beer company, even though legislation permits the association.

During which marketing phase can a licence be used?

It is necessary to take into account the various marketing phases of a product and precisely define to which phase the licensing agreement is applicable. Licences may be granted for any one or all of these stages. Product life cycle stages are not necessarily carried out by the same entity. It is possible to grant a licence to various licensees for the same product but in different stages of marketing.

For instance, an event rights owner can grant a licence to a football manufacturer to place the logo of the event on footballs. The rights owner may then grant another licence to a distributor for it to ship the footballs to Asia. Yet another licence can be granted to retailers for exclusive rights to sell the footballs.

From the perspective of the event organizer, it is much easier to grant one licence to a company and give it a right to sublicense certain operations to other companies. Although the granting of sublicences is more common than secondary licences, the event rights owner is under no legal obligation to grant any sublicences.

The contract must define the terms of licence use for the following phases:

- design;
- production;
- distribution;
- sale.

The event owner must take into account that each of these phases may also be managed separately if it proves more beneficial for achieving the communication and marketing strategies and for generating more revenues.

The design of the licensed product associated with the name, mark and/or event, either generically or with exact specifications, must be stipulated in the contract.

Entities seeking to obtain a licensing agreement are generally product manufacturers who are willing to pay royalties in exchange for associating their product with a sporting event with a view to increasing sales or justifying a higher price for their product. It is thus necessary to specify whether the licensed product was being produced prior to the partnership with the event, in which case the manufacturer will apply the name/trademark/logo of the event on the previously manufactured product, or whether a new product will be manufactured only for the duration of the event. Likewise, special edition versions of a previously manufactured product may be produced for the event.

Communications and sales strategies are developed in collaborative modes, considering the importance attached to the type of products associated with the sporting event. From a legal point of view, there is no restriction regarding the strategy that sponsorship partners may wish to develop. In all cases, the contractual agreement relates to a contract of authorization for the use of a trademark, name or image related to the right of the intellectual property.

There can be confusion about who actually holds the intellectual property for the design and creation of the product when a product is specifically designed to be exclusively associated with an event. Legally, it belongs to whoever registered the copyright for the product. However, given that both the event organizer and the manufacturer have certain limited rights regarding the intellectual property, the contract must identify to whom the intellectual property actually belongs.

It is necessary to specify each benefactor of various intellectual property rights of a licensing agreement involving any given patent, industrial design, trademark, copyright and/or trade secret (confidential information).

It is advisable to include a clause when the intellectual property on the design of a new product is shared. Otherwise, the manufacturer could be considered the sole intellectual property holder of the product due to the fact that it is manufacturing the product. In the absence of a shared property clause, the event organizer must stipulate the term and limits imposed upon the use of the licence, as well as a liquidated damages clause providing for compensation and/or penalties in the event of a breach of contract. This stipulation is important to prevent the manufacturer from marketing the same product once the event is over and the licence has expired. Furthermore, the contract should include a provision whereby the event rights owner holds a right of veto, or their compulsory agreement is required for the originally licensed product to be modified or used to develop new products. Additionally, the contract should contain a provision whereby the manufacturer is obligated to either cancel or modify the registration of the licensed product upon the expiration of the contract.

Lastly, and always in relation to the content, it is necessary to deal with the question of the amount that the company must pay for a licence relating to a sporting event. Three variables serve to establish the price of a licence:

- exclusivity characteristics;
- the scope of any exclusiveness (i.e. term, territory and content);
- the type of product or service concerned.

The nature of the product or service licensed also influences the price of the licence and its profitability. Therefore, the price of a licence also depends on the following five factors based on the nature of the products or services:

- the value of the brand of the event;
- product/service characteristics;
- market characteristics (mass market versus niche market);
- profitability forecast;
- the scope of exclusiveness.

Models of authorization

Like the contracts of audiovisual transmission, the contracts of 'licensing' are conditioned by various factors. Licence agreements can be exclusive or non-exclusive. Exclusiveness can be applied to a particular product and/or product line, as well as to a particular territory and/or worldwide.

The geographical area, as well as the duration of the licence, must also be specified in the contract. Moreover, the term of the various elements of the agreement is the most significant component to consider when drafting a contract. It is also necessary to determine whether the use of names, trademarks, logos, etc., is granted for one staging of the event, or for subsequent stagings too.

Characteristics of products and/or services

In the context of sporting event management, a licence agreement is a permission to use the name, trademark or logo of the event on a product or service. The event organizer assumes the majority of the risks in terms of image management when engaging in a licensing agreement. Consequently, it must be vigilant to ensure that the characteristics of the products and services it authorizes to be associated with the event are compatible with it.

Therefore, it is necessary to examine the characteristics of the product for which a licence is requested – including the price, sales and distribution channels of the product, and the quantity to be marketed. Licensed products have distinct characteristics appealing to different people. One can certainly imagine that the licensing agreement will differ based on the size of the target audience. Football fans, for example, typically represent a broader target than golfing fans. Similarly, the characteristics of the product should also be compatible with the target audience. Thus, one would not expect the English Football Premier

League to grant a licence to an elite perfume company such as Chanel, or the British Golf Open to grant a licence to a milk distributor.

Each type of event has its own potential in terms of what type of licence it can concede. In the contract, it is advisable to define the classification of the products concerned, which can be established from the following criteria.

Product features

It is important to describe the design features of the product, including the components used to manufacture the product, the system of production, the quality controls that the product is subject to and its technical specifications, as well as the format, colour and texture of the product, etc. In addition, it is necessary to write a detailed description of the final product, and include, if possible, the drawings, photographs and/or models used to develop it.

Price

The contract must indicate the authorized minimum and maximum price for which the product can be sold. The licensor can also make provisions, for example, to prohibit sales promotions, discounts, and tie-ins with other promotions. Without such provisions, the product manufacturer will be in total control of the sale of the product.

Sales and distribution channels

Likewise, the contract must specify the distribution and sales channels used to supply and sell the product. This specification must be coherent with respect to the image and positioning of the event. The licensor may conceive a particular marketing obligation, whereby the product must be displayed in a particular way, or in spaces assigned exclusively for the sale of event-related products. Such requirements must be explicitly defined in the contract.

Quantity

The event rights owner can also control the quantity of products to be put on the market. Again, it is possible to conceive of various marketing strategies. The product can be mass marketed, or sold to a niche market whereby the product is scarce and thus more valued. The licensor must stipulate the conditions regarding the number of product items to market in the contract.

Exclusivity

Exclusivity is an essential element in all the contracts related to the event. The exclusive rights granted by a licence grant the licensee the exclusive ability to take certain action. Therefore, exclusiveness is another key element, which must be defined in terms of scope, term, territory and content.

Scope

As mentioned earlier, competition authorities impose restrictions and limitations in relation to exclusive media rights. Licence agreements, however, are subject to fewer restrictions and limitations.

Ultimately, the granting of exclusive licences depends solely on the commercial and marketing strategies adopted by the rights owner. The licensor can subsequently decide to grant a licence applicable to all or some of the products and/or services associated with the event. In the absence of legal provisions in this regard, the marketing strategy of the event rights owner actually serves to determine whether exclusiveness is concentrated and conceded to only one partner, or else is bundled in various packages to engage several partners.

There is no legal basis for preventing a company from holding an exclusive licence for the purpose of distributing and selling entry tickets to a sporting event, and for simultaneously arranging transportation and lodging surrounding the event. However, European competition authorities do not set any restriction on the distribution of exclusive licences, nor do they impose a series of limitations with regard to the marketing of licensed products/services.

In Europe, what is incompatible with competition law is the situation in which these two elements are joined together and when the purchase of one is a condition of the purchase of the other. For example, it is forbidden to tie the acquisition of a sporting event entry ticket to the purchase of a travel ticket or the booking of a room at a particular hotel. More to the point, it is prohibited to associate ticketing services with a travel agency, when the purchase of an entry ticket requires the purchase of a particular package, as that would arguably restrict free competition.

Term

With the view to maintaining market competition, it was mentioned earlier that the term of exclusiveness is a key factor in exclusive TV exploitation rights contracts. With regard to licensing agreements, however, competition law is less likely to help determine a reasonable term for the granting of a licence.

The rules or limitations applicable to exclusive licences differ according to the type of sporting event. UEFA, which grants licences concerning a competition running every year over a 10-month period, does not concede the same exclusiveness as the IOC does with the licences it grants in view of the Olympic Games.

The European competition authorities consider that exclusive licences must not last more than three or four years. However, it is worth noting that the OCOG can logically grant licences to market some products for a period of six to eight years – that is, the licence is granted two years before the start of the Olympic Games and it lasts until two years after the end. Hence, the type of event is an important criterion used by competition authorities for establishing the term of an exclusive licence.

We consider that the main difference between one model and another is related to the criterion making it possible to fix the utilization period of the licence. This will involve a differentiation on the level of the legal treatment applicable to the temporal limits of exclusiveness.

If the period of contract validity is simply fixed according to the duration (e.g. two or three years), the rules relating to the right of the competition can fix temporal limits perfectly (e.g. maximum four years). On the other hand, if this period is fixed according to the moment when the sporting event is organized, it appears logical to think that the company which obtained the licence can make use of it until the event has taken place, whether within a two-months period or eight years.

Territory

With regard to the applicable territory over which the licence applies, the contract must define what the licence is specifically granted for (i.e. a product or a service, or both), but also specify whether the licence relates to the design, creation, distribution and sale of the product/service, or to only one of these elements.

The territorial range of an exclusive licence is allowed according to the type of product and/or service licensed and the type of market in which the product/service is introduced.

When a particular product can only be delivered by a multinational corporation that has a global presence, that corporation can obtain an exclusive licence applicable worldwide. By contrast, when several companies can deliver the same product, competition law requires that exclusive licences be granted to several entities, thereby limiting the range of territory for which exclusiveness is conceded (i.e. an area, a country, a group of country, a continent, etc.).

When the licence relates only to products, and more particularly if they are specific (according to the definition given previously) it can be granted worldwide. On the other hand, when they are services or non-specific products and there is no multinational able to produce them worldwide, it can be possible to grant several exclusive, but geographically limited, licences.

Content

Suffice it to mention that exclusive licences can be granted for products or services – or both, if they share common characteristics.

Sublicence agreements

Another very important element with licence agreements is whether the licensee has a right to sublicense to a third party the marketing rights obtained through negotiations with the licensor. It is prudent for the rights owner to stipulate in the contract any restriction on sublicences.

The rights owner can authorize the licensee to transfer the rights in their entirety to a third party. Alternatively, the licensor can choose to limit the transfer of those rights to a given territory, and/or during a certain period of time, and/or to certain products, services or distribution channels only.

When a licence agreement does contain any provision regarding sublicensing arrangements, it is considered that the transfer of the licence to a third party is not authorized, unless, however, the presence of certain facts or evidence pertaining to negotiations is seen in the wording of the contract that supports the notion that authorization is granted.

In some cases, the licensee can transfer the rights only after demanding and receiving the written authorization of the rights owner of the event. Similarly, sublicensing can be subject to any type of condition agreed upon by the parties. For instance, the licensor may request some guarantees regarding the quality of products and services to be sublicensed in order to ensure that the third party delivers quality products/services.

Quality assurance management

In the context of sports event management, quality assurance (QA) management is one of the major elements to consider with licensing agreements. QA covers all activities associated with the event, including design, development, production, installation, servicing and documentation. Additionally, QA includes the regulation of the quality of raw materials, assemblies, products and components, as well as services relating to production management and inspection processes.

Licensing agreements must state, if possible, the quality assurance processes put in place for guaranteeing that the contractual association remains beneficial for all partners and does not produce any negative effect on the event. Quality assurance management is carried out in the mutual interest of the parties and must be applied at all levels of improvement. The sale of counterfeited products with the logo of the event (i.e. non-licensed products), for example, is detrimental both to the company authorized to market these products (i.e. the licensee) and the event organizer (i.e. the licensor). Counterfeiting issues are on the agenda of governments and legislators worldwide. Despite the fact that current anti-counterfeit legislations are incomplete, insufficient or simply not effective in some places, the two parties should conceive adequate procedures to ensure that products and services, which are associated with the event and may be sublicensed to third parties, fulfil or exceed customer and partner expectations.

There are various elements of quality control, which can and should appear in the contract. It is typically easier to ensure QA with products than with services. The following discussion on QA relates to any product associated with a sporting event.

Labelling, moulds and patterns

In general, products have a label or barcode whose purpose is to identify them or their contents, particularly in clothing products. It is increasingly frequent that the organizer is the person in charge, or the owner, of the labels attached to the product. Frequently, however, neither the rights owner nor the licensee is responsible for manufacturing labels. Instead, they opt to buy and monitor labels jointly. A third party is utilized to manufacture and distribute labels. Many football clubs manage sublicensed products that way. In all cases, it is judicious that the purchase and the quality control of the labels are done by mutual agreement and are supervised by the two entities concerned (i.e. the organizer of the event and the company having obtained the licence).

Quality assurance directives must find ways to avoid, or reduce the number of counterfeited licensed products on the market.

Likewise, the contract should specify who owns the patterns (e.g. plastic patterns or CAD software) used in apparel designs and the moulds used to produce event-related products (e.g. keyrings). Ideally, the rights owner of the event must have proprietary rights on moulds and patterns because it is arguably the best way to avoid the manufacturing of counterfeited products after the contract expires.

Consequently, the contract may include a provision whereby the licensee is obliged either to give back the moulds and patterns to the rights owner of the event, or to produce proof that they have been destroyed at the expiration of the licence agreement.

Production scheduling system and inventory management

During the term of the licence agreement, it is very important for the event organizer to have a follow-up on production across the manufacturing, distribution and sales processes, as well as on product inventories.

Therefore, it is preferable to incorporate a clause whereby information on regional sales and inventories is shared. Sharing this information is essential for product-distribution sales revenues, especially when the price of licensed products, or a percentage of it, is based on the number of products sold at any given time.

The contract should mention that access is granted to company-operated and licensed facilities where products are manufactured, stocked and distributed from. Additionally, the two parties may wish to agree on a penalty in the event where access to these facilities is refused.

Inventory management is especially critical near and at the end of a licence agreement. When the licence agreement concludes, licensed products are often still in a warehouse. The contract must address how stocks are to be disposed of, and whether the licensee can continue to sell these stocks when the contract expires. There are two alternatives for remaining stock items:

- excess inventory can be destroyed to ensure it is not marketed in the future;
- excess inventory can be sold through specific distribution channels only (e.g. specialized stores).

External audit companies

Licensing agreements often contain a provision whereby the event organizer is given the freedom to examine the financial information of the licensee. This possibility is often considered when the price of the licence is based on the number of products sold by a licensee. It thus aims to create accurate financial reports that are useful to the licensor and other stakeholders as well.

It is often useful to include in the contract the possibility for the parties to resort to an outside firm (which must be accepted by both) to carry out the control of the products. Licensing partners often secure an external auditor to monitor the products that are manufactured, distributed and sold under licence. In this context, the independent auditor will examine a licensee's financial statements in order to express a reasonable opinion regarding adherence to generally accepted accounting principles (GAAP). In the case of recourse, the contract must specify which party is responsible for the auditing costs.

Homologation

Certain products must be approved before they are marketed. Homologation or certification is sometimes required to ensure that licensed products meet standards for such things as safety and environmental impact. In the event of a public agency or sanctioning body requiring that event-related products or equipment be homologated, the contract must specify which party has the responsibility to homologate, which is generally the company that obtained the licence.

Responsibility for damage

In this section, responsibility for damage does not refer to a breach of a contractual obligation. Instead, it refers to a liability for any damage a third party may suffer as a result of using or because of licensed products. Damage responsibility includes physical, mental and financial damage.

From a legal perspective, it is important to stipulate which party assumes the responsibility for damage caused by licensed products, as well as for any legal claim or judicial action. A subscription to a civil liability policy is recommended to cover any accidental damage that licensed products may cause. The contract must specify which party is responsible for contracting the insurance, or specify if the parties will split the cost of such a civil liability policy.

Marketing and commercial obligation

From a marketing point of view, the name and image of the event must be promoted in various places and locations. Likewise, the marketing of licensed products must begin prior to the commencement of the sporting event for it to be effective. A provision in the contract must guarantee that the marketing of the licensed products is carried out according to the terms provided for in the contract.

Complex contracts

We consider that it is more relevant to analyse each type of contract separately. Nevertheless the majority of the contracts concluded with regard to sporting events are a digest, or a combination of some of them. These can, or must, be linked to the expected economic and marketing results.

The contractual analysis completed in this chapter involved a review of the main contracts associated with sporting events, which reveals that economic partners involved in the sporting event have several rights and obligations towards one another. Consequently, contractual relationships are complex and often intertwined with various stakeholders.

For example, sponsors would not be interested in investing large amounts of money to support a sporting event if their publicity could not appear on television, or if their advertising campaigns run a high risk of being ambushed by competitors. In the same manner, it is not conceivable that a company pays for the right to manufacture sporting goods with the logo of the event and that the main sponsor can offer to its customers shirts made by another manufacturer.

Economic partners, therefore, increasingly construct more complex contracts aimed at creating favourable conditions to ensure a worthwhile return on investment. The principal interrelationships that can be established from the various types of contracts examined in this chapter are presented in the following sections.

The rights and obligations of the contracts of audiovisual transmission, of licensing, sponsorship and advertising thus today are often associated and coordinated. This is why more and more frequently complex or compound contracts are employed which incorporate aspects of those types of contract introduced in earlier sections of this chapter.

Content

Without claiming to be exhaustive, the principal interrelationships which can be established between these various types of contracts are introduced below.

TV exploitation rights contracts

TV exploitation rights contracts may contain special provisions on commercial advertisements, whereby event sponsors are given a discount and/or preference for buying advertising slots. Similarly, this type of contract can be conceived to exclude competitors during the broadcast of the sponsored event. For instance, the contract can stipulate that competitors are not allowed opportunities to buy certain TV advertisement slots. Restrictions are most often placed on commercials. Such provisions, however, can only be imposed on particular programming segments of the broadcast of the event. For example, sponsors may insist that competitors are not to be allowed to buy any advertising slots during the entire broadcast of the sponsored event. The same request could be applied before and/or after the broadcast of the event. In this case, the restriction can only be imposed for a specific period, such as a minimum of five minutes and up to a maximum of 30 minutes.

When the said limitations are significant, the TV operator has less freedom for selling commercial slots. As a result, he or she will negotiate to pay a lower price for TV exploitation rights. Because of that, the price paid for securing TV exploitation rights is the result of negotiation – it is a balancing point between the economic interests, market power and communications strategies of the parties concerned. From a strategic perspective, the event organizer can agree to reduce the price of TV exploitation rights when it is offset by the commitment of sponsor partners, and if the development of the event is guaranteed.

In the event where the TV exploitation rights franchise holder was also the holder of publicity rights for the event, the same type of limitations and conditions could be imposed. In other words, the TV broadcast obligation stipulated in complex contracts is subject to conditions envisaged in the contract. This obligation aims at preventing any prejudice to sponsors and advertisers.

Likewise, advertising obligations can also be introduced in the sponsorship contract. When a TV operator must reduce advertisement airtime, or has to refrain from selling slots to certain companies, he or she usually asks for a concession to compensate for lost opportunities. Therefore, it is important that the event organizer produces a clause to offset the TV operator's lost opportunities. Furthermore, sponsorship contracts must include a clause that obligates sponsors to purchase advertising slots with the TV exploitation rights franchise holder.

Sponsorship/publicity contracts and licence agreements

Sponsorship and publicity contracts, as well as licence agreements, participate in collaborative actions in two ways. First, licence agreements often interact with sponsorship contracts. For instance, when a sponsor has the right to use the name, trademark or logo of the event on its products, this authorization is limited to certain types of products/services, with a view to not causing prejudice to other licensing actions. The licence agreement concerns products/services related to core operations of the company sponsor. This licensing agreement serves to prevent competitors from obtaining the right to market similar products/services in association with the sporting event.

Second, contracts of this nature often contain an obligation to collaborate with other economic partners engaged in the event. For example, when a company sponsor wishes to integrate its communication campaign with a particular product that is also licensed by the event organizer, the company sponsor is obliged to obtain that product from the franchise company, as specified in its contract. In turn, the franchise company is obliged to sell the said product to the sponsor at a price and quantity that is predetermined in its contract with the event organizer, hence fulfilling its communication campaign (this mutual obligation must be stipulated in the licence agreement).

Shared responsibility or ownership

There are types of event sponsorship which go beyond advertisement insertion, licence use and public relations, which adds to the complexity of relationships between various contracts. For instance, when an event sponsor or broadcaster holds partial rights associated with the event or assumes certain responsibilities derived from the organization of the event, the contractual configuration differs from contract models discussed previously.

In addition, sponsorship contract configuration also differs with title sponsorship. In this case, although the rights owner of the event reserves the ownership of the event, the event bears the name of the naming sponsor. Naming rights sponsorship benefits the company sponsor by providing an opportunity to build and deepen relationships with current and potential customers as well as business partners and associates. Through activities at and around the sporting event venues, the naming rights sponsor can reinforce its corporate identity by associating with the values exemplified by athletes. The sponsor can promote understanding of its corporate identity through television slots aired during the broadcast of the event. Advertisements also help strengthen connections with specific audience segments.

On these assumptions, it is necessary to pay very detailed attention to the writing of the contract binding the parties, while delimiting and defining, in a very clear way, the responsibilities for each entity intervening with respect with the third parties. Even when these responsibilities are perfectly defined in the contract, the courts and the judges have the possibility of interpreting these clauses, and of determining responsibilities not envisaged with the contract, following complaints formulated by third parties for damages. Thus, it is not surprising that a third party having suffered an injury brings proceedings for damages caused because of an event. Let us take the example of the Nike Challenge Cup. The third party can think in good faith that Nike is the owner of this event (let us imagine that the owner of this sporting event is insolvent and that the company sponsor is not) and that the third party may ask compensation for the damages which it underwent with this company.

Conclusion

In summary, the most common sporting event contracts relate to audiovisual rights, advertising, sponsorship and merchandizing licences. Individual analyses of these various types of contracts have been made in this chapter. Although each type of contract has differentiating features, all contracts must include the following key elements:

- the identity of each party;
- information defining the contractual relationship;
- the rights, obligations, duties and responsibilities of each party;
- governing law and dispute resolution mechanisms.

Among the general characteristics shared between the various individual contracts, certain features such as definitions of content, price and the extent of exclusivity have an immense effect on the overall impact of a contract. However, the exclusivity of a contract has the greatest influence on other characteristics of a given contract. There are four defining factors determining the degree of exclusiveness:

- content (i.e. type of rights, products and/or services);
- scope;
- term;
- territory.

It is imperative that all provisions in any given contract are precisely and explicitly defined. This attention to detail will help to alleviate disputes between contracting partners. However, disputes may still arise over payment terms, the various obligations of the parties, representations and warranties, liability issues, remedies and termination rights. Arbitration courts or courts of jurisdiction are utilized to settle claims brought forth from third parties or disputes between contracting parties.

It is important to note that most sporting-event-related contracts are typically established with interconnectivity between a combination of sponsorship, publicity, licence and TV contracts in order to achieve satisfactory economic and marketing results. The basic contractual agreements examined in this chapter frequently interrelate to form complex contracts due to the overlapping rights and obligations of various contracting parties.

5

Case study: 'Perrier Fluo Beach Volleyball Experience'

In this last chapter, the sponsorship processes explained in this book are illustrated with a case study of an event simulation referred to as the 'Perrier Fluo Beach Volleyball Experience'. The event simulates an unofficial sporting competition of beach volleyball, which is theoretically organized by the French Federation of Volleyball (FFVB). The event occurs in Paris on City Hall Square during August of each year. The organizer of this event aims to bring together the best men's and women's teams originating from five continents for the competition. The rights owner of the event is the FFVB, which also serves as the event organizer.

The case study develops the strategic and operational aspects correlating to the initial phases of a sponsorship operation, which includes the analysis of the fit, conceiving and developing the sponsorship strategy, identifying prospective sponsors, and the designing of a customized offer. Legal analysis must be integrated into the marketing move during these phases of operation. However, aspects relating to trade negotiations are not incorporated into the case study due to their case-specific nature. The activities developed by the various parties involved culminate with the signing of a certain number of contracts. Models of a sponsorship contract, a TV contract and a licence merchandizing agreement are presented in Appendices 1–3 respectively.

The case study is divided into five parts. In the first stage, the essential components of the strategic diagnosis that the FFVB would perform are presented with a view to showing that organizing such an event facilitates the development of the federation. In the second stage, the characteristics of the event are defined, which takes into account the marketing objectives of the FFVB and the existing legal framework, as well as the media and sponsorship strategies. In the third stage, the strategy relating to the prospecting for a main sponsor whose brand will be included in the name of the event (i.e. naming right sponsor or title sponsor) is elaborated further. An analysis of the fit with the prospective sponsor is conducted in order to validate the sponsor selection and to conceive a satisfying customized offer. The prospective sponsor for this analysis is Perrier (belonging to Nestlé Waters) who owns the Perrier Fluo brand. In the fourth stage, the strategic analysis of the FFVB is compared with that of Perrier Fluo in order to study strategic and operational fits between the two entities. In the last stage, the sponsorship mix of the offer, price, sale and communication is presented, from which the structure of the sponsorship and proposal of the partnership is specified.

Note: for this case study we develop an event-driven project to avoid confidentiality issues and to ensure autonomy of analysis. Publicly available methods of data collection, such as the Internet and personal interviews were utilized to respect confidentiality concerns. This project epitomizes and exemplifies a possible event-driven strategy by the FFVB developed for organizing a stage of the FIVB Swatch World Tour (a competition integrated in the FIVB Grand Slam) in Paris during August 2007.

FIRST STAGE: STRATEGIC DIAGNOSIS OF THE FFVB AND BEACH VOLLEYBALL

The FFVB was created in 1936. It unites people and companies whose primary and instrumental goals are the practices of volleyball, beach volleyball and associated disciplines. The FFVB is affiliated with the International Federation of Volleyball (FIVB) and is a member of the French National Olympic Committee (CNOSF). Its mission is to organize, develop and regulate the practice of volleyball in all its forms in France, and in French territories.[1]

A strategic diagnosis was conducted in order to define a marketing strategy contributing to the success of the mission and development plan of the FFVB. Focus is limited to the significance of the organization of such a sporting event.

SUBSTAGE 1: INTERNAL DIAGNOSIS OF THE FFVB

The internal diagnosis of the FFVB will be carried out based on the following dimensions: mission, strategic orientations, project development, service offer, internal culture, organization, human resources, financial resources and brand equity. The essential elements of this diagnosis appear in Table 5.1.

SUBSTAGE 2: THE BRAND EQUITY OF BEACH VOLLEYBALL

As mentioned earlier, beach volleyball is integrated into the FFVB in France. Beach volleyball possesses distinctive brand equity, as shown in Table 5.2.

SUBSTAGE 3: EXTERNAL ANALYSIS OF THE FFVB

The SWOT external analysis highlights the opportunities and threats in the market facing the FFVB. Relevant data are presented in Table 5.3.

Table 5.1 Summary of the internal diagnosis of the FFVB

Dimensions		Strengths	Weaknesses
Mission		The FFVB mission is in line with the attitude of the newly formed management team and the expectations of the main stakeholders	
Strategic orientation and project development		The strategy and development project of the FFVB are well structured and realistic	The gap between the current and the projected situation requires management of changes and the development of resources
Internal culture		Shared values such as achievement, motivation, autonomy and friendship	The managerial culture must be developed
Organization and human resources		A coherent project of reorganization Competences in sports and education	There is a need to change the structure of the organization due to a deficit in managerial competences
Financial resources		The budget is balanced	No resources are available for investing
Brand equity	Stakeholders	Subsidies from the ministry of sports Solid bases at club and league levels Balanced combination of male and female participants	Sponsors and media are not involved adequately
	Foundations	The vision and identity of the new management team is coherent with the values shared by main stakeholders	There is a need to adapt to the environment and to competition
	Legal protection	Delegate federation[a] 'Beach Volleyball Experience' is trademarked	
	Knowledge	Strong brand awareness in the sports sector	The social awareness of the FFVB is weak. Volleyball and beach volleyball are indiscernibly associated with the federation. The image of the FFVB is tied to sport and tradition
	Experience	106,000 members (46% women) The foremost direct stakeholders are satisfied with its action in the sports sector	Critiques of the development, promotion, communication and corporate design of the FFVB
	Relationships	The FFVB developed programmes in collaboration with clubs, schools, local authorities, etc.	Association with the FFVB occurs primarily for functional reasons

a The FFVB received authorization from the French minister of sport to organize the official competitions (e.g. French championships).

Table 5.2 Brand equity dimensions of beach volleyball

Aspects of the brand equity of beach volleyball	Strengths	Weaknesses
Stakeholders	Olympic sport, FIVB, international events with strong media impact, influential sponsors involved	Seasonal sport not played worldwide
Foundations	Emerged in the 1920s on California beaches; it is now an Olympic discipline	
Legal protection	The FIVB is the rights owner of the most prestigious events, i.e. World Championship and World Tour	
Knowledge	Strong brand awareness Gravitational image encompassing components of the leisure sports culture	
Experience	The stakeholders are satisfied with this technical, sport dimension	
Relationship	Beach volleyball provides its stakeholders with functional, emotional, socio-cultural and psychological benefits	The stakeholders are not typically engaged in programmes of collaboration

SECOND STAGE: STRATEGIC CHOICES OF THE FFVB

This stage examines decisions pertaining to the purpose and future of the FFVB and the way in which it responds to pressures and influences identified in the strategic analysis (e.g. human resources, stakeholders, economic and competitive environment, legal framework, etc.). The process involves matching the FFVB's strategic advantages to the business environment facing the organization. Strategic decisions involve the generation of options and their evaluation, both of which are influenced by the missions and objectives of the FFVB. The strategic choices of the FFVB are based on its corporate, business and functional strategies.

SUBSTAGE 1: THREE LEVELS OF STRATEGY

The corporate strategy establishes the spheres of activity of the organization. It serves to determine which sector the FFVB should be in or withdraw from in order to constitute a balanced portfolio for the organization. The management team of the FFVB validated the choices laid out in the strategic diagnosis, which indicated that the FFVB desired involvement in volleyball and beach volleyball at the competitive, leisure and educational levels.

The competitive or business strategy defines the operations the FFVB must implement in each sphere of activity in order to forge sustainable advantages over competitors. For that purpose, the FFVB has outlined five areas where it wants to differentiate: brand awareness, attractiveness, education, more opportunities for female participation, and accessibility to the public.

The functional strategies correlate to the development and implementation of the competitive strategy on various functions of the organization such as marketing, human

Table 5.3 Summary of the external analysis of the FFVB

Dimensions	Opportunities	Threats
Overall economic outlook and economic significance of the sport in France	Consumption growth in sports and events Strong involvement of the community Sustained growth in sponsorships	Domination of football and sports such as tennis, rugby and Formula 1
Competition	The broad base of participants allows for a growth in the number of new members Strong growth in the number of young members aged 12–17 years Attractive sport for both women and men	Large federations (e.g. football and tennis) dominate in terms of number of registered members Unregistered participants appear to prefer practising other sport activities such as walking, swimming, cycling, etc. Low rate of volleyball participants aged 12–17; only a small percentage of the 12–17-year-old participants subscribe to FFVB clubs Volleyball is a niche sport on television (low public interest) Dominant sports and events tend to capture most sponsorship opportunities, thus increasing their impact
New trends	Beach volleyball appeals to people who like to just have fun and participate in social events	Problem of inconsistency and disengagement between the mission and management of the FFVB Several 'fun' and entertaining sports compete with volleyball to secure the participation of young people aged 12–17
Technological innovations	An investment in new information technologies would allow: • communication of customized messages to the target • improvements in the quality of the service delivered to stakeholders • new services for involving the stakeholders to be developed	Equal opportunities for competitors
Regulations (legal framework)	The FFVB is a delegation appointed by the Ministry for the youth and sports, responsible for the organization of beach volleyball competitions in France Monopoly for the organizing of official competitions Legal capacity to register the brands related to beach volleyball in France Favourable existing regulations	The development of volleyball at the international level is controlled by the FIVB, which involves stakeholders from various countries with different legal systems Ambush marketing possibilities exist due to few safeguards

resources, finance, etc. The marketing strategy is one of the essential elements that the FFVB must use to stimulate the growth of volleyball in France. The marketing strategy will help generate new resources for developing the impact of the FFVB and its member clubs by increasing the number of members, media exposure, events, etc.

The executives of the FFVB wish to revamp the marketing of the federation and its associated clubs with a view to satisfying the stakeholders. Thus, marketing efforts are concentrated on the professional and associated clubs, beach volleyball, children aged 6–10 years, women, new participants, sporting authorities (FIVB and National Federations of Volleyball), sponsors and the media. Beach volleyball is the cornerstone of the enticement strategy to attract new participants.

SUBSTAGE 2: POTENTIAL BENEFITS FROM THE INTERACTION BETWEEN THE BRAND EQUITY OF THE FFVB AND BEACH VOLLEYBALL

The new marketing direction of the FFVB intends to leverage its brand equity with beach volleyball in an effort to ensure further growth. Figure 5.1 shows the interrelationship between the components of this strategy.

The organization of an international event is utilized for the case study in order to demonstrate the full benefit that can be achieved from the brand equity of beach volleyball. The envisioned event would be an unofficial tournament approved by the FIVB, whereby the requirements imposed by the FIVB are easily applied for this case study. As such, the organization of this unofficial tournament can be utilized as a model for organizing a stage of the FIVB World Tour in Paris.

In the event that the FFVB succeeded in achieving its goals of integrating its brand equity with beach volleyball, the FFVB would achieve the following benefits:

- reinforce participative and business values;
- develop its brand identity to an association with beach volleyball ('branding');

Figure 5.1 The interaction between the two entities at the brand equity level

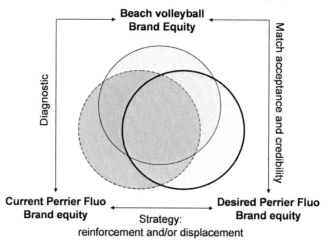

- reposition its image as festive and innovating;
- improve the perceived quality of beach volleyball and the FFVB;
- create value-adding partnerships and opportunities with stakeholders;
- facilitate the recruitment of new members.

Thus, the development of the FFVB will rely on a beach-volleyball-oriented, event-driven strategy for this case study.

SUBSTAGE 3: DEFINITION AND CONFIGURATION OF THE RIGHTS OWNER OF THE EVENT

When the organization of an event results from a set of initiatives taken by a group of people or a sporting movement, it is necessary to define and configure the entity recognized as the owner of the event. The various stages are summarized in Table 5.4.

The registration process for the case study is not necessary because the project is initiated and owned by the FFVB, which is already registered. However, the FFVB could contract a third party to organize and/or market its rights. In this case, the FFVB is the sole rights owner and organizer of the event. An internal marketing strategy will allow the FFVB to:

- develop internal competences;
- motivate the individuals responsible for the decisions;
- capitalize on the personnel experience of the event;
- show credibility and sincerity in the eyes of the stakeholders;
- direct contact with people involved with the event;
- allow better understanding of the needs and expectations of stakeholders;
- develop an entrepreneurial and marketing culture within the federation;
- control how strategies are implemented;
- reduce intermediaries (and commissions to be paid);
- develop contacts and networks;
- ensure the values and missions of the federation are respected;
- improve the image of the federation and its perceived quality.

Table 5.4 The legal and marketing functions required for establishing the rights owner of the event

Legal function	Marketing function
Creation of the organizing entity of the event (e.g. private company, association, foundation, etc.)	
Examination of the legal protection required for the name of the entity	
	Design of the corporate identity of the entity, i.e. logo, symbols, image, etc.
Registration of the name of the entity	

SUBSTAGE 4: BASIC STRATEGIC DECISIONS CONCERNING THE EVENT

The organization of the event-driven marketing strategy can effectively contribute to the growth of the FFVB. It is necessary to define the characteristics of the unofficial competition of beach volleyball by taking into account all the sporting, logistic, financial, marketing and legal functions required for the success of the event and the sponsorship operation. Only the aspects of marketing pertaining to legal ramifications are addressed at this stage (Table 5.5).

- From a marketing point of view, it is important to define the characteristics of the event in relation to the main stakeholders and prioritize them in a manner to satisfy their expectations.
- From a legal point of view, it is crucial to protect the brand of the event by registering it within the private[2] and public legal frameworks.

Marketing perspectives

The FFVB must define the concept of the event by making decisions with regard to which strategy to employ, stakeholders to collaborate with, positioning of the event, competitive advantages to develop and business moves to implement.

Which stakeholders should the event seek to satisfy?

The event is primarily intended for the satisfaction of the participants, clubs and regional leagues. However, it also seeks to satisfy two additional categories of stakeholders. On the one hand, it seeks to entice potential participants and spectators as well as professional players invited to the event; on the other hand, it seeks to fulfil the expectations of the town of Paris, the FIVB and the media, as well as current and prospective sponsors.

Which generic strategy to employ?

The FFVB should use a strategy of differentiation with the concept of the event, personnel, location, stakeholders and the image. These five aspects will be expanded upon in the following stages.

Which competitive tactic to implement?

The FFVB should not seek an innovative competing strategy, but rather adopt 'a follower' tactic, i.e. imitate successful processes that have already been used elsewhere. In this case study, the FFVB emulates the World Tour concept developed by the FIVB.

Which competitive advantages should the FFVB develop?

The competitive advantages of the FFVB take into account the expectations of the main stakeholders and the aforementioned differentiation strategy. The business advantages that are beneficial to develop are:

Table 5.5 Legal and marketing functions during the design and definition phases of the characteristics of the event

Legal function	Marketing function
	Defining the initial concept of the event (i.e. format and general characteristics in relation to the strategy of the FFVB and the interests of the main stakeholders) Choosing the name (i.e. Beach Volleyball Experience) and the corporate design (e.g. logo) of the event
Registering the initial name (i.e. Beach Volleyball Experience) and the corporate design (e.g. logo) of the event	
Collecting and analysing regulations applicable to the event: public and private (i.e. sport association) requirements; both generic and detailed specifications pertaining to the sport	
Drafting a report specifying what is legally binding and what is not for the attention of other departments in the organization	
	Outlining the original ideas for organizing the event whilst taking into account the legal framework (this should be done in collaboration with the sports and operations directors)
Format shaping of the event Type of event Type of participants Choice of where the event takes place Specification of the system of participation Specification of the rules of the game Specification of publicity and broadcasting regulations	
Preliminary prerequisites: • securing the use and availability of selected facilities (i.e. to obtain the administrative authorization, contracts, etc.); • securing the authorization of the FIVB (e.g. inclusion of the event in the international calendar of the FIVB); • securing the authorization of public authorities to organize the event (i.e. a public event); • securing housing for athletes, technicians, federation delegates, referees, judges and other sports authorities or public officials	
Regulations: • establishment of the competition standards, publicity regulations and TV broadcasting regulations; • development of sports-related regulations, such as disciplinary and doping sanctions if it is necessary to do so	

- the event is based on a unique concept associating empathy, responsiveness, trust and reliability;
- the event will take place on exceptional sites (i.e. in Paris on City Hall Square and on the banks of the River Seine);
- the event will stage the world's best beach volleyball players originating from five continents;
- the equipment and corporate design of the event are coherent with the desired positioning.

What is the desired positioning of the event?

The desired positioning of the event is defined by answering the three key questions appearing in Table 5.6.

Which identity should the event communicate?

The identity for the event will be a unique sporting and festive event celebrating beach volleyball at an exceptional site. Thus, the event will be called 'The Beach Volleyball Experience'.

Definition of the main characteristics of the event in relation to key stakeholders

A sporting event is essentially a service offer aimed at satisfying the expectations of the stakeholders for which the event was conceived. Therefore, it is important to specify the dimensions constituting the event.

Intangible aspects

Intangible aspects essentially refer to the concept of the event. In agreement with the requirements of the FIVB, the event is an unofficial sporting competition where the ten best men's and women's teams, originating from at least five continents, will compete on 18 and 19 August 2007.

The first day of competition will be devoted to the preliminary rounds where teams will be divided into two pools of five teams each. The second day will be reserved for the semi-finals and the finals.

The 'prize money' will be $100,000 for men and $100,000 for women.

Furthermore, given the synergy between the 'Paris Beach Project' (the man-made beach along the River Seine) and the will of the FFVB to involve its clubs and leagues, the event

Table 5.6 Positioning statement of the event

Questions	Elements
What is the event?	The best of beach volleyball in Paris
Whom is the event intended for?	For all those who enjoy a festive and sporting lifestyle
Why should people be interested in the event?	It offers a unique physical experience in a friendly and exciting environment

will incorporate peripheral events that consist of a tournament reserved for non-member players and a second tournament reserved for teams belonging to member clubs.

Physical environment

The tournament will take place in Paris on City Hall Square and on the banks of the River Seine. The sites will be arranged according to the specifications of the FIVB World Tour,[3] which include:

- one main sand court with a 4,000-seat platform equipped with a giant screen;
- three sand courts for warm-ups;
- a village for sponsors and partners;
- concessions with points of sale (POS) of associated products.

Associated products

Associated products relate to the merchandise derived from the licence agreement. The 'Perrier Fluo Beach Volleyball Experience' product line will include the following:

- clothing (i.e. T-shirts, tanks, shorts, bathing suits, caps and sun visors);
- accessories (i.e. bags, sunglasses, keyrings, volleyballs, etc.);
- collectors' items (e.g. 'Perrier Fluo Beach Volleyball Experience' bottles).

Stakeholders

The service provision within the framework of the event aims at satisfying various stakeholders, including the public. The event will be organized in collaboration with the city of Paris, which is the organizer of the previously mentioned Paris Beach Project, which offers free entertainment to the public, particularly to those who do not leave the city during summer holidays. In 2004, three million visitors enjoyed and relaxed on the man-made beach that will be used for the event.

Legal considerations concerning the sporting event

The legal department must collaborate with the marketing department for designing the characteristics of the event (Table 5.7).

Regulations

It is necessary to comply with private and public regulations.

Private regulations

The organizer must take into account the statutes and regulations of both the FIVB and the FFVB.

Table 5.7 Event's characteristics

Sports activity	A commercially characterized, unofficial sporting competition, which accounts for its realization with the authorization of the FIVB
Type of competition	International
Sport	Beach volleyball
Owner of the event	FFVB
Organizer of the event	FFVB
Place	City Hall Square and the banks of the River Seine in Paris
Day and time	18 and 19 August 2007 from 10:00 AM to 11:00 PM
Participating teams	10 men's teams and 10 women's teams composed of the world's top players originating from 5 continents, who are invited by the organizer
Sponsors	Naming rights (title) sponsor and official suppliers

Statutes and regulations of the International Federation of Volleyball

The FFVB wants to organize an event that is sanctioned by the FIVB. Therefore, the FFVB must comply with the requirements outlined in the WT/04b[4] application form of the FIVB.

Statutes and regulations of the French Federation of Volleyball

It is mandatory for the FFVB to comply with its own standards and those of the FIVB in regard to the configuration and organization of competitions, events and other activities.

Specific regulations for competitions

The FFVB must establish specific regulations for the event competition[5] concerning the rules of the game and disciplinary standards. For such a large-scale international event, the following regulations constitute just the bare minimum that need to be established:

- rules of the game (i.e. system of participation, registration, system of competition, scoring system, classifications, prize money and bonus pools, etc.);
- advertising regulations;
- TV broadcasting guidelines.

For a more detailed example, the FIVB Handbook of the World Tour can be consulted, which is available on the website of the FIVB.[6]

Public regulations

It is essential to take into account certain standards and regulations enacted by the European Union, the state, or, in certain circumstances, the region and/or the community in which the event is held. These can be differentiated according to their nature.

General regulations

All general regulatory standards are applicable to any type of social or economic activity (commercial law, civil law, labour regulations, insurance standards, fiscal regulations, broadcasting law, etc.).

Fiscal regulations

The 'Perrier Fluo Beach Volleyball Experience' unites various parties of various geographical origins (i.e. athletes, referees, sponsors, broadcasters, advertising agencies, licensees, etc.). Therefore, it is necessary to take into account the taxation that is applicable to each of them.

Regulations concerning public spaces

This event is scheduled to occur on public property where its usage is regulated. Therefore, the FFVB must research whether or not there are any specific regulations applicable in connection with the environmental protection or preservation of the selected site.

Regulations concerning public events

The 'Perrier Fluo Beach Volleyball Experience' event will be regarded as a public spectacle. As a result, the event is regulated by standards for public events such as safety precautions and measures, crowd capacity, security, emergency services, etc.

Specific sports regulations

There is a set of regulations emanating from public authorities in charge of regulating various sports activities, public spectacles or sporting events. These regulations encompass a broad range of issues that can arise during the event such as doping, insurance coverage for athletes or the event, liabilities for organizers and promoters, image rights, TV broadcasts, etc.

Trademark registration considerations

The owner of the event must adequately protect the names and symbols associated with the competition. Who must register trademarks and what must be registered is addressed in the following sections.

Who must register the trademarks?

The owner of the event is typically responsible for registering the trademarks, industrial designs and domain names of the event with the respective authorities. However, certain situations are more complex when certain rights are shared by various entities and when certain intellectual properties (e.g. trademarks registered before the event) existed before the commencement of the event. This case study is built on such a complex scenario.

The scenario is facilitated if the marketing actions carried out by a sponsor are strictly limited to advertising insertions (e.g. billboards in stadiums), public relations or product promotions associated with the event. In this case, the event organizer could easily register the trademarks, industrial designs and domain names. Furthermore, the event organizer can enter into merchandising licence agreements with a third party which would likely use, for example, the industrial designs of the sponsor on the mascot or logo of the event.

The registration of the mark of an event is much more complex if the name of the event incorporates the name of a brand or product(s) registered by the sponsor before the commencement of the event. In this second case scenario, both the sponsor and the organizer could legitimately claim the rights ensuing from the registration of the mark. In this case, there are two alternative solutions:

1. The owner of the event registers the brand and enters into merchandising licence agreements with the sponsor(s).
2. The owner of the event and the sponsor jointly register the trademark.

The FFVB, for the purpose of the case study, should use the second option. Hence, integration of the second option is incorporated into the sponsorship contract model by means of the joint creation of a commercial company whose purpose is the ownership and the exploitation of the brands, symbols and domain names that can be created specifically for this event.

What should be registered?

Chapter 2 revealed which characteristics of the brand should be protected. Three mechanisms will provide legal protection:

- trademarks and/or industrial design patents registration;
- intellectual property (e.g. non-denominative logos) registration;
- domains and domain names on the Internet registration.

These mechanisms are compatible. Therefore, it is advisable to use all three means to ensure the best possible legal protection.

Protection of trade names and industrial designs

The organizer and rights owner of the event must create unique trademarks for the event and protect them adequately. The protection of a trademark needs to be secured before the commencement of the event and before it gains brand popularity.

To ensure the legal protection of a trademark, an application for the registration of the trademark must be filed with the appropriate national or regional trademark office. This constitutes the best guarantee for the rights owner of the event to exploit other economic aspects of the event that are not strictly related to sport.

Nevertheless, the scope of protection depends on the budget available for taking legal actions in case of trademark infringement, and on the location where the event takes place because the effects of registration are limited to the country or countries concerned.

The application must also contain a list of goods or services to which the trademark would apply. A trademark or industrial design can apply to goods or services belonging to only one class of the list. There are 45 distinct classes on the list. Therefore, to cover the totality of goods and services envisaged under a particular trademark, it would be necessary to fill in 45 distinct classes.

It is thus necessary to be selective and register only those categories of products or services for which there is a reasonable potential for merchandizing and brand development. Likewise, it is prudent to register only in the countries where the exploitation of the event can generate an economic benefit.

Therefore, the organizer of the event must precisely appraise the three following aspects that need to be protected:

- trade names and industrial designs;
- classes of goods or services;
- territorial effect according to the countries where the protection of the products is deemed relevant.

Trade names and industrial designs to be protected
As merely a brief example, as a minimum the following trade names, industrial designs or signs of the event should be registered:

1. Name of the organizing entity: Nominative.

In many countries, the name of national sports federations is legally protected to ensure that their names can only be used by the authorized entity. The name of a sport federation is automatically protected nationally, but not internationally.

2. Generic name of the event: Nominative.
3. Name of the event for each year (e.g. 2007): Nominative-Figurative.
4. Logo of the event: Figurative.
5. Name of the event with the logo: Nominative-Figurative.
6. Mascot of the event: Figurative.
7. Name of the mascot: Nominative.

Classes of goods or services to seek protection for
The distinctive marks and signs selected must be registered under a certain number of classes. This constitutes the second aspect that requires specific protection.

The 'Nice Classification' consists of a classification of goods and services for the purposes of registering trademarks and service marks. The classification consists of a list of classes and an alphabetical list of the goods and services. According to that list, the most relevant classes regarding the 'Perrier Fluo Beach Volleyball Experience' are:

- *Class 6:* metals and their alloys; goods of common metal not included in other classes (e.g. badges, key rings, trophies, etc.).
- *Class 14:* precious metals and their alloys and goods in precious metals or coated therewith, that are not included in other classes; jewellery, precious stones; watches and other chronometric instruments.

- *Class 16:* paper, cardboard and goods made from these materials, that are not included in other classes; printed matter; bookbinding material; photographs; stationery; typewriters and office requisites (except furniture); instructional and teaching material (except apparatus); plastic materials for packaging (not included in other classes); printers' type; printing blocks.
- *Class 18:* any kind of bags, suitcases, umbrellas and parasols.
- *Class 24:* textiles and textile goods not included in other classes; table covers and e.g. flags that are not made out of paper.
- *Class 25:* clothing, footwear, headgear.
- *Class 28:* games and playthings; gymnastic and sporting articles not included in other classes.
- *Class 32:* beers; mineral and carbonated waters and other non-alcoholic drinks; fruit drinks and fruit juices; syrups and other preparations for making beverages.
- *Class 35:* advertising; business management; business administration; office functions.
- *Class 38:* telecommunications.
- *Class 41:* education; providing of training; entertainment; sporting and cultural activities.

The following classes are also useful for the organizing of sporting events: 3, 20 and 21.[7]

Territorial effect according to the countries in which the protection of the products are needed

The third aspect to take into account is the scope and effect of the protection. There is no single register that is valid and applicable worldwide. Nevertheless, the Paris Convention for the Protection of Industrial Property is designed to help people of one country obtain protection in other countries for their intellectual creations in the forms of industrial property rights, i.e. patents, trademarks and industrial designs. Each of the 169 countries adhering to the Paris Convention is obligated to grant nationals of other signatory states equal treatment with regard to the protection of industrial property. No requirement as to domicile or establishment in the country where protection is claimed may be imposed upon nationals of countries belonging to the Union for the enjoyment of any industrial property rights.[8]

There are also bilateral agreements between certain countries that allow a citizen of one country to register a mark in another country. However, these bilateral agreements do not fall within the scope of the Paris Convention. Thus, the organizer of the event will need to determine in which countries it is preferable to register its mark(s) and verify whether these countries are signatories of the Paris Convention, of the Nice Agreement and/or of any bilateral agreement.

The Paris Convention and most bilateral agreements establish that any person who has properly filed an application for the registration of a trademark in one of the countries belonging to the Union shall enjoy, for the purpose of filing in the other countries, a right of priority, insofar as subsequent filings are made within six months following the date of filing of the first application (the day of filing shall not be included in the period).

A second mechanism of international protection of the marks is the Madrid System for the international registration of marks. As of 22 September 2005, 78 countries had signed the Madrid Agreement, which is applicable in all the countries adhering to the protocol. As a result of the international procedural mechanism, the Madrid System offers a trademark owner the possibility to have its trademark protected in signatory countries by simply filing one application directly with its own national or regional trademark office. An international mark registered in this manner is equivalent to an application or a registration of the same mark effected directly in each of the countries designated by the applicant. If the trademark office of a designated country does not refuse protection within a specified period, the protection of the mark is the same as if it had been registered with that office. The Madrid System also greatly simplifies the subsequent management of the trademark, since it is possible to record subsequent changes or to renew the registration through a single procedural step.

Similarly, a directive of the European Union established a European Community (EC) system offering a trademark owner the possibility to have his trademark protected within Member States of the European Union by simply filing one trademark application.

With regard to the 'Perrier Fluo Beach Volleyball Experience', it is sufficient to register the mark with the EC system. It may be necessary later to register the trademarks of the event in the United States, Japan, China, or other countries depending on the audience and media impact of the event elsewhere.

Conditions of registering a trademark

It is necessary to fulfil a series of conditions for obtaining trademark protection, such as:

1. submit an application for the registration of a trademark with the appropriate national or regional trademark office;
2. identify the applicant(s);
3. produce a clear reproduction of the trademark filed for registration, including any colours, forms or three-dimensional features;
4. provide a list of goods or services for which the trademark is to be used.

Detailed information on all the treaties administered by the World Intellectual Property Organization (WIPO) and derived from the international protection of the intellectual property is available at: www.wipo.int/treaties.

Trademark law treaty forms are available online at: www.wipo.int/treaties/en/ip/tlt/index.html.

The directory listing of members of the Paris Convention is available online at: www.wipo.org/members.

There are some restrictions with the registration of trademarks. For instance, it is not possible to register a trademark with:

- no distinctive character;
- a sign or indication which has become customary in the current language or in the legitimate and established practices of the trade of the country where protection is claimed;
- state emblems, official hallmarks, and emblems of governmental organizations.

Registration procedures

1. Submission of the trademark application to the Trademarks and Patents Office.
2. If the trademark is properly registered, the International Bureau will publish the information in a monthly periodical for public information.
3. If the trademark is not refused or invalidated, it is officially registered.
4. If a request is made for the cancellation or the prohibition of the use of a registered trademark, the dispute will be solved with legal intervention.

The registration of a trademark is initially limited to 10 years. However, registrations can be renewed.

Protection of industrial designs within the framework of Intellectual property registration

In addition to the protection of trademarks with the Intellectual Property Register, it is equally important to register industrial designs. 'An industrial design is the ornamental or aesthetic aspect of an article. The design may consist of three-dimensional features, such as the shape or surface of an article, or of two-dimensional features, such as patterns, lines or color'.[9]

The owner, i.e. the person or entity that has registered the design, is assured an exclusive right against unauthorized copying or imitation of the design by third parties. In most countries, industrial design protection occurs under industrial design law whereby a certificate is issued to the owner of an industrial design. The following goods are examples of industrial designs which can be licensed to third parties:

- emblems;
- insignias;
- logos;
- mascots;
- other symbols or creations in two or three dimensions which do not bear the name of the event or of the organizer.

It is important to verify whether the name of the event is the work of the organization itself or the work of a specialized agency or designer. If a third party developed and conceived the name of the event, the organization will need to request the transfer of the intellectual property rights for the name of the event.

Important: the owner of an intellectual property is always the originator of that creative work (i.e. emblem, insignia, logo, mascot, etc.). Consequently, the owner of the event is seldom the initial owner of such creative works. Therefore, the owner of the event must reach a contractual agreement with the originator (e.g. designer or agency) before any creative work is achieved on its behalf. The owner of the event must secure the exclusive intellectual property rights of the creative work to be able to exploit those rights. In this type of contractual agreement, it is possible to incorporate a clause whereby any modification or change of the original creative work is forbidden without the written consent of the originator of the creative work.

The Bern Convention is especially concerned with the international protection of literary and artistic works. The aim of this convention is 'to help nationals of its member

States obtain international protection of their right to control, and receive payment for, the use of their creative works'[10] in the signatory countries. For more information about the content of the Bern Convention, consult:

www.wipo.int/treaties/en/ip/berne/index.html
www.wipo.int/treaties/en/ip/wct/index.html

Registration of domain names

The organizer of the event must also register the domain names of the event with an ICANN (Internet Corporation for Assigned Names and Numbers) accredited registrar. It is important to do this before any public announcement regarding the event. Registering the domain names of the event before they become known reduces the risk of 'cyber squatting' activities. Cyber squatters could strategically register the domain names associated with the event in order to own the rights to the domain name. The purpose of this strategy is to seek payment from those wishing to use the domain names. Thus, a cyber squatter holds the event organizer to ransom.

As previously discussed, it is important to decide what types of products need to be registered for trademark protection on a territorial and categorical basis. However, it is not necessary to follow the same process with the registration of domain names.

Since the domain name registry is not structured by any product category, it is impossible to register a trademark with an Internet registrar. Nevertheless, one can reserve a domain name with an accredited registrar, which will be applicable worldwide without any restriction on territory. The registering of a domain name does not confer any particular right of ownership other than a 'reservation' right on it based on applicable national and/or international laws.

There are two elements to take into consideration when registering domain names:

1. The exact determination of the domain name(s) or combination of names which one wishes to register, taking into account that the name of the event can include many different parts, which users can type in their browser when researching the website of the event (e.g. perrierfluo).
2. The type of domain in which the name(s) will be registered. A top-level domain (TLD) is the extension of a domain name. Domain names can be divided into two main categories: generic top-level domains (gTLD) such as '.com', '.biz', '.org', '.edu', '.net', etc., and country code top-level domains (ccTLD).

The Domain Name System or Domain Name Server (DNS) is a system that stores information associated with domain names in a distributed database, on networks such as the Internet. The DNS associates many types of information with domain names, but most importantly, it provides the IP address associated with the domain name. DNS is useful because it makes it possible to attach hard-to-remember IP addresses (e.g. 243.121.261.192) to easy-to-memorize domain names (e.g. 'perrierfluo.org').

ICANN is currently responsible for managing and coordinating the assignment of domain names and IP addresses. Created in 1998, ICANN is a non-profit corporation headquartered in California, whose role is to oversee a number of Internet-related tasks, including:

- distribution of unique IP addresses and domain names, so that users of the Internet can find all valid addresses;
- maintenance of the DNS root zone file;
- establishment of IP protocols.

In this context, the first step to safeguard the image of the event is to secure a unique domain name for the event. Hence, it is prudent to register several names in connection with the event in an effort to prevent third parties from ambushing the event. The registering of domain names must be in balance with the needs, resources and objectives of this communications platform.

For the purpose of the 'Perrier Fluo Beach Volleyball Experience', the following list of domain names would be registered.

1. Perrier Fluo Beach Volleyball Experience 2007
2. Perrier Fluo Beach Volleyball Experience
3. Perrier Fluo Experience
4. Beach Volleyball Experience
5. Perrier Beach Volleyball
6. Perrier Fluo Beach Volleyball
7. Fluo Beach Volleyball
8. Fluo Experience
9. Beach Volleyball Experience
10. PFBVE
11. The name of the mascot

Given that the name of the event includes the name of the title sponsor, it is important to stress that this list of domain names can be registered only after the signing of the contract with the title sponsor.

It is also very important to stress that domain names must meet with a number of technical requirements. For instance, they must contain a minimum of two and a maximum of 63 characters. To verify whether a given name is available, one can use the WHOIS search function by typing 'WHOIS' in any Internet-browser search engine.[11]

The second element to take into account when registering domain names corresponds to the determination of the categories (TLDs) in which the names or the combinations of names will be registered. In general, it is advisable to register one gTLD and one ccTLD based on the country where the event is celebrated.

Domain names are allocated on a first-come-first-served basis. Therefore, the event organizer should register the domain name of the event in all of the following currently available gTLDs:

- .com (commercial organizations);
- .net (network-oriented entities);
- .org (miscellaneous organizations).

Registration must be performed online with an ICANN-accredited registrar. The list of accredited registrars is available at: www.icann.org/registrars/accredited-list.html.

Considering that the simulated event will be held in Paris, the event would also be registered in the ccTLD for France (.fr).

The ccTLD registration would also be performed online like the gTLD. Each country has established specific regulations in this field of registration. In this case study, the country code registration is done with the France top-level domain, in accordance with the French rules governing jurisdiction and applicable laws.

In the case of abusive registration and use of the Internet domain name of the event, the registrant of the gTLD of the event (i.e. the rights owner/event organizer) can effectively defend the trademark in which it has rights. Pursuant to the ICANN Uniform Domain Name Dispute Resolution Policy (UDRP), this can be achieved by lodging a complaint with the WIPO Arbitration and Mediation Center. The UDRP ascertains the resolution of disputes between a domain name registrant and a third party. For instance, the said policy gives the legal resources required to nullify and block the abusive registration of domain names. For more information, one can consult: http://arbiter.wipo.int/domains/index.html.

Rights of individuals

Establishing a balance between an individual's rights and the will and the capability of the organizer of the event to market or yield the images of the event is often complicated. It can prove to be useful and necessary to distinguish certain legal problems arising from possible infringements upon the rights of an individual that result from organizing an event. Subsequently, it is advisable to prepare a means for the organizer to obtain appropriate permission from individuals, whether it is a sportsperson, technician, official or spectator.

Spectators

It is advisable to obtain the consent of spectators for the recording of images and their commercial exploitation. However, this consent is generally neither explicit nor implicitly formulated upon the purchase of an entry ticket to a public event.

Therefore, a solution for obtaining this consent consists of inserting a clause on the back of entry tickets to the event, whereby the condition of entry is subject to the terms and conditions contained in the said document of entry. In essence, the spectators would thus be 'agreeing' to an adhesion contract with the event organizer, although the guarantee of its validity is vulnerable.

As an example, the following terms and conditions of sale and use of the 'Perrier Fluo Beach Volleyball Experience' tickets could be written on the back of entry tickets to the event.

> The acquisition or possession of this entry ticket is subject to the terms and conditions contained herein. As the holder of this ticket, you declare to have read and accept, and agree to comply with all the said terms and conditions, including: giving your consent to be photographed, filmed, or taped by the Perrier Fluo Beach Volleyball Experience event organizer or third parties appointed by it. The event organizer or the third parties appointed by it can broadcast, publish, and use any photographs, film, recordings, or images of you without any compensation.

Participants (athletes, coaches, umpires, volunteers, employees of concessions, etc.)

It is recommended that similar consent is obtained from the various people participating in the event. Based on an analysis of the main possibilities for conflicts of interests' legalities with athletes/coaches/umpires/volunteers/employees of concession contractors, etc., the most important potential conflict corresponds to the recording and broadcasting of the event. In this case, the event organizer could obtain the consent of the participants through a written contract that authorizes the recording and broadcasting of images. The event organizer could require participants to sign the said contract prior to granting them their accreditations to the event. Consequently, the accreditation giving them access to the event could include the terms of consent. For example:

> I, _____ (name), *taking part in the Perrier Fluo Beach Volleyball Experience, in the capacity of _____* (athlete/coach/umpire/volunteer, etc.), *consent to be photographed, filmed, or taped by the Perrier Fluo Beach Volleyball Experience event organizer or third parties appointed by it. The event organizer or the third parties appointed by it can broadcast, publish, license and use any photographs, film, recordings or images taken at the event without any compensation requirement.*

Legal issues can arise when the individual rights of the participants clash with the conditions imposed by the event organizer. The significance of such conflicts depends on two variables: existing advertising regulations in connection with sporting event management and the use by the organizer of images in which athletes appear. Generally, the event organizer explicitly requires that an athlete comply with certain obligations prior to registering or inviting an athlete to partake in a competition, such as:

1. to adhere to the rules of the game and the rules of competition approved by the organizer;
2. to act with diligence and conscientiousness throughout the event while participating per se in the competition, as well as in the athletes' village and other installations set up for the event;
3. to subject oneself during the extent of the event to any doping control initiated by the organizer, the sporting federation concerned, or the public authorities;
4. to agree to submit any type of litigation or legal conflict which may arise with the event organizer, other athletes, sponsors and/or other participants to the arbitration of an arbitration court, such as the Court of Arbitration for Sport in Lausanne, or to a similar court of arbitration in the country of the athlete, where such a court exists.

In addition to these general conditions, which are typical in most sporting competitions, the event organizer can include additional specific obligations in the contract it concludes with the athlete. These particular obligations can vary according to the characteristics of the event, the obligations of an athlete and/or the agreements the event organizer made with third parties for the purpose of developing the event.

In the case of the 'Perrier Fluo Beach Volleyball Experience', the event organizer will require the written consent of the athlete. Furthermore, athletes must also consent to the following TV broadcast and advertising activities.

1. Images of the event will be transmitted on television and through other types of broadcasting platforms. Photographs, films and/or recordings of these images may be commercialized in DVDs, video games, etc.
2. Athletes will be required to wear apparel displaying publicity, such as T-shirts, shorts, pants, socks, jerseys, etc. This apparel will be distributed to them by the event organizer.
3. Athletes will need to use the sport bags or duffel bags, towels, caps, etc. showing publicity. This merchandise will also be provided by the event organizer.
4. Athletes will be provided with bottled beverages with publicity (e.g. mineral water) to consume, which are exclusively distributed by the event organizer. In addition, athletes must agree not to make any public appearance with beverages distributed by competitors of the event sponsors.
5. Athletes must commit not to use equipment, nor wear any garment, within the event venues, on which the name or marks of a competitor would appear.
6. Athletes must agree not to make any public statement against the sponsor or its products. Likewise, they will have to commit to not making any act or gesture showing contempt with respect to the trademark of the sponsor or its products.
7. Athletes, especially the semi-finalists and finalists, will be required to attend the press-room after their matches when the media request an interview with them.

The acceptance of these conditions presupposes that the athlete must sign, before the commencement of the competition or prior to obtaining an accreditation, the document in which these conditions are declared. It is increasingly frequent to have such advertising-related obligations in contracts signed by athletes, whereby athletes accept advertising insertion and/or image rights transfers. In exchange, the event organizer generally provides athletes with certain compensations, such as a fixed amount for participating in the competition, a stipulated bonus based on performance, or another form of remuneration such as a car awarded to the winner of the tournament.

SUBSTAGE 5: DECISIONS CONCERNING THE MEDIA AND SPONSORSHIP STRATEGIES OF THE EVENT

This substage focuses on defining a sponsorship strategy that is coherent with the concept of the event and the partnership with the media. Pursuant to the concept developed for the 'Perrier Fluo Beach Volleyball Experience', the following questions must be addressed.

• Which media partners should the FFVB associate with?
• Which production system should be used to broadcast images of the event?
• Which types of potential sponsors should the FFVB try to engage first?
• How should the FFVB structure its sponsorship offer?
• Which processes should the FFVB implement to manage the sponsorship operation?

Media partnership strategy

Based on the concept of the 'Perrier Fluo Beach Volleyball Experience', the characteristics of the targeted audience (which is presumably an audience of teenagers and young adults with a dynamic and festive lifestyle) and the limited impact of the Swatch Beach Volleyball Tour with the French media, the FFVB has an opportunity to produce the premier beach volleyball event in France. To do so, it will entrust the production of images to a specialized company by entering into a TV broadcast contract with the French TV operator 'M6' for transmission in France. Additionally, given that 'EUROSPORT' is the broadcast partner of the FIVB and of the French national volleyball team, the FFVB will also conduct a partial transfer of its media rights with 'EUROSPORT' in order to exploit the event in the broader European market. Furthermore, secondary media exploitation rights could be sold to 'France Televisions' and 'TF1', whereby highlights of the event would reach more people. The French 'Europe 2' radio and 'VSD' magazine have been loyal supporters of the Adia Beach Volleyball Tour. Consequently, it is advisable to develop relationships with them in view of their traditional support of beach volleyball. Lastly, the event organizer will negotiate a partnership with JC Decaux is one of the world's largest outdoor advertising groups.

Structure of the sponsorship offer and the selection precedence of prospective sponsors

Taking into account the brand identity of the FFVB and the exposure it seeks to achieve, it would be judicious to attract and secure companies whose brands are synonymous with the lifestyles of the targeted audience, such as festive, healthy and athletic. Likewise, the sponsorship offer must also engage key media partners and official suppliers who seek a unique opportunity in associating with beach volleyball. Since the sponsorship strategy of the FFVB aims at giving precedence to the title sponsor, the sponsorship offer will contain three levels of sponsorship:

1. naming rights (title) sponsor;
2. media partners: television, radio and printed media;
3. official suppliers in the following categories: sports clothing and equipment, volleyball manufacturer, Internet and data processing equipment.

Operational sponsorship management of the FFVB

The processes implemented by the FFVB to manage the sponsorship operations must take into account the legal and marketing requirements. Figure 5.2 describes the various necessary processes.

Thus, this management of sponsorship operations is divided into six steps:

1. structuring the offer;
2. establishing a pricing policy;

Figure 5.2 Marketing and legal processes required for targeting prospective sponsor

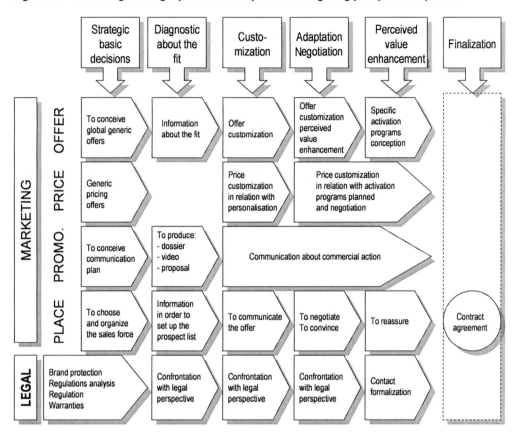

3. developing a message to attract potential sponsors;
4. choosing and building the sales force;
5. conducting a legal analysis;
6. signing the contract.

Again, the legal functions and marketing must collaborate to work out and implement this process. Table 5.8 shows how the FFVB will commercialize the 'Perrier Fluo Beach Volleyball Experience'.

SUBSTAGE 6: LEGAL CONSIDERATIONS REGARDING COMMERCIALIZATION RIGHTS

This substage focuses on aspects related to the transfer of audiovisual, sponsorship and licensing rights.

Table 5.8 Collaboration of the legal and marketing functions for the commercialization rights of the event

Legal function	Marketing function
	Search for media partners
	Negotiations with media partners (rights, responsibilities, duties and obligations)
Legal advisement	
First draft of the media partnership	
Second draft of the media partnership (if needed)	
Third draft of the media partnership (if needed)	
	Marketing of the sponsorship offer
Review of the final draft, formalization of the sponsorship contract	Negotiations and amendments to the sponsorship offer (rights, responsibilities, duties and obligations)
Legal advisement	
First draft of the sponsorship contract	
Second draft of the sponsorship contract (if needed)	
Third draft of the sponsorship contract (if needed)	
Review of the final draft, formalization of the sponsorship contract	Negotiations of TV rights (rights, responsibilities, duties and obligations)
Legal advisement	
First draft of the TV contract	
Second draft of the TV contract (if needed)	
Third draft of the TV contract (if needed)	
Review of the final draft, formalization of the sponsorship contract	
Review of the final draft, formalization of the TV contract	
	Licensing negotiations
Legal advisement	
First draft of the licence agreement	
Second draft of the licence agreement (if needed)	
Third draft of the licence agreement (if needed)	
Review of the final draft, formalization of the licence agreement	
Registration of trademarks, industrial designs, drawings and patents (if needed)	

Aspects regarding the cession of audiovisual rights

The principal aspect to consider regarding the transfer of audiovisual rights is securing ownership of the intellectual property rights of images produced during the event. As mentioned earlier in Substage 4, that can be achieved via the authorization or consent of third parties.

In this case study, the FFVB will have to obtain an authorization for the recording, broadcasting and marketing of images with various participants, including beach volleyball players, coaches and umpires, as well as the consent of volunteers, spectators and concession employees involved in the event.

The second aspect to consider relates to the communication strategy of the event. The FFVB must determine whether the sale of TV rights primarily serves to finance the 'Perrier Fluo Beach Volleyball Experience' or to communicate the event to its targeted audience. The FFVB wishes to retain the intellectual property rights of television materials produced during the event; that requires a particular legal framework and difficult negotiations due to the fact that the FFVB must combine its own communication strategy with those of its media partners and sponsors.

Before introducing media exploitation rights packages to potential media partners, the FFVB must analyse the following points.

1.   What is the position of the 'Perrier Fluo Beach Volleyball Experience' within the sponsorship network? There are at least two possibilities. A media sponsorship offer can be lucrative when an event has a strong position within the sponsorship market, or because several TV operators are interested in acquiring the media exploitation rights of the event. On the other hand, the value of media sponsorship offers decreases when the sponsorship market is saturated and demand is weak.

In this case study, the event organizer needs a TV partner in order to strengthen and better position the 'Perrier Fluo Beach Volleyball Experience', to leverage the sponsorship/ publicity/licensing offers, and to promote the event and the sport to a large audience. Thus, the FFVB must determine the role of its media partners: should this role be strictly limited to the production and broadcast of images of the event, or should media partners be largely involved in the development of the event?

Clearly, in this case, developing a solid partnership with audiovisual companies is arguably the most advantageous solution. In selling media exploitation rights to the event, the FFVB is not solely interested in money, but more importantly, in the methodical and widespread broadcast of the event.

2.   The second aspect to analyse is how to keep control over the intellectual property rights of images produced during the event. Thus, the FFVB must determine how much control it wishes to retain. Bearing in mind the quality of any audiovisual product depends on its conception and production, a decision must be made in this regard. To increase positive awareness about the 'Perrier Fluo Beach Volleyball Experience', the FFVB must ensure the product is well developed. For the event organizer, the solution consists of either being responsible for the development of all images produced during the event, or relying on the expertise of a specialized company. There are two ways to retain certain control over the final product:

- by establishing broadcast guidelines for the production, transmission and distribution of images, which TV operator partners must comply with;
- by developing the entire visual product in-house, from conception to production and distribution, whereby it is possible to guarantee that every image will be selected to deliver the desired message established in the communication strategy.

There is a vast range of solutions and budgets pertaining to project management for all events. It is not solely events such as the Olympic Games, Formula 1, UEFA Championship and the Tour de France that have the means to be broadcast on television. Smaller sporting events can also be transmitted, including the 'Perrier Fluo Beach Volleyball Experience'. In this context, the FFVB will choose to negotiate and establish broadcast guidelines for the production, transmission and distribution of images of the sporting event.

3.   The third element to consider is the transfer of media exploitation rights, in particular, the sale of exclusive rights to television networks, Internet providers and mobile phone operators. The exclusive sale and/or lease of media exploitation rights are always subject to the approval of the competition authorities concerned. In a sporting event of short duration, such as the 'Perrier Fluo Beach Volleyball Experience', the sale of exclusive media rights would be possible without violating competition law.

Aspects regarding sponsorship

As with the transfer of audiovisual rights, the FFVB must determine whether its sponsorship approach contributes to the communication strategy of the event or if it is only a source of financing.

Previous chapters stressed the importance of integrating and balancing the interests of various stakeholders in an effort to enhance the event. Therefore, publicity, sponsorship, licensing and broadcast approaches of the FFVB must be integrated into its own communication and marketing strategies, as well as into those of various partners.

Advertising and sponsorship agreements must be formalized in an official document (contract) that explicitly defines the agreements reached in negotiations. Thus, the sponsorship contract must be an indicator of the communication strategies that the event organizer and the sponsor intend to implement jointly. These communication strategies include:

1. Joint operational and communication strategies. For the 'Perrier Fluo Beach Volleyball Experience', a brand development approach is vital for the successful marketing of properties such as brands, industrial designs, domain names and other distinctive signs of the event. Thus, the sponsor and the event organizer will choose to engage in a joint venture by means of the creation of a commercial company of equal capital.
2. Operational and communication strategies that are incumbent to the event organizer can refer to, for example, extra space to set up an exhibit or to display signs and banners, to make public address announcements, or secure media recognition in which the event organizer will authorize the sponsor to associate its name or brand with the 'Perrier Fluo Beach Volleyball Experience'.
3. Operational and communication strategies that are incumbent to the title sponsor can refer to, for example, the acceptance of the title sponsor to promote the event in the media and through particular channels of its own. Similarly, the title sponsor may take advantage of regular communications to promote the event and thereby make it known to the public.

In order to provide customized activation platforms, sponsorship packages (title sponsor, official suppliers, etc.) must be based on exclusive product categories to avoid disputes between sponsors. Furthermore, the overall sponsorship offer must be coherent with the philosophy and objectives of the event.

Aspects regarding licences

The rights owner of the event can establish licensing agreements with a third party concerning the use, exploitation and marketing of the brands, associated products or given services derived from the event. The primary element that the event organizer must account for prior to transferring any rights is to ensure that the registration of all the trademarks, signs, industrial designs and domain names in connection with a licence are properly filed. In the case of the 'Perrier Fluo Beach Volleyball Experience', the following properties will be registered:

- the name and logo of the event;
- the name and image of the mascot (and all the possible variations);
- the Internet domain name of the event (and all the possible variations).

As previously mentioned, the sporting event will bear the name of the main sponsor. The commercial rights derived from the event will be registered under a commercial company with limited liability, where each of the participating parties (i.e. the organizer and the title sponsor) will contribute to its formation equally.

Thus, the licensor will be the newly incorporated commercial company, whereby it will be in a position to licence the commercial rights to any company interested in associating itself with the 'Perrier Fluo Beach Volleyball Experience'. Under this legal structure, commercial rights can be conceded via:

- a general licence to one company, for all types of products and services;
- several limited licences to various companies, i.e. per product and service categories, territory, and/or sales and distribution channels.

In this case study, the licensor (i.e. the event organizer and the title sponsor) chooses the option of distributing several limited licences, one per product and/or service category.

While structuring licensing opportunities, the licensor must decide which legal properties it wishes to assign rights to. This must take into consideration the current event, as well as any subsequent events in the future. The organizer will have to determine, before the negotiation and the formalization of any licensing contract, the following various aspects:

- a definition of product and service categories;
- the type of licence granted and its characteristics: exclusive, non-exclusive, general, limited, transferable, non-transferable, etc.;
- the validity period of the licence, including possible renewal options;
- a detailed definition of the products and/or services pertaining to a licence;
- definition of the distribution channels in circumstances of limited licences;

- definition of sales channels in circumstances of limited licences;
- conditions of use (e.g. can licensed products be sold at a discount?);
- definitions of possible limits on pricing and quantities to be sold;
- whether the licensee is to be responsible for the manufacturing, distribution and sale of licensed products, or whether it can contract the services of a third party for those purposes;
- specifications about sublicences (i.e. can the commercial rights be sublicensed? If so, what are the conditions?);
- definition of technical specifications of licensed products (e.g. colour, size, quality, etc.);
- specifications about the advertising campaign (i.e. is the licensee allowed to implement an advertising campaign in connection with the event because it holds a licence?);
- licence fee (e.g. fixed amount, based on a percentage of sales, etc.); note that it is possible here to include a provision whereby the licensee is entitled to return excess licensed products at the termination of the agreement;
- terms and schedule of payments;
- rights, responsibilities, duties and obligations of each party;
- definition of how inventory stocks are disposed of, and whether the licensee can continue to sell these stocks when the contract expires (e.g. must remaining stock items at the point of sale be returned, destroyed or sold?);
- conditions for withdrawing products off the market at the expiration of the contract (e.g. certificate proving that the moulds which served to manufacture certain licensed items have been disposed of or destroyed);
- process monitoring (i.e. does either the licensee or licensor have an obligation to produce a sales report at given intervals?);
- audit (i.e. is there a right to have an audit clause, whereby the licensor can have access to documents, warehouses, and/or manufacturing plants?);
- liquidated damages clause (i.e. is there a liquidated damages clause, which establishes damages to be paid to one party in the event where the other party should breach the contract? For instance, in the event where the licensee illegally transfers licensed rights to a third party);
- insurance (i.e. is the licensee obliged to subscribe to a civil liability insurance policy? If so, for what amount of damage protection?);
- procedures for registering trademarks, patents, or drawings to ensure proper protection of the licensed products;
- homologation (i.e. do licensed products have to be homologated, labelled or barcoded? Which party has the responsibility to fulfil these requirements?).

SUBSTAGE 7: STRUCTURING THE SPONSORSHIP

The marketing-mix approach to sponsorship consists of blending various factors in such a way that organizational and partner objectives are attained. This is achieved through structuring the offer by establishing the price of sponsorship levels, selecting the sales force and maximizing commercial actions.

Developing the sponsorship offer

Taking into account the structure of the sponsorship programme, the FFVB must develop various sponsorship offers corresponding to the following categories: title sponsor, media partners and official suppliers. Thus, each category and level of sponsorship will be differentiated through the following opportunities.

A. Branding with the 'Perrier Fluo Beach Volleyball Experience':

- sponsorship levels (i.e. naming rights sponsor, official supplier, etc.);
- exclusive product categories;
- preferential opportunities to purchase advertising spaces with media partners;
- website.

B. On-site identification opportunities:

- advertising spaces;
- contests;
- display of product and product samples.

C. Benefits of official naming rights:

- boards, hoardings, flyers;
- magazines, letterheads;
- licensed products.

D. Hospitality and public relations:

- spaces designed to carry out public relations (e.g. village, VIP lodges, etc.);
- VIP accreditations;
- provision of preferential seating and/or preferential ticket purchase rates;
- parking;
- 'Perrier Fluo Beach Volleyball Experience' lounge.

E. Other institutional and commercial opportunities:

- conferences and press releases;
- presence of players and/or officials during public relations and commercial operations.

F. Opportunities linked to organizational and marketing operations:

- services of personnel (e.g. hostesses);
- impact study following the event;
- consultancy.

Establishing the price for sponsorship offers

In Chapter 3, a model for establishing the price of various sponsorship packages was introduced. Keeping in mind that it is essential to perform a complex deliberation that takes into consideration several variables concerning the sporting organization, the environment and competition, and potential company sponsors, the FFVB now has to establish the price of various sponsorship packages accordingly.

To achieve this, the event organizer must compose the content of various sponsorship offers while taking into account the overall strategy of the FFVB and cost constraints with a view to optimizing cost parameters that control minimum and maximum budget levels required to deliver each offer.

From a strategic point of view, the FFVB's main pricing objective is merely to cover the expenses related to the event. The organization is not interested in assuming great financial risks. The organizer desires to propose attractive sponsorship offers with a favourable price/quality ratio.

The title sponsor package grants tangible and intangible benefits. Tangible components of this package include on-site brand exposure, hospitality at the sporting venues, public relations opportunities, and an organizational and marketing platform for brand activation across corporate and commercial communication channels. Intangible elements include a series of opportunities such as naming rights and exclusive use of the name and logo of the event.

Based on the cost parameters and the audience projection, the FFVB can justify the price of the following sponsorship offers (Table 5.9).

Designing a communication plan for the commercial action

When developing a new event, it is judicious to promote the event across various communication channels to optimize the commercial action and profit from the media campaign. Several advertising venues can be used to accomplish this function on the site of the event and elsewhere, including, but not limited to: public relations, publicity, Internet, sales promotion, direct marketing, press releases, radio and newspapers.

Given the specificity of sponsorship, the FFVB would build its communication plan around the following components (Table 5.10).

Table 5.9 Price of various sponsorship offers

Category	No.	Price (euros)	Memo
Naming rights sponsor	1	300,000	
Media partners	3	N/A	Exchange of services
Official volleyball supplier	1	40,000	Supplies volleyballs
Other official suppliers	4	40,000	

Table 5.10 Methods used to implement the commercial operation

Means	Purpose
Press relations	A press conference two years before the launching of the project at the City Hall in Paris
	A press conference upon the signing of the contract with the title sponsor
Internet	Launching of the 'Perrier Fluo Beach Volleyball Experience' website
	Newsletters
Public relations	Public relations campaign during the FIVB Swatch Beach Volleyball World Tour in Marseilles (France); showcase of top-level players during the Paris Beach Show
Other	Promotional video of the event
	Sponsor kit (to give to prospects)
	Sales kit (to sell sponsorships of the event)
	Letterhead, flyers, posters

Choosing the sales force

The FFVB will hire experienced professionals to develop the event in an effort to inter-
nalize the functions of marketing and selling sponsorships. Thus, the organization enjoys
the following competitive advantages: continued development of internal competences and
relationships, a stronger commitment to the project, direct interface with partners and
direct responsibility for executing the terms of the contract.

Legal action

From a legal and strategic perspective, the FFVB will have to seek the protection of
properties associated with the event in two phases. First, it will need to register the primary
name of the event, i.e., 'Beach Volleyball Experience'. When the title sponsor is secured,
the two parties will formalize their partnership by incorporating under a commercial
company with each party contributing 50 per cent of the holdings. The event will need to
be re-registered in the second phase under the name 'Perrier Fluo Beach Volley Experience'.
In addition to these phases, the FFVB will need to examine various sets of regulations in an
effort to draft the regulations that will govern the event.

THIRD STAGE: STRATEGIC ANALYSIS OF PERRIER AND THE PERRIER FLUO BRAND

According to the Perrier story,[12] Perrier was originally positioned as a top-notch product
to entice British consumers. At the dawn of the twentieth century, Perrier's management
team promoted its bottled water by highlighting its virtues – elegance, festiveness – and
introduced this product as the 'champagne of table water'. In 1992, following an initial
public offering (IPO), Perrier became part of the Nestlé SA group and thus fell within the
management of the Nestlé Waters division. In 2005, Nestlé was the world's largest food
and beverage company, with factories or operations in almost every country. The growing

and varied demand for drinking water has given Nestlé an opportunity to develop its commercial activities while satisfying the expectations of many consumers. Meanwhile, Perrier's environmental concerns are apparent in a multitude of initiatives in many areas, and the standards set by the company are even more stringent than those set by European legislators. Today, the Perrier brand is still praised for the same prestigious qualities, yet it is also focuses on three core elements:

- water is a element vital to all types of activities, and water resources are subject to sustainable management policies;
- packaging is one of the key factors to differentiate a product;
- consumers are concerned about health issues.

Since the turn of the twenty-first century, Perrier has leveraged its image and the brand has utilized new formats to appeal to a wider audience. In 2002, Perrier unveiled the Perrier Fluo brand. Mindful of the specificity of national cultures, Perrier ads currently feature local humour while offering a blend of the products' original values. Currently, the Perrier Fluo brand enjoys market strength on both the sparkling water and soft-drink markets. The Perrier Fluo brand is intended to reinforce the Perrier product line. Table 5.11 synthesizes this strategic analysis between Nestlé Waters and Perrier Fluo.

SUBSTAGE 1: EXTERNAL ANALYSIS OF PERRIER AND THE 'PERRIER FLUO' BRAND

To understand external forces, the FFVB must analyse the environment and market in which Perrier Fluo is positioned. Taking into account relevant factors in the business environment, this external analysis focuses on the following dimensions: the economic situation, consumption trends, sparkling water and non-alcoholic drink market segments, competitors and market legislation in France. Table 5.12 summarizes the external analysis.

At this point, attention will be focused on the most relevant information useful for the marketing of the 'Perrier Fluo' brand in the context of the event. In this case study, the following strategic conclusions regarding the 'Perrier Fluo' brand were made by the FFVB and Perrier.

1. The targeted audience comprises people aged 15–35.
2. 'Perrier Fluo' is an innovative soft drink whose unique taste produces sensory and emotional reactions.
3. Perrier Fluo's identity is communicated through the following slogans:[13] 'Perrier Fluo: It's Perrier by Perrier, a soft drink with Perrier's signature style'; 'A techno-colored blend that's 100% Perrier'; and 'Taste buds beware: Perrier Fluo is a totally new sensation'.
4. Perrier Fluo's competitive advantages are tied to the prestigious Perrier brand umbrella and the perception that 'Perrier Fluo' is a cool, healthy soft drink presented in an attractive, convenient water bottle.
5. As a market leader, Perrier is using a differentiated marketing approach to implement and develop its 'Perrier Fluo' brand in two overlapping market segments.

6. 'Perrier Fluo' is positioned at a junction between the soft-drinks market segment and the mineral water market segment. The product is offered in three flavours and colours: 'Glacier Blue' for peppermint, 'Spicy Yellow' for lemon juniper, and 'Acid Pink' for cherry ginger. It is sold in the new, convenient PET[14] plastic bottle developed by Perrier itself.
7. 'Perrier Fluo' is distributed through traditional channels and in the tertiary market.
8. 'Perrier Fluo' is sold at a competitive market price in the first and second markets, but at a higher price than competition in the tertiary market.

Table 5.11 Synthesis of the SWOT internal analysis of Nestlé Waters, Perrier and 'Perrier Fluo'

Dimensions		Strengths	Weaknesses
Strategies	Nestlé SA	Nestlé and Nestlé Waters (Perrier) have global operations with diversified operations. Market is expanding	
	Competitive advantages	Market leader Diversified portfolio	
	Operational marketing	Nestlé has integrated and rationalized key strategic functions (production, distribution, marketing, financial, HR, etc.)	Complex difficulties due to diversity of operations
	Perrier brand	Strong customer loyalty in Europe Innovative and diversified	Must regain consumer confidence in the United States (after benzene was found in its bottled water in 1990)
	Perrier Fluo brand	Message focused on current issues (health, fun, and the environment) aimed at consumers in search of an experience. Relevant brand positioning	The product is positioned in two different market segments: soft drink and sparkling water
Mission and ethics		Corporate mission and business policy show consistent awareness of corporate social responsibility.	
Company values		Strong managerial staff	Since Nestlé's acquisition, the relationships with CGT labour union have been strained Relationships with Perrier employees need to be restored
Organization and human resources		Nestlé has rationalized its operations according to local environments, market situations and corporate strategies	Perrier has to restructure its operations in order to attain the performance expectations of Nestlé Waters
Financial resources		Highly profitable company	Nestlé Waters divisions are less profitable than Nestlé Food divisions. Perrier's profitability remains weak

continued

Table 5.11 *continued*

Dimensions		Strengths	Weaknesses
Perrier Fluo brand equity	Stakeholders	Economic and institutional power of a worldwide group that is composed of 77 brands. Perrier is the No. 1 brand worldwide in the bottled sparkling water market	Disputes between the powerful trade union, employees and management
	Legal protection	Registered in countries where the brand is distributed (France, Europe) Knowledgeable legal team	
	Image	Perrier maintains favourable brand awareness. Consistent with socio-cultural trends (environment, festive/humour, health)	The disparity between Perrier's image and Perrier Fluo's. Perrier Fluo's festive image may appeal more to teenagers than to young adults: the offer may be too segmented
	Brand awareness	Leveraging of Perrier's existing strong brand awareness. Diversified targets: festive, innovative, trendy consumers	The disparity between Perrier's image and Perrier Fluo's. Inconsistent results on brand awareness tests
	Perceived quality	Some people enjoy the product Fashionable design, handy	Some people dislike the product May be priced too high, especially in the tertiary market
	Value relationship	Systematic repurchase. The brand has a reputable name with distributors and nightclub owners, and in the media	Loyal customers are few and young. A large percentage of customers are disappointed by the product, therefore will not repurchase it. Many customers only buy the product occasionally

9. Perrier Fluo's publicity is designed to increase sales and build brand loyalty. It is carried out through above-the-line and below-the-line advertising venues, and is reinforced by repetitive promotional campaigns (e.g. free samples, discounts). Its primary targets are people who like and enjoy music (i.e. festivals and nightclubs alike), as evidenced by: 'Pleasure peaks late. Under black light, Perrier Fluo is phosphorescent, lighting up the party'.[15]

FOURTH STAGE: ANALYSIS OF THE FIT BETWEEN FFVB AND THE 'PERRIER FLUO' BRAND

This stage is an analysis of the fit between FFVB and 'Perrier Fluo' brand. It is achieved by comparing the previous SWOT analysis of the FFVB, including its 'Beach Volleyball Experience' trademark, and that of Perrier and its 'Perrier Fluo' brand. The analysis of the fit is carried out with a view to investigating the convergences between these two entities. It includes the five following key points:

Table 5.12 Synthesis of the SWOT external analysis of Nestlé Waters, Perrier and 'Perrier Fluo' in France

Dimensions	Opportunities	Threats
Economic situation and consumption trends	Increasing demand for cool, healthy soft-drink option, and convenient, transportable bottled water products	Consumption is falling. Consumers rationalize consumption
Sparkling water and soft-drink market segments	Soft drinks represents 1/3 of the global bottled water market Bottled water sustained an annual growth of 9%[a] in the years 1999–2004 71% of the 18–34-year-olds prefer non-alcoholic drinks; 48% like trying new non-alcoholic drinks Innovation a key factor of success	Soft-drinks market grows more in volume than in profit value
Competitors	Introduction of Perrier Fluo favourable on the market Perrier Fluo's differentiated positioning is a key factor of success: sensation and innovation	Saturated market for offers. 'Coke' is the No.1 brand in the soft-drinks market
Technological factors	Soft-drinks brands must combine design, health benefits, sensation and convenience to achieve success	Lengthy research and development period (e.g. it took 11 years of investment in R&D to develop the innovative PET bottle
Market legislation	Nestlé Waters and Perrier amalgamate to develop healthy soft-drink options, increased social responsibility, and sustainable developments	Stringent legislation imposed to promote public health and sustainable development

a http://www.the-infoshop.com/study/zi35094-bottled-water.html

- the potential sponsor partner and the brand concerned (i.e. Nestlé Waters, Perrier and 'Perrier Fluo');
- the rights owner and organizer of the event (i.e. the FFVB);
- the social event being sponsored (i.e. Beach Volleyball Experience);
- characteristics of the sponsorship offer;
- competitors of the potential sponsor partner (e.g. Coca-Cola).

Strategic analysis of the fit between the prospective sponsor and the brand concerned

A series of strategic and operational criteria must be used to identify which competitive advantages will be developed via the sponsorship proposal.

Analysis of the fit at the strategic level

A summary of the said criteria is presented in Table 5.13.

The FFVB must then validate the fit between the components of the brand equity of 'Beach Volleyball Experience' and 'Perrier Fluo' respectively. For this purpose, it will analyse the interaction of qualitative components of each entity's brand equity, with a view to identifying similarities and differences. This task will make it possible to evaluate possible effects of the sponsorship operation, whether it is one of reinforcement or of a transfer of some characteristics. An in-depth analysis of this is summarized in Table 5.14.

It is important to recognize that certain components of brand equity such as image, perceived quality and value relationship are repetitive. Furthermore, the quantitative components of each entity's respective brand equity must be considered while evaluating the convergence of 'Perrier Fluo' and 'Beach Volleyball Experience' (Table 5.15).

Strategic and operational synergies

From a strategic and operational perspective, it is judicious to combine the brand equity of these two entities for the purpose of developing a synergy. Based on the marketing objectives of each party, a synergy would allow:

*   reinforcement of each respective brand identity;
*   collaboration with distribution and sales promotions;
*   developments with the partnership strategy within the music industry;

Table 5.13 Criteria used to analyse the fit at the strategic level

Criteria	Characteristics
Entity concerned	Perrier Fluo brand
Strategic and marketing objectives	Both Nestlé Waters and Perrier use a differentiated marketing approach to grow. They seek growth in prospective markets by exploiting certain markets such as their position overlapping market segments of soft drinks (soda) and mineral water. From a marketing point of view, establishing 'Perrier Fluo' as the leading brand in this overlapping market segment is the primary goal. To achieve this, they need to match the demographic profile of the target market (15–35 years old) to the demographic profile of the sponsorship and advertising medium. Their publicity must enhance brand awareness and develop consumer loyalty. Prior to building brand loyalty with consumers who dislike 'Perrier Fluo', they must work on improving perceived quality to create a positive opinion of the product.
Marketing target	The targeted audience is composed of people aged between 15 and 35 years.
Positioning and identity	'Perrier Fluo' is an innovative soft drink whose unique taste produces favourable sensations. Perrier Fluo's identity is communicated through the following slogans: 'Perrier Fluo: it's Perrier by Perrier, a soft drink with Perrier's signature style'; 'A techno-colored blend that's 100% Perrier'; and 'Taste buds beware: Perrier Fluo is a totally new sensation'.
Term	Short and medium marketing terms, with a particular focus on summer.

Table 5.14 Analysis of the qualitative fit between 'Perrier Fluo' and the 'Beach Volleyball Experience' respective brand equity

Dimensions	Components specific to the 'Beach Volleyball Experience'	Common components	Components specific to 'Perrier Fluo'	Possible and desirable effects for 'Perrier Fluo'
Values	Self-determination, friendship, altruism	Achievement, ambition, competence, stimulation, hedonism, loyalty, environmental protection	Responsibility, social influence, honesty, creativity and wisdom	Reinforcement of common components and transfer of friendship to the 'Perrier Fluo' brand
Mission	Development of all types of volleyball	Acquire and increase leverage in a competitive environment Integrate corporate social responsibility	Grow and remain world leader by managing water resources in a sustainable fashion	Reinforcement of common components
Image	Olympic sport, accessible to all, event, leisure, music, dance, world's most beautiful beaches, sun, river, athletic participants	For loyal users: festive, fun, connected, sympathetic, colourful, vivacious, exhilarating	Loyal users: genuine, fashion savvy, 'cool', colourful, different, astonishing, special Critics: it has a disagreeable taste; it is mass produced, unusual, and has an arrogant image	Reinforcement of common components with respect to loyal users Image transfer with both groups of buyers: enjoyable and enticing; skilled, healthy and energetic Image transfer with critics: festive, fun, connected, sympathetic, energetic, exhilarating
Perceived quality	Spectacular, entertaining, high-level competition, excellent physical condition, provision of services equates to quality	Innovative Unexpected Attractive corporate design	Loyal users: refreshing, unique taste, low sugar content, made of natural products Critics: disagreeable taste, too much sugar and carbonates All agree that 'Perrier Fluo' is a convenient and practical product	Reinforcement of common components
Value relationship	Athletic individual, skilful, health, enthusiasm, peaceful world, aesthetic, excitement, a sense of belonging to a group, achievement, freedom, performance, mental stimulation, self-expression	Loyal users: joy, fun, sensation, unexpected. 'Pop' culture, exciting life	Loyal users: refreshing, adequately sweetened, trendy Critics: disappointment, dislike, arrogance	Loyal users: reinforcement of common components. Critics: transform opinion to a 'cool', exciting lifestyle
Stakeholders	100,000 members, clubs, leagues, FIVB, volunteers, youth movements, schools, local authorities, the Paris Beach Project and its 3 million visitors, M6, Eurosport, Europe 2, VSD	15–35-year-olds	Nestlé Waters: 77 brands. Suppliers, service providers, millions of customers, local authorities	To reinforce and increase awareness with the 15–35-year-olds. Create and nurture loyalty with people interested in the 'Beach Volleyball Experience'

Table 5.15 Quantitative analysis of the convergence of the 'Perrier Fluo' brand equity to that of the 'Beach Volleyball Experience' brand equity

	'Beach Volleyball Experience'	'Perrier Fluo'	Desirable and possible outcome for 'Perrier Fluo'
Brand awareness	Normal to above-average brand awareness with the targeted audience of 15–35-year-olds	Weak to below-average brand awareness with the targeted audience of 15–35-year-olds	Brand awareness development
Attitude	Favourable	Range from 'favourable' to 'very unfavourable'	Favourable opinion reinforcement; favourable opinion transfer to consumers with unfavourable opinion
Customer satisfaction	High	Range from 'high' to 'low'	Customer satisfaction reinforcement; enhance customer satisfaction with the negative segment because of a satisfactory experience
Loyalty	Strong	Strong and weak	Enhance consumer loyalty because of a satisfactory experience

- promotion of the sport and 'Perrier Fluo' in collaborations with strategic stakeholders, such as volleyball clubs and leagues, the FIVB and the Paris Beach Project organizer.

In-house acceptance of the sponsorship operation

At Nestlé Waters, this sponsorship operation will likely have a positive impact on the company, since the sporting event embodies values shared by company employees. At Perrier, the partnership may help alleviate tensions between management and some company personnel by uniting them to develop the 'Perrier' brand.

Cost of the sponsorship operation

It is premature at this point to address the issue of an actual cost for the sponsorship proposal because neither a customized proposal nor an activation strategy has been presented yet. It is, however, relevant for the FFVB to update its provisional budget with the information collected during the validation of the synergy process. The FFVB can conclude that there is a strong fit between its brand equity, strategies and operations with those of the prospective sponsor. Moreover, it can forecast certain revenues and expenses that can be generated via its partnership with the Paris Beach Project. For example, taking into consideration that the Paris Beach Project generally attracts more than 3 million people to the beach volleyball exhibition each year, the FFVB can project that a marketing investment of €600,000 equates to a €0.20 investment per direct contact.

Capability to manage the sponsorship programme

Although Perrier belongs to Nestlé SA, a group with strong financial stability, which typically spends sizeable amounts on communication campaigns to develop the brand equity of its products, it does not necessarily retain the human and technical resources required to manage a sponsorship operation. Therefore, the FFVB must arrange to have an adequate management system and structure to support its sponsorship programme. Thus, the FFVB must guarantee the delivery of a quality provision of service directly or indirectly through the services of a specialized third party in order to secure the sponsorship commitment of Perrier.

Competitive advantages created by the sponsorship operation

By speculating about competitors, based on their sponsorship operations and advertising campaigns, the FFVB can assert that its sponsorship operation will create the following competitive advantages:

- favourable strategic and operational fit;
- excellent brand equity fit;
- internal acceptability of the sponsorship campaign.

Convergence with components of the sporting event

Once the essential components constituting the 'Beach Volley Experience' have been accounted for, the FFVB must then analyse the concept, characteristics, positioning, acceptance and recognition, and brand identity of Perrier with strategic stakeholders.

Concept and characteristics

The 'Beach Volleyball Experience' is a tournament where the world's best players can display their talent. It is also a festival for celebrating beach volleyball on Paris beaches, in the heart of the French capital at the peak of the summer holidays. Therefore, the 'Beach Volleyball Experience' is a unique event in which anyone can take part, either as a spectator or participant.

Positioning and brand identity

The event positioning envisioned by the FFVB corresponds to a unique sporting and festive experience. The event brand identity revolves around the following components: innovative, sporting, competitive, stimulating, festive and universal.

Acceptance and recognition

The results of two preliminary surveys on the acceptance and recognition of the event prospect are positive. The first survey was carried out with a focus group composed of FFVB players and leaders. The second survey was conducted with people aged between 15 and 35 who are interested in the 'Perrier Fluo Beach Volleyball Experience'. In both cases, results show that the 'Perrier Fluo' brand is well accepted in the context of this event. The respondents consider 'Perrier and the event share the same expressed values' and that '"Perrier Fluo" and the "Beach Volleyball Experience" associate well together'. Likewise, they feel 'it is logical why Perrier would sponsor the event'. It is difficult to assess recognition, since the 'Beach Volleyball Experience' is only a simulation at this point.

Convergence with the sponsorship programme

To validate the convergence of the sponsorship programme, the FFVB must evaluate a number of variables, such as:

- the structure of its sponsorship programme;
- the importance of other sponsors and partners;
- the reliability of data contained in the impact report the FFVB will provide to sponsors after the event;
- the communication plan and media partners involved in the sponsorship;
- the sponsorship activation platform;
- the package of rights and legal protection granted;
- the resources and competences of the FFVB;
- the quality management and price of the offer;
- the opportunities and competitive advantages it will create.

Structure of the sponsorship programme

The structure of the sponsorship programme is conceived in a way to promote a title sponsor and prevent conflicts between various product category sponsors. As such, the structure of the title sponsorship offer is a unique opportunity for Perrier to develop its 'Perrier Fluo' brand.

Other sponsors and partners

In addition to the previously mentioned entities having an interest in the brand equity of the 'Beach Volleyball Experience', there are a number of other entities which also have an interest. The sponsorship offer should state that the FFVB has signed supplemental agreements with, for example, some media partners (i.e. M6, Europe 2, VSD), product category sponsors, such as Mikasa (official supplier of volleyballs) and Cébé (official supplier of sunglasses), the city of Paris and the Paris Beach Project organizer.

Likewise, the FFVB sponsorship proposal should state that it is engaged in regional volleyball leagues and clubs, as well as the Ministry of Youth, Sports and Community.

Evaluation management system

In an effort to add value to the sponsorship offer, the FFVB should establish a management system and structure to evaluate the impact of the event after it occurs. Although previous analyses of fit provide a significant part of essential data required for achieving the initial analysis, it is limited by:

- lack of available data on the 'Beach Volleyball Experience' since it has never previously taken place;
- current data on the 'Beach Volleyball Experience' are the result of surveys and interviews, and hence do not have the validity compared with an *ad hoc* study.

Consequently, the FFVB will establish a management system and structure to evaluate the characteristics and impact of the 'Beach Volleyball Experience' by enlisting the services of a specialized agency to analyse the media effects of sponsorship in an effort to better understand and promote the sporting event with sponsors and key partners. In addition, the FFVB will request three in-depth studies within the framework of a partnership with the French National Institute of Sport and Physical Education (INSEP) in Paris. Table 5.16 outlines the main elements of the in-depth studies that the FFVB will request from INSEP.

Additionally, the FFVB reached an agreement with M6 and Europe 2 to obtain the audience reach and profile of the event. Furthermore, the FFVB will assign personnel to collect TV footage and newspaper clips of the event in order to determine and/or compare the impact of various partners.

Communication plan and media partners

The choice of media partners was based on the fact that the targeted audience of 15–35-year-olds is typically closely connected to M6, Europe 2 and VSD. The communication plan extends to the FFVB members and volleyball fans, as well as to the Paris Beach Project visitors. Specifically, the communication plan will have the following agenda:

1. Build and reinforce the relationship with the audience. This will be achieved through mass communication, customized communication and experiential operations.
2. Adjust to corporate and commercial interests.
3. Combine push and pull marketing strategies: a push strategy whereby the FFVB, media partners and Perrier will use their sales force to develop, promote and sell the event and 'Perrier Fluo' to the audience; a pull strategy whereby the FFVB will use advertising and promotion to persuade consumers to ask for 'Perrier Fluo' and/or information about the event.

Table 5.16 Outline of the in-depth studies to be conducted by INSEP

Respondents	When?	Data collection	Method
Paris Beach Project Visitors	Before and after the event	Socio-demographics Consumption trends	Survey
Spectators	During the event	(including Perrier Fluo)	Survey
FFVB licensed members	Before and after the event	Brand awareness, image, perceived quality, attitude and purchase intention	Internet survey on the FFVB's website

Therefore, the communication plan will be a combination of above-the-line and below-the-line advertising based on the eight following components: public relations, press relations, publicity (via M6, Europe 2, VSD, and INSEP), flyers, the websites of the event and FFVB, sales promotion, direct marketing and peripheral events in association with the Paris Beach Project. The communication plan, in a nutshell, is depicted in Figure 5.3.

The sponsorship proposal

Presentation software, such as Microsoft PowerPoint, will help the FFVB make a simple, clear and efficient sales presentation to Perrier executives. Table 5.17 is an outline of the FFVB presentation demonstrating that 'Perrier Fluo' and the 'Beach Volleyball Experience' are compatible. A promotional video highlighting the 'FIVB Swatch World Tour' will also be introduced to give a preview of what the 'Beach Volleyball Experience' could become if Perrier decided to engage in a partnership. Furthermore, it is stressed in the proposal that the official name and logo of the event will be designed in a distinguished manner that emphasizes the partnership with Perrier.

Aspects of the preliminary activation platform

At this stage, the FFVB will present the main components of the activation plan proposed to the title sponsor. In accordance with the communication plan, the activation programme

Figure 5.3 Structure of an above-the-line and below-the-line advertising mix

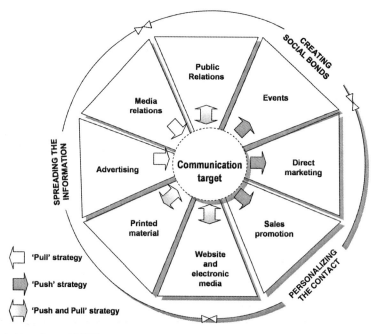

Source: Adapted from Ferrand (2004)

Table 5.17 Structure of the sponsorship proposal

Outline view	Contents
1st slide	Title of the presentation (name of the event, name of the rights holder, date)
2nd slide	Purpose of the presentation (concept, impact, etc.)
3rd slide	Outline of the presentation
4th slide	Positioning and brand identity of the event
5th slide	Sales kit (calendar, location, potential audience reach, etc.)
6th and subsequent slides	Presentation of the FFVB, rights owner of the event
	Presentation of the brand equity of the 'Beach Volleyball Experience' and justification for the convergence with 'Perrier Fluo'
	Programme of on-site activities and the Paris Beach project
	Marketing and communication plan
	Budget of customized proposal
	Proposed activation plan
Last slide	Contact information

will suggest a variety of operations to activate the 'Perrier Fluo' brand. It is possible that the sponsor will choose not to participate in all of the operations proposed, but agree to certain provisions. Therefore, the activation plan and cost will need to be renegotiated.

Table 5.18 provides a series of examples that are often used as a basis for negotiations in a contract proposal. Upon validation of the activation plan, the details of each operation will be defined and planned.

Transferred rights and legal protection mechanisms

Appendices 1–3, which present the sponsorship, television and licensing contracts, give details of specific types of rights that would be transferred to respective sponsors. Additionally, the safety devices needed to deliver these contractual rights are also presented. Thus, specific legal attention must be given when forming any contract to protect the rights of individuals that are subject to the terms of a contract. Furthermore, having a strong legal team is necessary for protection of exclusively transferred rights when ambush marketing threatens to encroach on these rights.

In an effort to balance the needs and level of protection requested by Perrier and other partners, the FFVB will request the assistance of a specialized legal advisor to ensure contract terms are executed as planned.

Quality management system

The management of the quality of the service delivered to sponsors depends directly on the organization and execution of various processes designed to ensure quality services. As a result, the FFVB will establish the following quality management (QA) programme in accordance with the model presented in Chapter 3:

- The following process supports will help implement the operational processes: IT system management, rights management, HR and finance management, and knowledge transfer management.

Table 5.18 Proposals for the activation of the 'Perrier Fluo' brand

Components	Examples
Public relations	Sessions where professional players and Perrier VIP guests meet at the FFVB village venue Host a Celebrity Tournament
Media relations	Press conference held at the 'Perrier Fluo Beach' on the opening day of the Paris Beach Project, including an exhibition tournament and contest with journalists
Advertising	50% discount on advertising spaces with media partners (M6, Europe 2, VSD) Sponsored ad of Perrier in the FFVB magazine
Flyers	3 million copies will be distributed to visitors to Paris Beach, as well as to FFVB members and spectators
Internet	E-mail newsletters to FFVB members Free download of a 'Perrier Fluo Beach Volleyball' game on the respective websites of the FFVB and the event
Direct marketing	Free passes to FFVB members who participate in the online game Online game winners will collect their prize (a coloured Perrier Fluo T-shirt) at the booth whose colour corresponds to the colour of the T-shirt won
Sales promotion	Distribution of free samples and reduced-price packs of Perrier Fluo at event venues
Peripheral events	Regional competitions in each league of the FFVB, whose finals will take place at the 'Perrier Fluo Beach Volley Experience' Contests during the Paris Beach Project (e.g. 'The Perrier Fluo Pro Am' where a professional player teams up with a spectator to participate in a contest) Free concert for the closing of the 'Perrier Fluo Beach Volleyball Experience'

- There will be three QA procedures: developing a strategy; communicating it to FFVB personnel, sponsors and partners; and verifying quality at every level of improvement.

Implementing and coordinating these types of processes will keep the FFVB focused on delivering quality services in a timely manner, and as guaranteed.

Resources and expertise provided by the FFVB

Since Perrier does not retain the human and technical resources required to manage its sponsorship operation, the previously mentioned QA processes will account for a certain number of technical and human resources provisions. Thus, the FFVB will facilitate the following:

- competition venues (in partnership with local authorities);
- sports executives (to manage peripheral events and contests);
- volunteers and paid employees (to run the event).

Furthermore, the FFVB will provide Perrier three employees (who will report to a project manager) to help the title sponsor manage the title sponsorship programme.

Price and trade negotiations

Taking into account the available information about 'Perrier Fluo' products, the FFVB established a price for the customized sponsorship offer.[16] Considering the components of the provisions, the FFVB priced the offer at €300,000, which includes €100,000 in prize money for the winners of the competition. In addition, Perrier will be responsible for an additional €300,000 for activating the sponsorship programme and covering administrative and technical expenses.

Therefore, the trade negotiation strategy will consist of highlighting key components of the offer, in an effort to justify the requested fee and to persuade the prospective sponsor that it is judicious to invest in this partnership. When the prospective sponsor indicates that it is interested in the offer, the next step is to tailor the sponsorship package according to the needs and expectations of the sponsor. Each new proposal must be reviewed and updated to reflect the addition or removal of certain provisions. The requested price must also be amended to reflect any changes made to the original proposal.

Benefits related to the strategic objectives and marketing

The primary marketing objective that Perrier seeks is to keep the 'Perrier Fluo' brand atop the market segment where it is currently positioned. In order to achieve that, marketing movements should act on the following sequence of objectives:

- establish the perceived value;
- increase brand awareness;
- develop the image;
- demonstrate perceived quality;
- generate a positive attitude;
- build a value relationship with the previously mentioned stakeholders.

Based on a careful examination of the content of the sponsorship package, the FFVB can presume that 'Perrier Fluo' will reap the following benefits should Perrier accept the proposal:

- reinforcement and development of its customer base, especially with the 15–35-year-old audience;
- reinforcement and positive transfer of loyalties and values;
- brand identity reinforcement with loyal customers of 'Perrier Fluo' products, and a favourable opinion transfer with consumers who currently have an unfavourable opinion of 'Perrier Fluo' products;
- perceived quality reinforcement of 'Perrier Fluo' products;
- reinforcement of value-adding partnerships with retailers and consumers;
- development of a value-adding partnership with the FFVB.

Persuasive experiential strategies can be executed to promote the title sponsorship package. It offers unique opportunities to implement experiential marketing strategies for reinforcing and developing value-adding relationships. Reinforcing favourable relations and improving weaker relationships through the experience of the event contributes to the expansion of the consumer base of Perrier, which is significant for the growth of the company.

Competitive advantages of the sponsorship offer

The competitive advantages created by the sponsorship offer relate to strategic and operational aspects of brand equity, positioning and brand identity, as well as the development and strengthening of internal resources and the increased contentment of its employees.

It is appropriate for the FFVB to emphasize that the content of the sponsorship offer will likely contribute to the success of Perrier Fluo's marketing and communication strategies.

Competitive advantage convergence

From a strategic point of view, Perrier must develop competitive advantages. It can do so by differentiating its 'Perrier Fluo' products, maintaining the positioning of 'Perrier Fluo', and monitoring industry competitors.

Differentiating 'Perrier Fluo' products

It is important to know the territory of competition in order to differentiate. Companies need to know what the market forces are, particularly the strength of their competitors. This requires the ability to identify threats of competing products and rivals in a given market segment. In this case, it is important to know where competitors position their products, and which communications and sponsorship strategies they engage in. The external analysis given earlier shows that 'Perrier Fluo' is positioned as a 'sensational and innovative' product. Competing products similar to the 'Badoit Vertigo' brand of water infused with various flavours such as mango–lemon, raspberry–apple, and lemon, may communicate the same message (i.e. festive, sporting and healthy), but do not engage in sponsorship activities. In this case, Coca-Cola is the major rival to compete with in this regard. 'Diet Coke' and 'Coke Classic' products communicate a similar message (i.e. fun, energetic, invigorating) as Perrier and are aggressively involved in many sponsorship activities. However, these previously mentioned products are not positioned within the same natural market segment. Furthermore, these rival products are not associated with any international event of beach volleyball managed by the FIVB. Therefore, the 'Beach Volleyball Experience' is a unique platform to differentiate 'Perrier Fluo' products from its competitors.

Maintaining and strengthening the positioning of 'Perrier Fluo' products

Certain companies may develop invasion plans to enter a given market segment. Although Perrier cannot predict which markets its competitors may venture into, it can conduct a market segment analysis periodically. At this point, the positioning of 'Perrier Fluo' products is not likely to be challenged by rival beverage products in the 'healthy' genre given their rather distant positioning. However, major rivals such as Coke and Schweppes may try to invade the natural market segment in which 'Perrier Fluo' is positioned. Therefore, Perrier must continually seek ways to maintain and strengthen its market position.

Strength of competition

Taking into account market forces, the FFVB must assess whether Perrier could sustain a segment invasion should its rivals decide to launch new products or if they engaged in ambush marketing. Based on previous analyses, the FFVB can assume that Perrier (Nestlé Waters) has the relational and financial power to resist competitors' moves.

Convergence with the rights owner of the event and/or the project manager

In the framework of an event-driven project, the rights owner of the event is the legal person or company who profits from the operations of the event. As for the 'Beach Volleyball Experience', the FFVB is responsible for organizing this event. This responsibility includes managing sponsorship activities. As the rights owner of the event, the FFVB can call upon the service provision of a third party, or project manager, to control the event in part or its entirety. For example, the rights owner of the 'Adia Beach Tour' entrusted the organization of this beach volleyball competition to the company MCO Sports. In this case study, however, the FFVB is the rights owner and the organizer of the event.

    Sponsors generally try to minimize their level of uncertainty and the risks associated with it as such. Therefore, they are interested in specifically knowing who owns and manages the event, because of the considerable risk that is inherent in a sponsorship operation. Sponsors will evaluate risk by examining the company seeking a sponsorship operation. This analysis will focus primarily on its operations, financial condition and sponsorship experience. From the sponsor's perspective, it is generally a lower risk to assume a partnership with an organization with significant sponsorship credentials than with one that has little experience of implementing sponsorship activities – irrespective of how auspicious a sponsorship package may appear. Therefore, Perrier executives will take into account FFVB's brand equity and their competences in sponsorship and event management in analysing a convergence with the sponsorship proposal. Table 5.19 shows the risk analysis of a partnership with the FFVB.

    The FFVB will need to demonstrate cohesive and competent skills in the field of event management in order to reassure Perrier Fluo that its risks are minimal with regard to a sponsorship agreement.

Assessment of the comprehensive analysis of the fit

As evidenced by the comprehensive analysis of the fit, the FFVB can assume it has a solid offer to present to Perrier executives. However, sponsors' expectations have the greatest influence on the attractiveness of an offer and will often influence decision-making.

Table 5.19 Risk analysis of a partnership with the FFVB

Components	Characteristics	Risk factors
Mission and project	The FFVB is governed by a group of delegates whose objectives are to develop volleyball and beach volleyball, particularly by organizing relevant events to revive the image of the sport in France	A report highlighting the revival of volleyball in France identifies various steps required to improve the situation of the sport in this country
Structure and values	Not-for-profit sport organization Values: achievement, inspiration, self-determination, friendship and altruism	There is a disparity between the philosophy of the new management executives and the mission of the organization
Strategic and marketing objectives	To reinforce the professional and federation clubs To develop beach volleyball and to revamp its image To launch and attract youth participation (6–10-year-olds) To revive and expand participation of girls and women To increase participation generally	Positive convergence
Strategic and operational synergies	Organizing the 'Beach Volleyball Experience' will facilitate cohesion between the FFVB and its members, thereby contributing to the achievement of the strategic objectives of the FFVB	The FFVB is disengaged with its members, clubs and leagues. The success of the event requires their involvement
Positioning and brand identity	Positioning: sport and tradition. Brand identity: innovation, organization and challenging/competitive	There is a disparity between the current positioning and brand image of the FFVB
Brand equity of the FFVB	Low level of brand awareness, image, perceived quality and value-adding partnerships with stakeholders (especially with the general public)	The 'Beach Volleyball Experience' should help reinforce the brand equity of the FFVB
Managerial capabilities: resources and competences	Excellent competences in sport management and training The new executive management team has vast experience in marketing and management of sporting events	The 'Beach Volleyball Experience' is a premier, spectacular event. The FFVB must show its competences on this level
Rights owner versus organizer of the event	The FFVB is both the rights owner and organizer of the event 'Beach Volleyball Experience'	Low risk

Figure 5.4 shows that the FFVB's title sponsorship package is well tailored to Perrier's expectations. In this figure, a web-like platform is used to assess the FFVB's sponsorship offer according to five key axes. The axes are scaled to show the perceived quality of the sponsorship offer. The dotted line reveals the prospective sponsor's expectations regarding priorities in the sponsorship offer. In this case, Perrier is primarily interested in associating with a brand equity that is compatible with its own.

Figure 5.4 Assessment of the comprehensive analysis of the fit between 'Perrier Fluo' and FFVB's 'Beach Volleyball Experience'

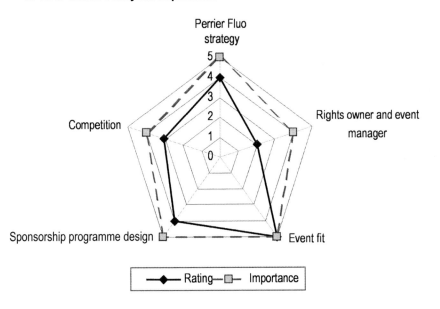

FIFTH STAGE: DEVELOPING A CUSTOMIZED PROPOSAL

Following the convergence validation between the 'Beach Volleyball Experience' and 'Perrier Fluo', the FFVB will prepare a customized sponsorship proposal. The sponsorship offer will need to be tailored to meet the expectations of the prospective sponsor according to its evaluation of the perceived quality.

Proposal

The following proposal includes a number of benefits to the title sponsorship proposal,[17] thereby adding value to the monetary contribution by Perrier towards a partnership between 'Perrier Fluo' and the 'Beach Volleyball Experience'.

Branding opportunities

Branding opportunities associated with the 'Beach Volleyball Experience' include:

- incorporation of the title sponsor's name in the name of the event: 'Perrier Fluo Beach Volleyball Experience';
- product category exclusivity in class 32;[18]
- licence exclusivity, including the permission to use the official logo of the event in any communications campaign;

- exclusive pre-emptive rights to buy advertising spaces/slots with media partners;
- presence of the 'Perrier Fluo' trademark on the official website of the event, including on web pages where the contest and video game are posted.

On-site branding opportunities

Predominant placement with 50 per cent exposure on:

- advertising spaces;
- billboards;
- flags in the sporting venues;
- banners in the press conference room and during interviews;
- podium;
- advertising spaces in the press centre;
- accreditations;
- two giant inflatable Perrier bottles positioned in the camera background shots;
- 12 cm × 5 cm logos on the edge of the net;
- two logos on the scoreboard;
- two logos on the giant video screen;
- two logos on the umpire's chair;
- two logos on the players' bench;
- logo on coolers containing beverages for the players;
- logo on personnel's apparel;
- sample products that can be distributed to spectators;
- logo on towels provided to players.

Branding opportunities in advertising insertions

- Name and logo on posters promoting the event;
- name and logo on the cover page of press releases, brochure, leaflets and programmes of the event;
- one page of colour advertising in the programme of the event;
- one page of colour advertising in the FIVB magazine during one year;
- name and logo on letterheads, envelopes, etc.

Hospitality and public relations opportunities

- One booth of 200 m² located in the centre of the village;
- ten VIP accreditations giving access to sporting events and ceremonies;
- 'Perrier Fluo Beach Volleyball Experience' lounge.

Other corporate and commercial opportunities

- Inclusion of a company brochure with the press releases;
- 'Perrier Fluo' representatives to present trophies during the award ceremony.

Benefits related to the marketing and organization of the event

- Provisional use of a project manager throughout sponsorship contract;
- provisional use of three employees during the week of the event;
- realization of an impact study (the methodology must be specified).

Proposal for activating the 'Perrier Fluo' brand

Given the marketing strategy adopted by the FFVB, the activation strategy is presented separately to the prospective sponsor. Components of the activation programme are priced after negotiations with the title sponsor. The FFVB will thus propose an activation programme based on the following initiatives:

Event-driven activation

Within the framework of the event

- Distribution of product samples at the 'PFBVE' concessions and lounges;
- organizing contests with spectators featuring licensed products;
- 2,000 accreditations for sponsors to the finals.

Within the framework of the Paris Beach Project

- Leveraging of the brand during beach volleyball activities;
- distribution of flyers.

Within the framework of peripheral tournaments organized by the regional leagues of the FFVB

- Title sponsor of each event;
- distribution of products;
- distribution of flyers;
- distribution of volleyballs and nets (in collaboration with the official volleyball supplier of the event).

Merchandizing

- Possibility of creating a derived product line with the name of the event, including volleyballs and nets with the official volleyball supplier of the event;
- sales of products during the main and peripheral events.

Public relations

- Public relations with participating volleyball players during the event;
- public relations with Team France volleyball players before and after the event (according to their availability).

- media and celebrity tournament;
- free concert on the beach at the end of the competition.

Direct marketing

Direct marketing opportunities with FFVB members through the FFVB directory.

Distribution network

Marketing operations at various points of sale are possible, including the launch of the new limited edition 'Perrier Fluo' label, promotional stands, discounts, etc.

CONCLUSION

For the purpose of this book, the development of an international event serves to illustrate several aspects of sponsorship. The case study is an illustration of strategic and operational components to consider while designing a sponsorship programme. In developing such a programme, it is always necessary to make a strategic diagnosis of the situation, define a comprehensive sponsorship strategy, identify prospective sponsors and develop customized offers. Equally important is the legal side of sponsorship, which must be consulted throughout the entire process.

The development of a customized sponsorship offer culminates with the signing of several contracts that are negotiated within the framework of a sponsorship. Models of the following three most common types of contracts associated with a sponsorship operation are found in the appendix:

- sponsorship contract;
- TV contract;
- licensing agreement.

Although the contract models contain detailed information pertaining to the case study, each respective model can easily be simplified and/or adapted to different sports and sponsorship situations. When conceiving and proposing a contract, irrespective of the sport and size of the event, it is imperative to tailor the offer according to the needs and expectations of a prospective sponsor.

A contract formalizes a series of agreements that are formed between two or more parties after a series of negotiations. Contracts often contain tangible and intangible components, which are defined within a legal framework. The signing of the contract will legally establish the agreement as binding and signifies the beginning of the sponsorship operation. However, the success of the operation depends solely on the proper execution of the provisions provided for in the contract. The following five dimensions of quality must be actualized in a successful sponsorship agreement:

- tangible and intangible components;
- reliability (i.e. the ability to deliver provisions in a professional and timely manner);

- responsiveness (i.e. the ability to understand and respond to suggestions, proposals and situations quickly and favourably for each party);
- reassurance (i.e. the ability to reassure the sponsor of adaptability if a situation requires it);
- empathy (i.e. the ability to identify, understand and meet the sponsor's expectations).

Securing the commitment of a sponsor to a sponsorship operation is often very difficult to do. It entails a complex series of negotiations that require the involvement of many stakeholders and various legal manoeuvres. As this case study demonstrates, the most important element of securing and implementing a successful sponsorship programme is identifying and fulfilling the expectations of the prospective sponsor.

Conclusion

This book establishes the various relationships between the stakeholders in respect of sports sponsorships and the event, sporting and territorial systems. The relationship between the sponsor and sponsored entity was analysed from strategic and operational viewpoints, which identified the foremost actors within the sponsorship framework. The legal and marketing dimensions relating to the management of the key variables of the sponsorship operation were also introduced. Furthermore, several strategic planning tools were presented for developing a sponsorship strategy to evaluate the external and internal forces affecting the sporting organization that seeks to engage sponsor partners in a particular event. Lastly, a selection of functional and operational procedures was proposed as a way to implement sponsorship activities and to evaluate their impact.

The sponsorship approach presented within the framework of this book is in respect of sporting events. The sporting event serves as an excellent example of what occurs before, during and after any sponsorship programme because it is easily identifiable and it embodies a significant source for this type of operation. However, the methods and planning tools presented in this book are applicable in other fields of sponsorship, including various organizations, clubs, athletes or artists, and event management projects. The said methods and tools can also be used in the context of sporting and technological venture projects, such as sailing on the banks of the North Pole, which Jean-Louis Etienne achieved aboard a high-tech igloo, or in breakthrough scientific research projects, such as the Solar Impulse project.[1] The Solar Impulse, a project initiated by Bertrand Piccard, is the first solar plane to fly around the world solely on renewable energy. The challenge consists in conceiving an airplane capable of taking off autonomously, then climbing to an altitude of 12,000 metres, and maintaining its flight for several days with no fuel, propelling itself by means only of the solar cells mounted on its wings. In addition, it will have to use the energy accumulated during the day, not only to maintain its flight, but also to recharge its batteries and to ensure its flight at night. The construction uses today's most advanced technologies and acts as a catalyst for scientific research in the field of composite structures, lightweight, so-called intelligent materials, and in ways of producing and storing energy. These results will be utilized as much in the construction of the plane, as later in various other applications useful to society. The pioneering features of this project provide unique opportunities for a research sponsorship based on a convergence with a company seeking to associate with the environmental benefits this project has to offer.

As discussed in Chapter 1, the business side of the sponsorship management system has evolved into a complex system of balancing various stakeholders' interests. Over the course of the past 30 years, sponsorship has developed both at the strategic and operational levels. In the 1980s, sponsorship was conceived as a communication technique with possible integration into the communication strategy of companies. Companies then began seeking ways to exploit synergies between their sponsorship strategy and other variables of the marketing mix in an effort to ensure the best possible return on investment. Currently, the sponsorship trend consists of integrating sponsorship into the various strategies of the company while giving branding opportunities to strengthen the corporate identity of the sponsor. The development of the 'Perrier Fluo Beach Volleyball Experience' case study serves to illustrate the current complexity of the methodology for managing a sponsorship programme.

The complexity of managing a sponsorship programme results from the combination and interaction of various elements within the systemic sponsorship system. In this context, the sporting organization must contend with uncertainty generated from the following risk factors:

- Sponsorship proposals involve complex negotiations. There is an inherent risk involved in determining the proper sponsor and the legalities associated with concluding a contract. It is imperative that careful and diligent analysis be conducted to minimize the risk factors of securing a sponsorship contract.
- Successful sponsorship operations are partly contingent upon the uncertainty associated with the elements of the event. Certain elements or occurrences, for example, can have positive effects, such as when Adidas sponsored the French national football team that won the 1998 FIFA World Cup, or negative effects, as with the Festina doping scandal, which resulted in the French team Festina's expulsion from the 1998 Tour de France.
- The interdependence between various partners (i.e. sponsors, media partners, official suppliers, etc.) can be perceived as an inherent risk to a particular sponsorship offer. For instance, should a TV operator decide to cancel the programmed broadcast of a sponsored event, the audience reach would be diminished. Other sponsors then receive a lesser impact on their sponsorship agreement.

In order to minimize complexity, it is necessary to establish a comprehensive methodology for managing various elements of the sponsorship systems. The sponsorship approach developed in this book addresses this complexity and proposes ways to reduce risks. The sports sponsorship market is a highly competitive and complex sector. Notwithstanding the difficulty of persuading sponsors to engage in a given partnership, the predominant challenge in the emergent sponsorship model consists of delivering the provision of services promised to the sponsor.

There are various levels of complexity related to sponsorship management. Based on the French proverb '*qui peut le plus peut le moins*' (i.e. 'He who can do more, can do less'), an intricate case study was developed that comprised a multifaceted, international sporting event involving negotiations with an international company, which is implementing a complex decision-making process based on precise data. This intricate case study allows for the more complex dimensions of this method to be presented in an operational manner. Consequently, it will be simple to use the same tools and principles consistently in a less complex situation. When conceiving and proposing a sponsorship, irrespective of the sport and size of the event, it is imperative to tailor the offer according to the needs and expectations of a prospective sponsor.

In today's environment, managing complexity involves developing in-house resources and competences. What is more, organizations seeking sponsorships must often create and sustain changes by developing a new managerial culture. Pinfield (1986) points out that a dual-management system exists within some organizations. While sophisticated tools for planning and coordinating a variety of processes have been developed, efforts still have to be made to actually implement these processes. Furthermore, these rational efforts inter-relate with emotional components where risks can be measured and evaluated. Insofar as sponsorship managers are concerned, they must continually strive to demonstrate the value-adding performance of sponsorship.

In addition, an overview of global sponsorship trends and management practices makes it possible to project three genres that will need to be reinforced in the future: quality management processes, the increasing implications of local authorities, and various systemic governance.

The topic of quality management was addressed in Chapter 3. Quality management is a systematic way of ensuring that the entire organization is mobilized for achieving all the activities necessary to develop and implement the sponsorship operation to secure the lasting satisfaction of the stakeholders. Quality management also ensures that the activities are performed in a cost-effective manner. A number of key principles were applied to quality management, whereby it is possible to categorize and prioritize various stakeholders and the processes required to satisfy these partners. Not all stakeholders have the same influence when prioritizing these processes. Large companies very often have a strong influence on sporting organizations, local authorities and event organizers.

Quality management is one of the key criteria of the convergence analysis, as it takes into account companies' expectations and makes it possible to improve certain processes with the delivery of provisions of services to sponsors. Various organizations produce worldwide industrial and commercial standards, with the foremost being the International Organization for Standardization (ISO[2]). While a number of sporting organizations and events obtain the ISO certification, others developed their own certification process. For example, Valais Tourism developed its own Swiss 'Valais Excellence'[3] certification, which is an innovative quality management system for introducing sustainable management within small and medium-size companies. The Swiss organizers of the Omega European Masters[4] (golf) and Cristalp Grand Raid[5] (mountain-bike race marathon) have received this particular certification. Developing standards serves two complementary purposes. First, it serves to establish standards among competing entities in a market, which will allow comparisons between the quality of various sponsorship programmes and services. This relates to the positioning of the offer (i.e. the price/quality ratio of the offer). In addition, it can also be viewed as a mechanism for optimizing the quality of processes at every level of the sponsorship operation. Increasingly, quality management constitutes a new way to create a significant competitive advantage.

Prior to 1982, many sporting facilities in Europe were traditionally owned by the State, with sport being developed by the government. Thus, sporting organizations and event organizers often had to cooperate with this authority. Since 1982, however, the European landscape has evolved, as State's powers have gradually been transferred to municipalities, departments and local regions (which have been provided with corresponding financial resources). Consequently, as Chappelet *et al.* (2005) and other authors point out, a number of regions have become interested in organizing major sporting events in an effort to boost the economy and tourism of their region. In recent years, a number of initiatives have been introduced to encourage organizers to incorporate the notions of sustainable development in the organization of their event. In 1996, the Olympic Charter was amended and the promotion of sustainable development became one of the tenets of the Olympic Movement. According to Chappelet *et al.* (2005: 23), 'these initiatives are designed to raise awareness of the harmful side effects an event may have, especially with respect to the environment, while encouraging organizers to reap the greatest possible economic and social benefits'. According to these authors, the sporting event market has exploded in the past 20 years, as characterized by the following:

- a growing demand for spectator sport and mass-participation sport;
- the development of a constant increase in the number and types of events;[6]
- the organization of sporting events has become a significant promotional tool and a window to showcase the local attractions of a given region;
- the creation of economic benefits related to the direct and indirect event-related expenditure in the region, and the development of the region's image, which encourages spectators and television viewers to visit the area before, during and after the event;
- the creation of social benefits, e.g. the acquisition of organizational skills and the development of inter-regional cooperation: acquisition of expertise, reinforcement of local identity and community pride, work experience and youth training. There is also a benefit from the event's legacy, which can be both material (i.e. sports facilities, general infrastructure, etc.) and non-material (i.e. increased participation in sports, reputation, etc.).

Local authorities engage in sponsorships in a prudent and strategic way. The involvement of local authorities is significant, since such a commitment promotes ongoing economic, social and environmental development.

Sporting organizations involved in sponsorship programmes often reform their mode of governance, i.e. they integrate more efficient, ethical managerial practices. Following the emergence of new managerial methods and tools, a number of sporting organizations restructured operations in order to adapt to a competitive sport market environment (Henry and Lee 2004). The current trend in the European sports genre is to integrate the marketing and sponsorship functions within one's own organization. This is evidenced by the respective moves of several sporting organizations of all sizes, including the IOC, UEFA, FIFA, FIVB and various professional and amateur sporting clubs.

However, the most noteworthy evolution in the European market relates to political governance and systemic governance. Political governance involves processes by means of which governments and governing bodies of sporting organizations influence, one way or another, the systemic approach of sponsorship. Indeed, governing bodies of the European Community, national governments, international and national federations use a number of levers to retain a certain control over sport and sponsorship, such as:

- lobbying (e.g. conventions, conferences, media campaigns, consulting, etc.);
- financial incentives (e.g. objectives contracts binding the Ministry of Youth and Sports to national federations);

- regulations (e.g. compliance to competition and technical rules with a view to making the sport more spectacular and to meet the expectations of sponsors and the media).

Lastly, systemic governance relates to competition or cooperation amongst political and business organizations, which strongly influence actors in the field of sports sponsorship. Within this sports sponsorship system, each organization has its own strategy. If one takes the case study of the 'Perrier Fluo Beach Volleyball Experience' as an example, systemic governance relates to managing internal and external forces within and between the FIVB, FFVB, leagues, clubs, professional players, the city of Paris, media partners, Perrier and other sponsors. Inevitably, the success of this event depends on negotiations and collaborations between these various stakeholders.

In this context, the rights of each stakeholder must be carefully considered and collaborative programmes developed to ensure the satisfaction of all stakeholders. Legal advice and procedures work in a proactive manner to minimize conflicts. This due diligence of procedures helps to avoid litigations between entities or individuals who have certain rights in connection with the event. For example, the legal function provides the legal framework for transferring the image rights of athletes to the organizer in an effort to develop the event and provides conflict resolution when disputes arise. Likewise, the legal function establishes the guidelines between the rights of a national federation and those of the international federation. It is essential to involve the legal function when determining the rights associated with the exclusivity granted with various categories of sponsorship packages, the media access right of broadcasters, the public's right to information, etc., to lessen the possibility of an infringement of rights. Each entity must therefore view sponsorship as a collaborative effort, whereby athletes, federations, media, clubs and the public are involved in a number of operations carried out to activate a successful sponsorship. Thus, the marketing function is to conceive and implement a programme to satisfy all the stakeholders' expectations.

Sports sponsorship must be managed with a collaborative approach. It must be rooted in people's preoccupations and stakeholders' expectations, and it must combine legal and marketing functions. It is important not to isolate technological and economic developments from sociological issues. Although this book examines each sphere of the sponsorship operation in an individual manner, it also establishes their amalgamation by providing the tools needed to implement a collaborative, systemic approach to sponsorship operations.

> A rich knowledge is not necessarily sophisticated, structured, or statistical, but obtained from the ability to connect information, data, and its substance within a given context.
>
> (Morin 1990: 32)

Appendix 1

Sponsorship contract

In Paris, at _____

Between

The first party, _____ (*name of the individual*) acting on behalf of the French Federation of Volleyball in the capacity of President by virtue of the powers granted to him by the statutes of the aforementioned Federation domiciled at _____.

The second party, _____ (*name of the individual*) acting on behalf of the company, PERRIER SA, in the capacity of General Manager, by virtue of the powers conferred to him by the statutes of the aforementioned company domiciled at _____.

Each party, as a respective representative, is recognized to have the legal authority to enter into this contract and perform its obligations, and for this purpose:

Declare

I.   That the French Federation of Volleyball (the 'ORGANIZER') possesses the ability and the faculty to organize, promote and develop all forms of operations, activities, competitions and sporting events associated with volleyball, for which the competitions and events of the 'Perrier Fluo Beach Volleyball Experience' are included.

II. That the French Federation of Volleyball is recognized by the governing body in charge of the sport in France as the only entity exerting a public service objective for all of the activities related to volleyball. Likewise, the French Federation of Volleyball is the sole entity affiliated with and recognized by the International Federation of Volleyball.

III. That PERRIER SA (the 'SPONSOR') is a universally recognized commercial organization, whose primary operations correspond to, among other things, manufacturing operations and the distribution, marketing and selling of non-alcoholic beverages, more specifically, of mineral water and other products originating from it or in association with it as such.

IV. That the French Federation of Volleyball desires to organize, develop and implement an annual international sporting event of beach volleyball, wherein players from around the world will participate in the event via the invitational system. This sporting event will proceed in the form of an unofficial competition with the benefits of recognition by the International Federation of Volleyball.

V. That the French Federation of Volleyball agrees to associating the name of this international sporting competition with the prestigious international brand 'PERRIER' by including the name 'PERRIER' in the title of the event and designating it as the only official SPONSOR of the competition.

VI. That PERRIER SA agrees to the association of its brand name 'PERRIER' with this sporting event in the broadest way possible as a SPONSOR of the event with the ability to execute further undertakings in connection with advertising, promotions of its products, and public relations.

VII. That by virtue of this which has been stated, each acting party hereby consents to the execution of this exclusive sponsorship contract, which will be governed by the agreements contained herein this document.

Agreement

First: Purpose

The purpose of this contract is to establish the collaboration between the ORGANIZER and the SPONSOR within the set of activities of sponsorship, advertising integrations, sales promotion and public relations of the SPONSOR, to establish any required fees, and to provide for the distribution of the sporting event through the advertising communications of the SPONSOR.

For this purpose, the two parties agree to implement a commercialized sporting event that will bear the name of 'Perrier Fluo Beach Volleyball Experience' which is characterized as an unofficial competition.

In this event, the French Federation of Volleyball is the sole 'OWNER' of the event, except with regard to aspects referring to the brand, the domain name and other distinctive signs of the event where the two entities will jointly act together; the Federation as owner of the event is considered the 'ORGANIZER' and PERRIER SA as the sponsor of the event is considered as the 'SPONSOR'.

Joint functions:

a. The two parties agree to form a commercial company with limited liability whose initial social capital equity will amount to €4000, in which each of the participating parties will contribute 50 per cent of the equity.

b. The company will be registered under the name 'Perrier Fluo Beach Volleyball Experience SA' and will take up residence in the headquarters of the French Federation of Volleyball.

c. The administrative body of the company will be formed by an equal number of members appointed by each of the parties (no less than 2 and no higher than 6).
d. The parties mutually agree on the nomination of a single administrator who will be in charge of the management of the company.
e. The company will have for its social and enduring purpose, the ownership and the exploitation worldwide of the industrial and intellectual property rights that will be derived from the event, particularly with regard to the ownership and the exploitation of the brands and the Internet domain name, either by itself, or by a third party through a transfer or a licence. For this purpose, the parties commit to register in a maximum number of countries, at least the following brands:

1. 'Perrier Fluo Beach Volleyball Experience' **Nominative.**
2. 'Perrier Fluo Beach Volleyball Experience 2007' **Nominative-Figurative.**
3. Logo of the event. **Figurative.**
4. Name of the event with the logo. **Nominative-Figurative.**
5. Mascot of the event. **Figurative.**
6. Name of the mascot. **Nominative.**

Additionally, the following Internet domain names:

1. Perrier Fluo Beach Volleyball Experience.fr
2. Perrier Fluo Beach Volleyball Experience.com
3. Perrier Fluo Beach Volleyball Experience.org
4. Perrier Fluo Beach Volleyball Experience.net
5. Name of the mascot.com; net
6. Perrier Fluo Beach Volleyball Experience2007.fr; com; org; net
7. Perrier Fluo Experience.fr; com; org; net
8. Beach Volleyball Experience.fr; com; org; net
9. Perrier Beach Volleyball.fr; com; org; net
10 Fluo Beach Volleyball.fr; com; org; net
11. PFBVE.fr; com; org; net

f. The parties accept and explicitly agree to execute, with impartiality and without having to pay any counter-benefit to a third party, all the acts, agreements and necessary documents for the new company to register and use the brands and other exclusively distinctive signs or symbols under its name, such as the domain names of each entity, when it proves necessary to register them.
g. The parties agree to the dissolution of the aforementioned company. They agree to distribute any existing assets equally between the parties when the company comes to dissolve or cease to exist for any reason that may be including the expiration of the validity period agreed upon and agree to the de-registration. Furthermore, they will not individually use any of the brands or domain names which were registered prior to the dissolution.

Functions of the Organizer:

The ORGANIZER will collaborate with the SPONSOR in the following operations:

Advertising sponsorship operations:

1. The ORGANIZER accepts and acknowledges that only the SPONSOR possesses the capacity to be associated with the name of the event, the logo, the mascot and other distinctive signs of the ORGANIZER, particularly, the products which it markets under the name 'Perrier Fluo'.
2. The ORGANIZER accepts and acknowledges that only the SPONSOR is given the authority to use the slogans: 'Perrier: Official Sponsor of the Perrier Fluo Beach Volleyball Experience' and 'Fluo Perrier: The Official Beverage of the Perrier Fluo Beach Volleyball Experience' for their use in all of its external communication strategies.
3. The ORGANIZER accepts and acknowledges that the SPONSOR has the faculty to use the slogan: 'Perrier: Official Supplier of the Perrier Fluo Beach Volleyball Experience' and to use it in its external communication strategies. PERRIER SA will be designated the only official supplier of the beverage sector.

Operations of advertising integrations:

1. The ORGANIZER agrees to exclude the brands, distinctive marks or symbols, products or services of any other company. The ORGANIZER agrees to only include the name of the SPONSOR and/or the name or distinctive signs and symbols of the product promoted by the SPONSOR in all facilities or media where it is possible that they could be integrated, particularly in the following (*here one should add an appendix, graphically describing each area subject to receive advertising integration, that will be an integral part of this contract*):

    a. In the entire advertising perimeter of each court, and especially within the television panoramic scope, with a minimum dimension of _____ (for example, 2×1 m²) for each of the advertising panels.
    b. On the vertical posts being used to hold the net dividing the court into two parts.
    c. On the metal structures of the platform used for the chair of the primary referee ('referee's chair').
    d. On the umbrella which may be covering the primary referee of the match.
    e. On the chairs of the auxiliary referees or the line referees.
    f. On the players' chairs where players rest during the time-outs of the match.
    g. On the front side of the players' uniforms of all the participating athletes whereupon the logo of the SPONSOR or the name of the promoted product will be imprinted with a maximum dimension of _____ (for example 200 cm²).
    h. On the back of the players' uniforms of all the participating athletes whereupon the logo of the SPONSOR or the name of promoted product will be imprinted with a maximum dimension of _____ (for example 180 cm²).
    i. On the running suits, the sweatshirts, the training equipment, etc.
    j. On the sporting bags or travel bags, a maximum dimension of 230 cm² is allowed; on towels, a maximum dimension of 500 cm² is allowed.
    k. On billboards that must be placed behind athletes in the pressroom or in the area intended for interviewing the participating athletes, a maximum of 3 columns of

advertising integrations will appear; the integrations will have a minimum dimension of 40×20 cm^2 each.

l. On the front side of the admittances or accreditations allowing access rights to the sporting event with a maximum dimension of 25 per cent of the total dimension or used as an integral background.

m. On the front side of the admission tickets or the accreditations giving entrance rights to the sporting event whereupon it can have a maximum area of 85 per cent of the total printed area.

n. At the back of all places or rooms where any act of communication of the event can be carried out, such as press conferences of the organizers, lottery drawings, etc. Similarly, on the frontal sides of platforms which must be located behind the people having to participate in the act of communication.

o. Two bottles of 'Perrier Fluo' will be positioned, one on each side of the main microphone in clearly visible locations, in all of the press conferences or other acts of communication involving the athletes participating in the event, the technical staff, the personnel of the organization, etc.

p. *It is possible to include the integration on all advertising billboards and on all the stationery of the organization such as envelopes, letters, faxes, press releases, etc.*

2. The ORGANIZER has the obligation to have a continually visible and sufficient reference to the SPONSOR and its promotional products on the official Web page of the event. Therefore, the continual existence of a visible link to the Web page of the SPONSOR must be guaranteed.

3. The ORGANIZER has the obligation to include the name and/or the identifying symbols of the SPONSOR in all publications, booklets, posters, etc., that it publishes, with it appearing on a minimum of _____ (*for example 5 per cent*) of each page or piece of document, except on posters where it will appear on a minimum of _____ per cent of the poster.

   The ORGANIZER has the sole and exclusive responsibility for all expenses deriving from the labelling, printing, placement and assembling of all the advertising means and structures.

Operations of collaboration for the promotion and direct distribution of the products of the SPONSOR:

1. The ORGANIZER grants the SPONSOR, in an exclusive way and for the entire validity period of the contract and its possible extensions, the capacity to manage, individually or through a transfer to third party, all the services of the cafeteria, points of sale of beverages and refreshments, as well as catering/foodservice which can be installed inside the sporting facility where the event takes place. The SPONSOR will not pay any additional fee to the ORGANIZER for this. Furthermore, the ORGANIZER will make available to the SPONSOR or to the company or the companies to whom the SPONSOR assigns this task, a minimum space of _____ (*for example: a covered area of __ m^2 of which one has a pre-installation of ____*). The SPONSOR is solely responsible for the operation and the management of the areas, either by itself or a contracted third party; it assumes all risks and operating profits of such activities.

2. The ORGANIZER has the obligation to provide the SPONSOR a covered area (*it is possible to determine an additional number of areas, if necessary, for distinctive purposes such as to have special guests, areas for product promotions, product storage, etc.*) with a minimum size of ____ m² and a maximum size of ____ m², and must be ____ (*for example 50 per cent*) larger than any other space which may be provided, for free or at a premium price, by the ORGANIZER to another company or third party inside the facility where the event takes place for its entire duration without any counter-benefit paid to the ORGANIZER. The SPONSOR may use this area for convenient purposes such as for promotions and the sale of products. This area must have the following minimum provisions: electric power supply of ____ watts, air conditioning, water supply, ____ telephone lines, as well as ____ Internet connections. In addition, this space must be located on the ground floor and must be directly accessible from the street for access without going through various spaces, passages, abodes or installations. The decoration and the arrangement of the area will be the sole and exclusive responsibility of the SPONSOR who thus assumes responsibility for all ensuing expenses, except for the cost of the water and electricity which remains the responsibility of the ORGANIZER.

3. The ORGANIZER agrees to facilitate the installations and consents, without limiting their number, to the arrangement of any stand, display unit, etc., of the SPONSOR inside the facility of the event for any promotional activities and sales of its products. In all cases, each stand will not exceed ____ m² of surface area and will not disturb the passageway of the spectators, nor shall it endanger the basic standards set forth for evacuation, safety and exiting from the sporting facility.

4. The ORGANIZER must provide the SPONSOR with an adequate number of passes and accreditations in accordance with its needs for the site in order for the SPONSOR, by means of his personnel or those contracted for such purpose, to develop its promotional operations, sales and public relations as it desires. The number of passes and accreditations must not be less than ____ (*for example, 30*) nor higher than ____ (*for example, 150*). Hence, three months prior to the event, the SPONSOR must provide the ORGANIZER with the agenda it expects to implement and the number of accreditations needed.

Other operations of collaboration:

1. The ORGANIZER will provide the SPONSOR with a minimum of ____ (*for example, 100*) free access passes to the event and ____ (*for example, 300*) time-specific passes for entry to the sessions of the morning or that of the afternoon, for the SPONSOR to distribute as it deems necessary. The SPONSOR must not sell any of the passes or receive any direct economic counter-benefit for them. If the SPONSOR requests a larger number of passes and time-specific entry passes than originally requested, the ORGANIZER will honour the request if the passes are available; however, the SPONSOR must pay the ORGANIZER a fee equivalent to ____ (*for example, 80 per cent*) of the selling price to the public. Consequently, the SPONSOR should request the number of passes and entries it will need to the ORGANIZER within four months prior to the commencement of the event.

2. The ORGANIZER will strive to have the athletes participating in the event visit the

area or room for which the SPONSOR establishes for the functions of the promotion and for public relations inside the facility where the event takes place. The ORGANIZER guarantees to have the champions as well as the finalists visit the aforementioned area upon completion of the competition.

3. Additionally, the ORGANIZER must strive to have the public authorities (national, regional and local) and the sporting authorities officially attending the event visit the aforementioned area or room of the SPONSOR.

4. Furthermore, the ORGANIZER guarantees it will organize the closing ceremony at the completion of the competition in the location the SPONSOR has set up for that purpose, to which all participating athletes as well as the public and sporting authorities will be invited.

Functions of the Sponsor:

The SPONSOR will collaborate with the ORGANIZER in the promotion of the event via the following functions:

a) The SPONSOR must label all beverage products with 'Perrier Fluo' and the slogan: 'Official Sponsor of the Perrier Fluo Beach Volleyball Experience' or 'Perrier Fluo: The Official Beverage of the Perrier Fluo Beach Volleyball Experience' on the various labels of its products.

b) The SPONSOR must include the 'Official Sponsor of the Perrier Fluo Beach Volleyball Experience' reference in all advertising campaigns it carries out two months prior to the commencement of the event and on all products it publicizes.

c) The SPONSOR agrees to implement an above-the-line advertising campaign in newspapers, specialized magazines, radio and television at the national level during the month prior to the commencement of the event, in which the product 'Perrier Fluo' will be exclusively publicized. In this publicity, a clearly visible or audible reference must be made that PERRIER is the 'Official Sponsor of the Perrier Fluo Beach Volleyball Experience' or that 'Perrier Fluo' is 'The Official Beverage of the Perrier Fluo Beach Volleyball Experience'.

d) The SPONSOR is obligated to make a reference on his Web page that PERRIER is the 'Official Sponsor of the Perrier Fluo Beach Volleyball Experience' or that 'Perrier Fluo' is 'The Official Beverage of the Perrier Fluo Beach Volleyball Experience' and must include a visible link to the Web page of the event.

Second: Description of the event

The event will bear the name 'Perrier Fluo Beach Volleyball Experience' and will correlate to a commercially characterized, unofficial sporting competition of beach volleyball, created with the authorization of the International Federation of Volleyball. The event will proceed according to the technical regulations of the International Federation.

The competition will occur, except in cases of uncontrollable causes or acts of nature, in Paris, at City Hall Square and on the bank of the River Seine, in August of each year.

The competition will have a minimum duration of two days and a maximum duration of six days. Additionally, it is mandatory for the men's finals and the women's finals to take place on a Saturday or on a Sunday.

A minimum of 10 men's teams and a minimum of 10 women's teams, originating from 5 continents, will participate in the competition. A minimum of _____ participating athletes must be classified in the top _____ positions of the FIVB ranking system.

The competition will take place in a maximum of three sporting stadiums, thus enabling the development of simultaneous matches on various courts. Beginning at the quarterfinals, however, the matches may not be scheduled simultaneously and it is mandatory that they occur on the same court.

It is sole and exclusive responsibility and task of the ORGANIZER to determine the regulations and competition format (*such as for the existence or not of preliminary phases, qualification tournament, seeds, wild cards, etc.*), respecting in all cases the competition standards set by the International Federation for these types of events.

The ORGANIZER will determine the match schedules.

The ORGANIZER may propose a modification to the location (*including the city or the country*) and/or the competition dates to the SPONSOR who must explicitly acknowledge acceptance of the modifications in writing. Failure of the SPONSOR to respond within 15 days following the notification will be considered as a non-acceptance of the modification.

The SPONSOR may accept the modification of the location or the date of the event without any reserve, in which case the contract will be maintained in force in all its components. Conversely, the SPONSOR may propose new modifications or alternatives to the initial proposal which can include a modification of the prize money paid by the SPONSOR and the obligations accepted in this contract. If the ORGANIZER accepts the modifications made by the SPONSOR, the contract will be maintained with the new modifications suggested by each party. In the absence of an agreement between the two parties, the conditions agreed upon in the initial contract must be maintained except when that is not possible due to uncontrollable causes (*for example, the unavailability of the area where the event must be held, the lack of authorization from the International Federation or when it is impossible to have the minimum number of participants who are ranked at the top of the FIVB system as previously stated due to an overlap with other official competitions on the same dates*), in which case the SPONSOR may choose between the maintenance of the contract, to suspend it up to a maximum duration of one year, or cancellation of the contract. If the SPONSOR chooses to cancel the contract, it must pay the ORGANIZER the sum of € _____ for damages.

Third: Validity

The parties agree this contract will have an initial validity period of four years, effective from January 1, 2007 until December 30, 2010.

At the end of this period, the SPONSOR may renew the contract as often as it deems appropriate. However, the contract must be renewed in two-year periods. Additionally, the SPONSOR must communicate his decision to extend the contract to the ORGANIZER at least four months prior to the term of each renewal or validity date of the contract.

Fourth: Consideration

For all the services and concepts provided for in this contract, the SPONSOR agrees to pay the ORGANIZER a total annual sum of € _____ (+ VAT or the equivalent applicable tax).

The payment is divided into instalments due on the following dates:

- On February 1, the sum of € _____ (+ VAT)
- On April 1, the sum of € _____ (+ VAT)
- On May 1, the sum of € _____ (+ VAT)
- On July 1, the sum of € _____ (+ VAT)

The sum to be paid by the SPONSOR is to be recalculated annually when there is a positive increase resulting from the application of the annual IPC (price index) calculated from January 1 to December 31.

Both parties agree the SPONSOR may need to increase the annual economic contribution it gives to the ORGANIZER equal to ____ (*for example, 50 per cent*) of the net benefit correlating to the SPONSOR for the distribution of the dividends with the companies in which the ORGANIZER and the SPONSOR have set up for the better management of the rights or assets that each one of them holds or may hold in relation to the event, and in particular, for the company which must be set up for the rightful ownership of the brands and domain names derived from the event stated in first clause (joint functions) of this contract.

Fifth: Non-concurrence clause

1. The SPONSOR and any other company from the same sector or product line for which it actively partakes in (*correlating to a minimum of 10 per cent of common stock capital*) agree not to patronize, sponsor, nor advertise at any other sporting event in the field of volleyball or beach volleyball (regardless if it is competitive or not, when the scope is of international dimension, independent of the country where it is held, or of national scope, and when it is held in France) during the validity of this contract or its possible extensions, as well as during the _____ (*for example, two years*) following its conclusion for all reasons to the effects of the contract, except when the French Federation of Volleyball has given its expressed written authorization to do so.

2. Furthermore, the SPONSOR and any other company from the same sector or product line for which it actively partakes in (correlating to a minimum of 10 per cent of common stock capital) agree not to patronize, sponsor, nor advertise at any sporting event (whether it is competitive or not), taking place on the beach or being played or held on a sand surface or on a similar surface regardless of the place or country where it takes place during the entire validity period of the contract and its possible extensions, and during the _____ (*for example, two years*) following its conclusion for all reasons of the effects of the contract, except when the French Federation of Volleyball has given its expressed written authorization to do so.

3. The ORGANIZER agrees, under any circumstance, not to contract with any other sponsor nor to contract advertising in any of the means or mediums for which it can

offer in all the activities (competitive or not) that it organizes, either itself or via a third party, during the entire validity period of this contract or its possible extensions, as well as during the _____ (*for example, two years*) following the conclusion of the effects of the contract, with any company or groups of companies which manufacture, market, distribute or sell mineral water and/or other products derived from or associated with it except with written authorization from PERRIER SA. This exclusion of concurrence is extended to the teams, the selection of national teams, and all the competitions depending directly on the Federation and in which it intervenes as the organizer or for which it holds the capacity to transfer it to a third party.

Sixth: Commitments and guarantees of the ORGANIZER

1. The ORGANIZER guarantees it is the sole entity with rightful ownership and responsibility for the sporting event which will take place; that it did not enter into an accord, agreement or contract with any third party in relation to the sponsorship and the advertising of the event or accompanying events. Likewise, the ORGANIZER guarantees that no third party holds a right which can disrupt the execution or the fulfilment of this contract or disturb its exploitation; most particularly, by the execution of operations by a third party based on intellectual property rights.
2. The ORGANIZER agrees to directly execute the organization of the event and to maintain the rightful ownership and must not transfer it to third parties without the expressed written authorization of the SPONSOR.
3. The ORGANIZER agrees to organize and develop the event, except in the case of major cause, for a minimum duration of _____ (*for example, the first two years*) of the contract, and, on the occasion where the contract would be extended, for a minimum duration of the first year of its renewal.
4. If the ORGANIZER comes to modify its legal status during the validity period of the contract transforming its status into any other form than the current one, the new entity will be subrogated to all the rights and obligations emanating from this contract, which will continue in all its effects in force where the SPONSOR requests this subrogation and the maintenance of the contract.
5. The ORGANIZER guarantees it will not organize by means of entities or companies depending directly, or indirectly, on it nor in which it takes part as a shareholder, any commercial event, unofficial event, national or international dimensional event of beach volleyball during the validity period of the contract and its possible extensions. Alternatively, the International Federation of Volleyball, as a federation exerting a public service mission, is able to authorize the organization of any event of a similar nature to this contract, when it has been requested to do so by an entity or a club affiliated with the aforementioned federation.
6. The ORGANIZER guarantees live broadcasts in France and in _____ (*other possible countries*), for a minimum of two hours daily, during a minimum period of two days, of the matches occurring during that time. The aforementioned broadcast is to be carried out between 3:00PM and 8:00PM.
7. The ORGANIZER guarantees the live broadcast of the event on free-to-air television on a state channel in France and in _____ (*other possible countries*) of the men's semi-finals and of the men's and women's finals.

8. The ORGANIZER guarantees the broadcast by 'pay-per-view' (PPV) or 'on-demand' for all of the matches that will be played during the event except for the ones presented on free-to-air television as described in the preceding paragraphs.

9. Likewise, the ORGANIZER guarantees in the transfer of audiovisual contracts, which may be executed for this event, that a clause will be inserted stating the SPONSOR has precedence over any other advertiser for television advertising breaks except for those subject to a special reservation in the manner of time or preferences on behalf of the ORGANIZER. For this purpose, the ORGANIZER must communicate that such a possibility exists to the SPONSOR and provide a detailed list of the time slots with their characteristics and which ones are being allotted to the SPONSOR, within a preliminary period of _____ days prior the commencement of the event. The SPONSOR must respond within a maximum of 15 days from the notification whether if it desires to use the right to this advertising integration and of its characteristics. The SPONSOR forfeits this right if it fails to respond within 15 days of notification.

10. The ORGANIZER is obligated to provide the following information to the SPONSOR without receiving any counter-benefit, and agrees to do so in a timely manner and always within 10 days of receiving the following information:

    • Means of relaying or distributing the images and/or the soundtracks of the events, acts and the supplementary activities.
    • Territories for the rebroadcast of the event, supplementary acts, and activities.
    • The viewing index of the broadcast, insofar as the ORGANIZER possesses this piece of information.
    • Information relating to the 'commercial breaks' of the matches relayed in the PPV mode.

    The SPONSOR must use this piece of information with the necessary confidentiality and to exclusively use it for purposes of study and internal development of the company.

11. The ORGANIZER is obligated to give the SPONSOR a copy of the audiovisual recordings of every match, as well as each act or activity that may have been recorded and/or relayed. The SPONSOR will not have to pay any amount in return for this but is obligated to use these recordings solely for its own internal usage or for institutional and promotional purposes in an effort to promote the sponsorship of the event; however, to do this, it must have the expressed written authorization from the company or organization having acquired the audiovisual rights. Nevertheless, it must not commercialize them nor transfer them to third parties.

12. The ORGANIZER guarantees the SPONSOR that the athletes will exclusively use the sporting attire, towels and sporting bags produced for the event and facilitated by the ORGANIZER throughout the duration of the event; furthermore, the athletes will not use outfits or accessories containing the advertisement of a direct competitor of the SPONSOR. Likewise, the athletes will not be allowed to publicly drink beverages not provided by the SPONSOR.

13. The ORGANIZER shall purchase a policy of civil liability insurance, with a minimum coverage of € _____, for any damage which may occur at the location of the event and during the event.

14. The ORGANIZER shall indemnify the SPONSOR, agreeing to avoid and, according to the situation, to be accountable for all legitimate legal complaints and out of court complaints for damages, and, as a general rule, for any disputes being brought forth to the SPONSOR, except for those arising from the services of cafeteria, of catering and of the beverages and refreshments points of sale. In this case, the dispute will be the sole responsibility of the SPONSOR. For the purpose of this clause, the term 'SPONSOR' includes the employees, directors, agents and other personnel dependent upon the SPONSOR, as well as with its respective subsidiary companies or subsidiaries. In any case, the SPONSOR retains the opportunity to directly respond to and execute all legal proceedings for which it regards as necessary for the protection of its interests. The SPONSOR assumes the court expenses in such a case and must inform the ORGANIZER beforehand of its intention to act.

Seventh: Commitments and guarantees of the SPONSOR

1. The SPONSOR is obligated to provide a minimum of _____ bottles of the product 'Perrier Fluo' and a minimum of _____ bottles of mineral water for the duration of the event for exclusive consumption by the athletes, technicians, officials, organizers and volunteers participating in the event. The ORGANIZER must not sell or distribute the products to anyone except the aforementioned individuals.
2. The SPONSOR acknowledges and accepts the rules of the game and of the competition, and anti doping regulations which are applied to this contract and may require the criteria established herein this contract to be modified accordingly.
3. The SPONSOR agrees to directly purchase from the companies which have been given licensing rights for all the products it uses for its promotional campaign and public relations. The SPONSOR must not sell or market the products except when they are associated with the bottles of drink marketed by the SPONSOR. The SPONSOR will be able to purchase unlimited quantities of these products at the best selling price previously established by the licensee in each territory where it will distribute the licensed products.
4. The SPONSOR guarantees all standards of hygiene, safety and labour safety in the cafeteria services, catering and the points of sale of beverages or refreshments will be respected; furthermore, it will obtain the administrative authorizations essential for executing these services to the public.
5. The SPONSOR guarantees it will assume all sanctions and responsibilities for the damages that may result from the management or the exploitation of the cafeteria services, catering or the points of sale for beverages and refreshments inside the facility of the event, thereby exempting the ORGANIZER of any responsibility in such matter.

Eighth: Penal clauses and breaches

1. If one of the parties commits a serious breach of one of the obligations stipulated in this contract, the party fulfilling its obligations (*the one acting in good faith*) must communicate to the offending party that such a breach has been committed, and if the breach persists (except in the event of non-payment on the date agreed upon in which

case they are allowed an extension of 5 days), the party in good faith can claim indemnification caused by the breach in a manner which it considers adequate. Additionally, the parties may demand under the established penal clause, the sum of € _____. The two parties accept that the amount of the penal clause may not be revised during the validity period of this contract.

2. Without any prejudice to what has been previously agreed upon, if the ORGANIZER prevents access into the facility where the event takes place to the employees of the SPONSOR thus preventing them from executing the activities of the SPONSOR for its promotional product sales or the cafeteria services, catering, beverages and refreshments distribution; moreover, if it allows unauthorized third parties to carry out the aforementioned activities, the SPONSOR has the right to receive compensation from the ORGANIZER, under the established penal clause, the sum of € _____, without any prejudice to compensation for the damage and harm that may have been caused.

3. Without any prejudice to what has been previously agreed upon, if the SPONSOR does not fulfil its advertising communication obligations by referring to the event during the period preceding it, the SPONSOR must compensate the ORGANIZER, under the established penal clause, the sum of € _____, without any prejudice to compensation for the damage and harm that may have been caused.

Ninth: Confidentiality

The parties agree to maintain the confidentiality of the terms and conditions of the contract and will not reveal, directly or indirectly, any type of data or information contained herein, and will adopt necessary measures to effectively guarantee this confidentiality, without prejudice to the legal assumptions imposed in accordance with the regulation in force.

Tenth: Public accounts

Each party commits to reviewing the public account of this contract at the request of either one of the parties with the expenses being the responsibility of the requesting party.

Eleventh: Expenses and taxes

Each party of the contract will assume the expenses and taxes resulting from the signing of the contract pursuant to what has been previously established by law.

Twelfth: Notifications and communications

All notifications required for this contract will be sent to the following places of residence:

•   For PERRIER SA, the address of notification: _____
    _____

•   For the French Federation of Volleyball, the address of notification: _____
    _____

The communications between the parties may be executed by any means for which the reception can be proven; thus, it is allowable to communicate by fax, COD letter, e-mail with acknowledgment of delivery or any other traditional mode of communication.

Thirteenth: Jurisdiction

With regard to the resolution of any divergence derived from the interpretation or execution of the contract, each party agrees to be subject to the arbitration of the Court of Arbitration for Sport (CAS) whose seat is located in Lausanne, Switzerland, while expressly renouncing any other jurisdictional appeal.

As proof of conformity, this contract will be written in as many copies as there are parties, at the place and on the date stated above.

On behalf of the French Federation of Volleyball _____

On behalf of PERRIER SA _____

Appendix 2

Television contract

In Paris, at _____

Between

The first party, the French Federation of Volleyball domiciled at _____,
represented by its President.

The second party, SPORTTV SA, domiciled at _____, represented by its
General Manager.

Each party, as a respective representative, is recognized to have the legal authority to
enter into this contract and perform its obligations, and for this purpose:

Declare

I.   That the French Federation of Volleyball is an entity possessing its own legal status,
     subject to French law, with the faculty to use whichever rights derive from the sport
     activity carried out, among which is the audiovisual rights arising from the exploitation
     of the 'Perrier Fluo Beach Volleyball Experience' as well as the sole and exclusive
     image rights of the athletes who participate in the aforementioned event. It is, therefore,
     the rightful owner of the name, logo, colours and other distinctive symbols of the
     event with the only limitations provided for herein this contract.
II. That SPORTTV SA is a commercial entity whose social purpose, among other things,
     is the acquisition of all forms of audiovisual rights by means of any technical standard
     of exploitation, with the ability to exploit them directly or to transfer them in whole or
     in part to a third party.
III. That according to the aforementioned information, both parties consent to the
     execution of this contract for the exclusive transfer of rights which will be governed
     according to the agreements contained herein this document.

Definitions

Event: the 'Perrier Fluo Beach Volleyball Experience' is a commercially characterized, unofficial sporting competition of beach volleyball, created with the authorization of the International Federation of Volleyball, where 10 teams originating from 5 continents are allowed to participate in the competition via the invitational system. The event will proceed according to the technical regulations of the International Federation.

Disclosure and publication: the right to make the original images, soundtracks and/or the audiovisual recordings accessible to the public.

Reproduction: the right to secure or partially secure all of the images, sounds and/or audiovisual recordings, through any platform or format of either provisional or permanent character, by any system or procedure that allows for their communication and/or for the ability to obtain copies of its entirety or in segments. The digitalization of the work, as well as the digital storage of an electronic medium, will be considered as an act of reproduction.

Distribution: the right to make the original, copies or reproductions of the images, soundtracks and/or audiovisual recordings available to the public which can be put into circulation as tangible objects on any platform or format including video, electronic and digital, and additionally by any system or procedure via their sale, rental, loan or any other form of permanent or temporary transfer of the property, possession or usage for any lawful purpose.

Public communication: this right relates to all actions (regardless of the platform or format) and any system or procedure, either analogue or digital, that allows a plurality of people to have access to the images, soundtracks and/or audiovisual recordings without previous distributions of samples, either free of charge, by means of pay-per-view (PPV) or subscription fee, requiring or not the payment of an entrance fee, or by means of any other free or conditional access system. Particularly, the following are considered as acts of public communication of the images, soundtracks and/or audiovisual recordings:

I.   The exhibition, broadcast or transmission in locations accessible to the public, regardless if a payment is required or not for admittance.

II. The broadcast by television, or any other audiovisual means or procedure being used for wave or cable distribution, via a terrestrial network, satellite or any similar system.

III. The transmission of the images, soundtracks, and/or audiovisual recordings by wire, cable, optical fibre or any other similar procedure.

IV. The transmission, simultaneous or not, by any procedure and organization other than that of the originator of the images, sounds and/or audiovisual recordings being relayed, transmitted or broadcasted.

V.   The broadcast or transmission in locations accessible to the public such as pubs/lounges, hotels, motels, ships, airplanes and public transportation, of the images, soundtracks and/or televised audiovisual recordings.

VI. The public availability of the images, soundtracks and/or audiovisual recordings by any other electronic system or wireless procedure so that each member of the public can have access to the same recordings, at any requested time, which includes the systems of pay-per-view (PPV), video on-demand (VOD) and near video on-demand (NVOD), incorporated to databases and other similar interactive or digital video systems.

Transformation: the adaptation or transformation of the images, soundtracks and/or audiovisual recordings for a realized form that is derived from other audiovisual recordings, or for the introduction of digitalized elements that can alter the integrity of the audiovisual recording.

Universal Mobile Telecommunications System: the third generation of mobile systems granted to third-party successions through corresponding administrative licences that permit the operation of these services.

Internet: Service for data transmission via communication networks using the TPC/IP protocol, whenever the end-user has exclusive access through the personal computer (PC).

Agreements

First: Objective

The objective of this contract is for the exclusive transfer of the audiovisual rights from the French Federation of Volleyball to SPORTTV SA, for all matches, acts, and activities carried out within the framework of the organization and the duration of the 'Perrier Fluo Beach Volleyball Experience' for the years _____ (*for example 2007, 2008, 2009 and 2010*).

Second: Scope of the transferred rights

a. The French Federation of Volleyball exclusively transfers the rights of exploitation to SPORTTV SA, including the ability to transfer these rights to third parties, via any audiovisual system or procedure of the matches, acts, and activities as well as the images and/or soundtracks obtained through such occasions.

b. It is agreed this transfer exclusively assigns the ownership of the aforementioned rights to SPORTTV SA with the faculty to commercialize and exploit the matches, acts and activities referenced in the objective of the contract via any audiovisual format, system or procedure obtained of the said events, whereby excluding any third party and also the French Federation of Volleyball of these rights.

c. The components of the event include all the matches of the competition during the celebration of the event, from the beginning until the end, while also including, if so occurring, according to a situation where matches were played as a prerequisite phase for classification in order to participate in this event.

d. The acts and activities of the event consist of all those being organized by the rights owner which adheres to a direct relationship with the owner, regardless or not if they are held within the facility designed for the purpose of the event. For example, the public presentation of the event, the drawing/lottery of the competition, the press conferences with the organizers, participants, officials and sponsors, the presentation of trophies/ awards, and acts of promotion are mere examples of such possible activities.

e. Included in the contract are any images and/or soundtracks derived from any act or activity provided for in this contract which takes place inside the facility, regardless of whether or not they are organized by the rights owner of the event, but only when it does not infringe upon the privacy rights of the participating athletes, organizers, officials, advertising sponsors, spectators or any other person within the facility where the event takes place.

f. Both parties explicitly accept and recognize that the possibility exists for limitations on the exclusive transfer of these rights in circumstances where the regulations of public ordinances may require the granting of certain images of the matches, acts and activities to other audiovisual companies in compliance with the standards of public information and the information rights which other audiovisual companies may hold while occurring at all times within the limitations established by the respective standards.

g. The exclusive rights of exploitation transferred by the French Federation of Volleyball to SPORTTV SA include the exploitation by SPORTTV SA, or third parties, of the images, soundtracks and/or audiovisual recordings of the matches, acts and activities determined in this contract, either live or deferred, in its entirety or in fragments, of any format or platform via any existing and/or not yet made available system, procedure, or means whether it be free or in exchange of a counter-benefit, private or public, and in particular, without limitations, the following rights:

- Disclosure and publication
- Reproduction
- Distribution
- Public communication
- Translation and subtitling: This right refers to the realization of necessary adaptations for the translation of the original idioms, versions or sounds to any other language or dialect.
- Transformation: Respect must be given at all times to any derived publicity that exists from the capturing of the images or from what appears in the original images and/or sounds, such as with fixed advertising, and the exposure of what appears on the athletes' and official participants' clothing.

Third: Description of the event

The 'Perrier Fluo Beach Volleyball Experience' is a commercially characterized, unofficial sporting competition of beach volleyball, created with the authorization of the International Federation of Volleyball. The event will proceed according to the technical regulations of the International Federation.

The competition will occur, except in cases of uncontrollable causes or acts of nature, in Paris at the City Hall Square and on the banks of the Seine River in August of each year.

The competition will have a minimum duration of two days and a maximum duration of six days. It is mandatory that the men's finals and the women's finals occur on a Saturday or on a Sunday. SPORTTV SA has the faculty to decide if the finals must be played on a Saturday or on a Sunday. To effectively ensure the right of selection regarding the day of the finals, it will be necessary to communicate the decision to the organizing federation no less than a minimum of six months prior to the beginning of the event. When this notification is not properly given, the organizing federation will have the complete freedom to decide the day of the finals.

A minimum of 10 men's teams and a minimum of 10 women's teams, originating from 5 continents, will participate in the competition. A minimum of _____ participating athletes must be classified in the top _____ positions of the FIVB ranking system.

The competition will take place in a maximum of three sporting stadiums, thus enabling the development of simultaneous matches on various courts. Beginning at the quarterfinals, however, the matches may not be scheduled simultaneously and it is mandatory that they occur on the same court.

It is sole and exclusive responsibility and task of the organization to determine the regulations and competition format (*such as the existence or not of preliminary phases, qualification tournament, seeds, wild cards, etc.*), respecting in all cases the competition standards set by the International Federation for these types of events.

It is mandatory that the match schedules be determined in agreement between the French Federation of Volleyball and SPORTTV SA In the absence of such an agreement, SPORTTV SA will determine a two-hour time span during which it will be mandatory that matches be played in all or some of the sporting courts, whereby the French Federation of Volleyball will have the faculty to determine the remainder of the schedule. Nevertheless, SPORTTV SA will determine the schedules of the men's semi-finals and finals as well as the women's finals.

The French Federation of Volleyball holds the faculty to modify the location, including a change of the city or the country, as well as the competition dates. To this effect, the Federation must notify SPORTTV SA of the changes at least six months in advance, whereupon the latter will have a period of 15 days to acknowledge the acceptance or not of these changes. If it communicates a non-acceptance of the change, this contract will become null and void and the French Federation of Volleyball must compensate SPORTTV SA a unique and fixed-price sum of €_____ as a result to the exclusion of any other indemnity based on any other reason.

If the French Federation of Volleyball must modify the place or dates of the event due to uncontrollable causes or in the absence of administrative authorization essential for occupying the space at the City Hall Square, yet the event still occurs outdoors and in the town of Paris, SPORTTV SA will be obligated to accept the modification and respect the agreements stipulated in this contract without being able to claim an indemnity from the event organizer.

If under any circumstance, the French Federation of Volleyball does not acquire the authorization of the International Federation of Volleyball for the organization of the event, or if the minimum number of participants, teams, countries or athletes depicted in the preceding subparagraphs is not available, SPORTTV SA will have the faculty to maintain the contract with the acceptance of these terms or make the decision to suspend this contract until the following year. In this assumption, the suspension of the contract will not result in any economic liability for either of the two parties.

Fourth: Validity period

The transfer of the rights of this contract pertains to the years _____ (*for example 2007, 2008, 2009 and 2010*).

This contract will come into effect on January 1, 2007 and will finalize on the last day of the event of the 'Perrier Fluo Beach Volleyball Experience' in the year 2010.

The exclusive rights transferred to SPORTTV SA, by virtue of the terms of this contract, relate only to the aforementioned years and may only be exploited by SPORTTV SA during a maximum period of two years after the conclusion of the event or act. At the conclusion of this time period, SPORTTV SA will be obligated to give all images, soundtracks and/or audiovisual recordings it would have in its possession to the French Federation of Volleyball. After the two-year period following the conclusion of the event, the rights to the archives belong solely and exclusively to the French Federation of Volleyball.

If this contract remains suspended by the will of SPORTTV SA for any circumstance stipulated in the Third section, the French Federation of Volleyball will have the faculty to freely contract, without any type of limitation, with any other company or audiovisual corporation that wishes to assume the audiovisual rights of the event during the period of suspension.

Fifth: Consideration

In exchange for the rights established in this contract, the French Federation of Volleyball will receive the following fixed amounts from SPORTTV SA:

1. For the year 2007, the sum of €_____ (+ VAT or any equivalent applicable tax substituting it) payable in three equal installments as noted below:

    *   On January 30th, the amount of €_____ (+ VAT).
    *   On June 30th, the amount of €_____ (+ VAT).
    *   On October 30th, the amount of €_____ (+ VAT).

2   For the year 2008, the sum of €_____ (+ VAT). (*Remaining years will follow the same model*)

    A percentage system could be established on the sale of the images and/or sounds via the PPV exploitations.

Sixth: Production and distribution of images and/or soundtracks

SPORTTV SA, and/or its assignees, is solely responsible for the recording and production of images and/or soundtracks before, during and after all matches, acts and activities for which it has acquired the rights, as well as the technical service expenses for signal transmissions to their production centres.

SPORTTV SA may exclusively record the warm-ups prior to each match and bring them into production with the purpose of obtaining images to enhance the broadcast of the matches. The company also holds the exclusive right to record and broadcast any type of acts or activities in connection with the event, be it before, during or after the celebration of the matches.

Within a minimum period of six months prior to the beginning of the 'Perrier Fluo Beach Volleyball Experience', SPORTV SA must send a 'Technical Plan of Production' to the French Federation of Volleyball with details on the location of the cameras within its facilities, the positioning of the commentators, and all the technical conditions that the French Federation of Volleyball must comply with so that SPORTV SA can properly carry out the recording of the matches and acts.

The 'Technical Plan of Production' must respect each and every one of the 'Standards of Technical Production and Audiovisual Broadcast' that have been approved by the French Federation of Volleyball for the production and broadcast of the event of which SPORTV SA declares to know and to accept and are included in appendix to this contract. (*Standards of technical production and audiovisual broadcast must be annexed to the contract.*)

The French Federation of Volleyball must take the necessary steps to ensure that the audiovisual and televised recordings and broadcasts can progress properly throughout the duration of the event, from either inside the facility where it takes place, or from any area or space where one or more of the activities organized by the rights holder in association with the event takes place. Consequently, they must give access to personnel to allow for the connection and placement of the technical equipment in the most optimal locations within a minimum period of 72 hours prior to the commencement of the event.

The French Federation of Volleyball must guarantee the supply of energy and the lighting required for the broadcast as established in the 'Standards of Technical Production and Audiovisual Broadcast' while assuring their maintenance and continuity.

The French Federation of Volleyball must make continual efforts to ensure objects and individuals who could prevent the optimal recording of the matches will not be located in front of the cameras.

The French Federation of Volleyball agrees to grant a minimum of _____ passes and accreditations to the personnel appointed by SPORTV SA for the realization of their functions while also facilitating the access of the cameras to the presidential tribune, the pressroom, the Village, the dressing room corridor, and other facilities except for areas or facilities where the privacy of the athletes, technicians and officials could be infringed upon, particularly in the dressing rooms, massage rooms, anti-doping control rooms, medical service stations, etc.; however, the sporting and safety regulations in force during the celebration of the event must be complied with.

The French Federation of Volleyball must make every effort to ensure that interviews can be carried out with the top-ranked athletes participating in the event, either on the court immediately following the match for a minimum duration of three minutes, or afterwards in the press room for a minimum duration of five minutes. Furthermore, SPORTV SA (or any other company it appointed or licensed for the production of images), agrees to interview an athlete on the court at the conclusion of the match only when it can take place located in front of an advertising banner or wall where the name or the logo of the official sponsor of the event is clearly visible, or in the press room when an advertising billboard is located directly behind the athlete.

Seventh: Access to information

The two parties agree that the authorization given to third parties for the recording of images of the matches, or acts and activities in relation to the event, can only be granted by SPORTTV SA. Furthermore, the exercise of the rights to information or news access can only be used by the third parties for their own use following the conditions stipulated by SPORTV SA in accordance with the regulations in force for the television broadcast of their own customary preference of reporting general information.

Eighth: Image, logos and brands of the event

The French Federation of Volleyball authorizes the exclusive use of the following to SPORTTV SA:

- The logos, distinctive signs and symbols, mascots, registered trademarks, and any other differentiating features of the event or of the rights holder.
- The names and images of athletes who have participated in the matches whenever they are developing their sports activity within the framework of the event, for a maximum period of one year from the day the images were acquired.

SPORTTV SA must use the aforementioned rights in the preceding subparagraph for the sole and exclusive purpose of exploiting the rights referenced in this contract such as for promotions, the producing of advertisements and/or sponsorships of the broadcast or recordings of matches, and of the contents and programming distributed by the licensees via any platform, medium or format.

Ninth: Advertising and Sponsorship

SPORTTV SA, and/or its assignees, may contract any type of advertisement, promotion or sponsorship to achieve the exploitation of the rights referenced in this contract, whether it is through television or any other audiovisual means or telecommunications, either before, during or after the transmission of the matches or the highlights of the competition via any technical means with the only limitations originating from compliance with the standards in force in connection with advertising and the limits stipulated in the following paragraph.

SPORTTV SA acknowledges and accepts the existence of a programme of sponsorship of the event, whose sole rightful owner is and always will be the French Federation of Volleyball. Additionally, SPORTTV SA, or any other audiovisual company to which it may have transferred its rights derived from this contract, must assure that the sponsor for the rights of broadcasting, transmission, etc., is not a direct competitor of the sponsor of the event; furthermore, SPORTTV SA is obligated to offer, in any territory or part of the world, a preferential right to tender to the company or the companies sponsoring the event so that they can also sponsor all the acts and activities derived from this contract. Likewise, the companies sponsoring the event will have a right of retraction regarding the sponsorship of the aforementioned acts or broadcasts.

The preceding paragraph is not prejudicial to the right of the French Federation of

Volleyball or of third parties to contract programmes of sponsorship which bear no relationship to the subject of this contract.

The French Federation of Volleyball is the sole rightful owner of all the advertising spaces which exist or can exist inside the sporting facility, thus SPORTTV SA and/or its assignees cannot claim any right, or royalty, by means of the broadcasting or distribution of the images it relays. Neither SPORTTV SA nor any of the assignees to whom they may have transferred the images and/or recordings of the images will be able to superimpose or modify the images for the inclusion in advertisements by means of digital systems or other technique that can be articulated in the future, without the express written authorization of the French Federation of Volleyball.

Tenth: Transfer to third parties

SPORTTV SA may transfer, sell or convey the rights and obligations that were transferred according to this contract to third parties, either exclusively or otherwise, in its entirety or portions thereof. Nevertheless, it is mandatory for the third party to honour all the terms of this contract agreed to by SPORTTV SA, particularly, the commitments for all the sales or transfers which may occur and the totality of the profits ensuing from these. (*Here, it is possible to set up an option whereby a percentage of the profit on all the sales and transfers would go to the owner of the event.*)

Eleventh: Commitments and guarantees of the French Federation of Volleyball

1. The French Federation of Volleyball assumes the direct responsibility for the 'Perrier Fluo Beach Volleyball Experience', and as a result, is accountable for the total organization of the matches, acts and activities linked to this event.
2. The French Federation of Volleyball declares and guarantees that it is the exclusive, rightful owner of the event possessing free disposition of all the rights transferred in this contract, for which there does not exist a possibility for the acquisition of those rights, nor for any right to tender or for retraction, contribution, taxation, limitation or claims of any kind, and that no third party possesses rights to prevent or condition the adherence or execution of this contract, or to disrupt its favourable exploitation. Hence, the French Federation of Volleyball can ensure the proficient and impartial use of these rights by SPORTTV SA or its possible assignees. Likewise, it declares and guarantees that, to the best of its knowledge, there is no dispute, litigation, arbitration, nor legal or administrative procedures against it for deeds or acts in relation to the fulfilment and execution of the transferred rights provided for in this contract.
3. If the French Federation of Volleyball changes its legal status during the validity period of the contract by transforming its status into any form other than the current one, the new entity will be subrogated to all the rights and obligations emanating from this contract, which will, in all cases, continue in all its effects in force when SPORTTV SA requests this subrogation and the maintenance of the contract.
4. In the event where the French Federation of Volleyball comes to modify the competition model, the type of sport activity, the name of the event, and/or any other essential aspects of the event which could lead to the dissolution of this contract, SPORTTV SA

will have the preferential right to tender and retraction rights over any other audiovisual company in the negotiation of the current rights concerning the new event organized by the French Federation of Volleyball, any of its subsidiaries, or by any other company that replaces it during the validity period of this contract.

Twelfth: Commitments and guarantees of the company SPORTTV SA

1. SPORTTV SA guarantees live broadcasts in France and in _____ (*other possible countries*), for a minimum of two hours daily, during a minimum period of two days, of the matches occurring during that time. The aforementioned broadcast is to be carried out between 3:00PM and 8:00PM.
2. SPORTTV SA guarantees the live broadcast of the event in France and in _____ _____ (*other possible countries*) of the men's semi-finals and of the men's and women's finals.
3. SPORTTV SA guarantees the broadcast by PPV or VOD for all of the matches that will be played during the event except for the ones presented on free-to-air television as described in the preceding paragraphs.
4. SPORTTV SA acknowledges and accepts the rules of the game and of the competition, and anti-doping regulations which are applied to this contract and may require the criteria established herein this contract to be modified accordingly.

Thirteenth: Advertising information, recordings and allotments

1. SPORTTV SA is obligated to facilitate information on behalf of the French Federation of Volleyball (including the potential transfer of that information to third parties) without receiving any counter-benefit, and agrees to do so in a timely manner and always within 10 days of receiving the following information:

   • Means of relaying or distributing the images and/or the soundtracks of the events, acts and the supplementary activities.
   • Territories for the broadcast of the event, supplementary acts, and activities.
   • The viewing index of the broadcast, insofar as SPORTTV SA possesses this piece of information.
   • Information relating to the 'commercial breaks' of the matches relayed in the PPV mode.

   The French Federation of Volleyball must use this information with the necessary confidentiality for internal, organizational and institutional aims except for information relating to the audiences which can be used for commercial or promotional purposes.
2. SPORTTV SA is obligated to give the French Federation of Volleyball a copy of the audiovisual recordings of every match, as well as each act or activity that may have been recorded and/or relayed. The French Federation of Volleyball will not have to pay any amount in return for this but is obligated to use these recordings solely for its own internal usage or for institutional and promotional purposes for the attainment of greater resources. Nevertheless, it must not commercialize them nor transfer them to third parties.

3. SPORTTV SA will allow the French Federation of Volleyball a maximum of 10 minutes for advertising allotments, each limited to 30 seconds, without receiving any counter-benefit, for the purpose of promoting the event and of making it known to the public. However, these allotments for informational or advertising purposes cannot be sponsored or patronized by another company or entity. Additionally, these allotments will not be broadcast during the 'prime time' schedule.

4. All the advertising sponsors and advertisers associated with the event are guaranteed to have rights to tender and of retraction for the aforementioned advertising allotments.

5. SPORTTV SA agrees to offer the companies sponsoring the event, or those who are participating directly in the event, all the advertising allotments that will be transmitted during the two minutes prior to the broadcast of the matches, throughout the broadcast during the commercial breaks, and during the two minutes following the broadcast of the matches or related acts of the event, all of which will be available at the fair market price. For this purpose, the French Federation of Volleyball, as organizer of the event, must provide SPORTTV SA, no later than two months prior to the event, a complete list of all the sponsorship companies and advertisers associated with the event. Failure to make this notification prior to the two-month period before the event, exonerates SPORTTV SA, or its assignees, from the obligation to offer preferential contracting for the aforementioned advertising allotments.

Fourteenth: Penal clauses and breaches

1. If one of the parties commits a serious breach of one of the obligations stipulated in this contract, the party fulfilling its obligations (*the one acting in good faith*) must communicate to the offending party that such a breach has been committed, and if the breach persists (except in the event of non-payment on the date agreed upon for which they are allowed an extension of 5 days), the party in good faith may request compensation for the damage and the prejudices caused by the breach in a manner which it considers adequate. Additionally, the respective parties may demand under the established penal clause, the sum of €_____ if the breach is caused by SPORTTV SA, and the sum of €_____ if the breach is caused by the French Federation of Volleyball. The two parties accept that the respective amounts of the penal clause may not be revised during the entire validity period of the contract.

2. Without any prejudice to what has been previously agreed upon, if the French Federation of Volleyball prevents the access of the cameras or their proper operation essential for the distribution or recording of the images of the event in the forms and terms stipulated in this contract, whether it is for the live broadcast, deferred broadcast, or for the highlights; additionally, if it allows third parties not authorized by SPORTTV SA to access the recording or the distribution of images of any match or act provided for in this contract, the French Federation of Volleyball will be required to compensate SPORTTV SA the sum of €_____ under the established penal clause without prejudice to compensation for the damage and harm that may have been caused.

3. Without any prejudice to what has been previously agreed upon, if SPORTTV SA does not carry out its obligations regarding the live and PPV broadcasts on the afore-mentioned days and schedules provided for in this contract, it will be required to compensate the French Federation of Volleyball the sum of €_____ under the

established penal clause without prejudice to compensation for the damage and harm that may have been caused.

Fifteenth: Confidentiality

The parties agree to maintain the confidentiality of the terms and conditions of the contract and will not reveal, directly or indirectly, any type of data or information contained herein, and will adopt necessary measures to effectively guarantee this confidentiality, without prejudice to the legal assumptions imposed in accordance with the regulation in force.

Sixteenth: Public accounts

Each party commits to reviewing the public account of this contract at the request of either one of the parties with the expenses being the responsibility of the requesting party.

Seventeenth: Expenses and taxes

Each party will assume the expenses and taxes resulting from the signing of the contract at hand pursuant to what has been previously established by legislature.

Eighteenth: Notifications and communications

All notifications required for this contract will be sent to the following places of residence:

• For the company SPORTTV SA: address for notifications: _____
_____

• For the French Federation of Volleyball: address for notifications: _____
_____

The communications between the parties may be executed by any means for which the reception can be proven; thus, it is allowable to communicate by fax, COD letter, e-mail with acknowledgment of delivery or any other traditional mode of communication.

Nineteenth: Jurisdiction

With regard to the resolution of any divergence derived from the interpretation or execution of the contract, each party agrees to be subject to the arbitration of the Court of Arbitration for Sport (CAS) whose seat is located in Lausanne, Switzerland, while expressly renouncing any other jurisdictional appeal.

As proof of conformity, this contract will be written in as many copies as there are parties, at the place and on the date stated above.

On behalf of the French Federation of Volleyball _____

On behalf of the company SPORTTV SA _____

Appendix 3

Licensing contract

In Paris, at _____

Between

The first party, _____ (*name of the individual*) acting on behalf of the company, PERRIER FLUO BEACH VOLLEYBALL EXPERIENCE SARL in the capacity of General Manager, by virtue of the powers conferred upon him by the statutes of the company domiciled at _____.

The second party, _____ (*name of the individual*) acting on behalf of the company, PROEVENT SA, in the capacity of Administrator, by virtue of the powers granted to him by the statutes of the company domiciled at _____.

Each party, as a respective representative, is recognized to have the legal authority to enter into this contract and perform its obligations, and for this purpose:

Declare

I. That the company, PERRIER FLUO BEACH VOLLEYBALL EXPERIENCE SARL (the 'RIGHTS OWNER') is the rightful owner of all the rights derived from the exploitation and usage of marketing, whatever the form of these rights adopted for their marketing or the characteristics of the product which is marketed, of the brands associated with the event 'Perrier Fluo Beach Volleyball Experience' and, in particular, the following brands:

A. 'Perrier Fluo Beach Volleyball Experience' Nominative.
B. (*Here should appear both the description of the name and the form of the name adopted by the event for the current edition*) 'Perrier Fluo Beach Volleyball Experience 2007' Nominative-Figurative.

    C. Logo of the event: Figurative.
    D. Name of the event with the logo: Nominative-Figurative.
    E. Mascot of the event: Figurative.
    F. Name of the mascot: Nominative.

II. That the company PROEVENT SA (the 'LICENSEE') is a commercial entity with established distribution and marketing channels worldwide whose social purpose, among other things, is the exploitation and the marketing of all types of products derived from brands, particularly in the field of sporting events.

III. That the RIGHTS OWNER is interested in having a third party exploit and market the rights derived from various products associated with the brands previously mentioned and that the LICENSEE is also interested in their exploitation by their broader distribution and territorial expansion in the common interest of the two parties.

IV. That by virtue of this which has been stated, each appearing party consents to the execution and the commencement of this exclusive licence agreement (the 'CONTRACT'), which is governed by the agreements contained herein.

Definitions

Event: the 'Perrier Fluo Beach Volleyball Experience' is a commercially characterized, unofficial sporting competition of beach volleyball, created with the authorization of the International Federation of Volleyball, where 10 teams originating from 5 continents are allowed to participate in the competition via the invitational system. The event will proceed according to the technical regulations of the International Federation.

Brand: any symbol or means differentiating the products or services of a corporate body from those similar to another legal entity.

Licence: the legal entitlement for a third party to use a brand while respecting the applicable legislation in each territory in which it will be used.

Exclusive licence by product: a licence granted to only one licensee which excludes all commercial exploitation of the same product line associated with the brand by the RIGHTS OWNER. Additionally, it prohibits the LICENSEE from transferring the licence to another given person.

Products:

- Keyrings: _____
- Badges: _____
- Hats: _____

(*Here it is necessary to define all the products or services which are the subject of the licence*).

Agreement

First: Purpose

The RIGHTS OWNER transfers partial usage of the brands described in the declarations to the LICENSEE, to the extent of their commercial exploitation and their distribution by itself or third parties when they are associated with the following products (*it is possible to choose the inclusion of the definitions in the preceding paragraph reserved to this end or to include the definition of each product in this part*):

For example and for the purpose of this company, the transfer relates to:

- Keyrings
- Badges or pins
- Hats
- Jerseys
- Bags, ties, scarves
- Umbrellas and parasols
- Pens, pencils, notebooks

Second: Scope of the transferred rights

1. The transfer of the rights provided for in this contract is characterized as one sole licence for all the products described in the preceding subparagraph, enabling them to associate with all the brands of the 'Perrier Fluo Beach Volleyball Experience' and for all the operations, manufacturing, distribution and sales models.
2. The transfer of the rights provided for in this contract is valid worldwide.
3. The transfer of the rights provided for in this contract relates to all the rights provided for in the declarations, but also to those which may develop during the validity period of the contract from the modification, the transformation, innovation or from a new creation within the framework of the event.

(*It is possible to specify in a non-exclusive way and/or only for the given countries or territories, or for specific distribution channels, and also various types of sales*)

Third: Validity

The transfer of the rights contained herein the contract is valid for the years _____ _____ (*for example 2007, 2008 and 2009*).

The contract will come into effect on January 1, 2007 and will terminate on December 30, 2009.

Without prejudice to the validity period established in this contract, the LICENSEE and/or any other third party having obtained a sublicence, whether it is for distribution or for selling, will be allowed to maintain the sale of the products which, on the day of the term of the contract, are still on the market for a period no longer than 30 days from the end of the contract, thus necessitating the need to withdraw from the market all products that are for sale prior to January 30, 2010. Hence, the LICENSEE must present to the

RIGHTS OWNER, prior to December 30, 2009, a certificate listing the products which it has in its capacity and those which were distributed or presented at points of sale.

From December 30, 2009, the LICENSEE will not be allowed to produce, manufacture, nor distribute any new products.

Fourth: Price

The RIGHTS OWNER, in exchange for the transfer of the commercial exploitation of the rights depicted in this contract, will be entitled to collect the following sums:

A. _____ per cent of the selling price to third parties, before tax, of all the products included herein this contract.
B. _____ per cent of the selling price to the public, before tax, of all the products included in this contract, whether the LICENSEE opts for the exclusive and direct sale of the products to the public, through its own channels of distribution or points of sale, or companies or groups of companies in which the LICENSEE partakes for a total value of 10 per cent of the capital.
C. Without prejudice to what has been previously stated, the LICENSEE must pay the RIGHTS OWNER the annual sum of € _____ (plus the corresponding tax, VAT, etc.), as a guaranteed minimum counter-benefit, except in the case where the latter would not have authorized any application that the LICENSEE presented to him to manufacture. Consequently, when the amount owed to the RIGHTS OWNER for each annual instalment, once the determined percentage is applied and based on the statement of the preceding subparagraphs, is lower than the guaranteed minimum quantity, the LICENSEE will not have any right to allocate previous payments in excess of the minimum standard already paid to the RIGHTS OWNER. Conversely, when the sum to be paid, with the application of the determined percentage and the statements made in subparagraphs A and B, is higher than the guaranteed minimum quantity, then following the term of each annual instalment, the LICENSEE will have to pay the RIGHTS OWNER the difference resulting in its favour prior to January 30.

The amount set in part 'C' as the guaranteed minimum counter-benefit must always be paid to the RIGHTS OWNER within the first 15 days of the annual instalment, i.e. before January 15 of each year.

The LICENSEE is also obligated to annually remit, prior to June 1, the number of all licensed products it has in its possession (*for example, 300*) to the RIGHTS OWNER, for which it will not have to pay the LICENSEE any compensation.

Pursuant to what was stated in the subparagraphs A and B of this agreement, it is established that the LICENSEE will be obligated to inform the RIGHTS OWNER of the actual quarterly sales, by necessarily differentiating each type of product and by country (*or by territory*) within 15 days following the conclusion of each quarter.

The LICENSEE accepts and grants the irrevocable entitlement for the RIGHTS OWNER to examine and verify quarterly and annual liquidations by way of an inspection by him or a duly accredited third-party auditor of the financial books of the business. As such, the LICENSEE will be obligated to place at the disposal of the owner or the auditor, at the address of the former, all sufficient accounting documentation to carry out the verification stated in this subparagraph. In any case, all expenses resulting from the audit of the accounting data is the responsibility of the RIGHTS OWNER, without enabling the LICENSEE to seek payment of any monetary amount for the verifications, nor for the provision of providing the necessary documentation.

Fifth: Production, distribution and sale of the products

1. The production, distribution and sale of the products subject to the licence correspond exclusively to the LICENSEE, or depending on individual cases, to individuals having obtained a sublicence according to the parameters stated in this contract.
2. All the expenditures ensuing from the production, the distribution and the sale of the licensed products will correspond to the LICENSEE or to a third party to whom the RIGHTS OWNER may have granted a sublicence.
3. The parties' consent that the design, the colour, the material and the application of the product are to be the responsibility of the LICENSEE, thus it assumes all costs resulting from it, even if the authorization of the owner remains essential for their manufacture and distribution. One will consider that there is an authorization when in the 15 days following the presentation of the product to the RIGHTS OWNER, the latter did not expressly submit its written refusal or proposed changes. Any modification of the product, in reference to its form, format, design, materials, etc., remains subject to the authorization of the RIGHTS OWNER.
4. The LICENSEE must always seek to use the same colours, formats, graphics and design as well identifiable visual symbols characterizing the event.
5. The LICENSEE, in the design of all the products, will have to take into account the following:

   a) In the presentation of the products, the inscription: 'Perrier Fluo Beach Volleyball Experience' will have to appear either on the packaging or on the product itself in an unambiguous way and in a sufficiently visible format without exception.
   b) The inscription quoted previously may be: accompanied with or without reference to the year of celebration of the event; with or without the logo of the event; with or without the image of the mascot; with or without the name of the mascot; with or without the name of the tenured federation of the event.
   c) When it is physically possible, whether it to be on the packaging, on the label or on the product itself (taking into account the format, the material or the characteristics of the product), the inscription: 'Produced under the official licence of the FFVB' or 'Licensed by the FFVB' will have to appear in a sufficiently visible place.

6. The LICENSEE is obliged to manufacture or to distribute and to sell to the public, directly or through a third party, a minimum of _____ units (annual/quarterly/ monthly) for each of the products (*it is possible to predict a minimum quantity of distribution for each product according to its characteristics or its commercial interests*) from which a minimum of _____ units will need to be distributed and marketed in France.

7. The LICENSEE will be allowed to manufacture and distribute the products listed without any quantitative limit (*if they are products for which one seeks a certain possession of exclusiveness, it will then be necessary to establish a maximum quantity of production*).

8. The LICENSEE will be able to use the distribution channels, up to the points of sale, which it considers adequate with the intention of obtaining the greatest possible effectiveness.

9. It is established that products included in this contract could be sold at all the points of sale _____ (*insert here a description of the points of sale: specialized stores, supermarkets/shopping centres*) without limits or conditions other than those provided for in this contract.

10. The LICENSEE or the third party having authorization to sell the products included in this contract will have to do it continuously and at a fixed price.

11. It is established that the minimum and maximum selling price to the public for each product is as follows:

- Keyrings: €_____ (*in general, a minimum of €2 and a maximum of €60, except in the European Union where this sum will have to be increased 50 per cent and in the United States, as well as in Japan, 100 per cent*)
- Badges or pins: €_____

The LICENSEE or the third party having authorization to sell the products included in this contract shall not do it in the form of sales, the form of remission, in batches or at cut prices, in association with other products or services, by the means of costly or free promotions, of the set/collection sales, except when the LICENSEE has been specifically authorized to do so by the RIGHTS OWNER.

Sixth: Transfers to third parties

The LICENSEE has the option to transfer to a third party, totally or partially, in exclusivity or not, the ability to distribute and/or to sell the products subject to the contract where, in all circumstances, the third-party distributors or salesmen meet the technical, distributional, or sales conditions established in this contract.

The LICENSEE is obligated to communicate to the owner, within 15 days from the signing of the agreement or contract with the third party, the existence of such agreement, as well as to give the RIGHTS OWNER a copy of the signed documents.

The LICENSEE does not have the option to permanently transfer to a third party the right to manufacture, all or in part, the products which are the subject of the contract, as its unique and exclusive competency is the manufacturing of the products by exclusive means of production or by companies in which the LICENSEE holds a minimum of 50 per cent of the common capital.

The LICENSEE is authorized to give responsibility to third-party companies to manufacture separate parts of the final product when it is necessary or appropriate for the best development of the product, but regardless of this, it may not give a company the responsibility for manufacturing or making the products in its entirety.

Seventh: Commitments and guarantees of the RIGHTS OWNER

1. The RIGHTS OWNER guarantees and commits to manufacture all the brands which are the subject of the partial transfer concluded in this contract.
2. The RIGHTS OWNER declares and guarantees to have exclusive rightful possession of, and has the freedom to relinquish, all of the rights transferred in this contract, for which there is no possibility for their acquisition, nor for preferential rights to tender or retraction rights, of contribution, of taxation, without restriction or claim of all types, and that there is no third party able to prevent or stipulate the commemoration or the execution of this contract, or to disturb the use of it, especially through interventions of a third party that are based on the rights of the intellectual property. Therefore, the RIGHTS OWNER will guarantee the free and impartial usage of the rights for the LICENSEE or possible assignees of these rights. Likewise, the RIGHTS OWNER declares and guarantees that to the best of its knowledge, there is no dispute, litigation, arbitration, nor legal or administrative procedures against itself for deeds or acts in relation to the rights being transferred in this contract.
3. If the RIGHTS OWNER comes to change its legal status during the validity period of the contract, transforming its status into any other form than the current one, the new entity will be subrogated to all the rights and obligations emanating from this contract, which will, in all cases, continue in all its effects in force where the LICENSEE requests this subrogation and the maintenance of the contract.
4. In the event where the RIGHTS OWNER comes to change the competition model, the type of sport activity, the name of the event, or other essential aspects of the event which could lead to the voiding of this contract, the LICENSEE will have preferential rights to tender and retraction rights in the negotiation, in relation to any other company wishing to have a licence for the rights provided for in this contract for the new sport activity, in situations where it would have similar characteristics, organized by the RIGHTS OWNER or any of its subsidiary companies or by any other entity being able to substitute it during the period of validity of this contract.
5. The RIGHTS OWNER guarantees that in all contracts of sponsorship, collaboration, publicity, or any other contract of similar nature concluded with third parties, a clause will be inserted to provide for the obligation of the third party to directly obtain the products of this contract from the LICENSEE when it wishes to use them for promotional or advertising purposes without having the option to sell them directly at any time, except if they are linked to a product or service specific to the subject of their contract.
6. The RIGHTS OWNER agrees to provide the LICENSEE a covered space of _____ ____ m² with electricity inside the facility where the event will take place, for the entire duration of the event, for which the LICENSEE must pay the RIGHTS OWNER the tariff stipulated for this space plus an additional _____ per cent (*for example 25 per cent*). For these purposes, the RIGHTS OWNER will communicate relevant information regarding this space to the LICENSEE, within a period of _____ days prior to the commencement of the event, whereupon the LICENSEE must respond if it desires to make use of this space or not within a maximum period of 15 days from the notification. The LICENSEE forfeits its right to the space if it fails to respond within 15 days of notification.

7. The RIGHTS OWNER accepts that the LICENSEE can publicize the licensed products by announcing that the company holds the licence of the RIGHTS OWNER or that it possesses a sublicensed product of the event.

8. The RIGHTS OWNER agrees to publicize the products of the LICENSEE, if requested by the latter, in all publications, booklets, posters, etc., published by the RIGHTS OWNER wherein it is possible to include such publicity. However, in situations where only the advertisement of the sponsor must appear, the LICENSEE must pay the stipulated tariff plus an additional _____ per cent to the RIGHTS OWNER for the advertising integration. In such a case, the RIGHTS OWNER will communicate to the LICENSEE the possibility for the inclusion and of its characteristics, within a minimum period of _____ days prior to the commencement of the event, whereupon the LICENSEE must respond if it desires to make use or not of this advertising inclusion and of the characteristics of the advertising, within a maximum period of 15 days from the notification. The LICENSEE forfeits this right if it fails to respond within 15 days of notification.

9. The RIGHTS OWNER agrees to advertise the products being sublicensed on the official Web page of the event and to include a link to the Web page of the LICENSEE to allow them the ability to sell the licensed products via the Internet.

10. The RIGHTS OWNER agrees to publicize the products of the LICENSEE, if requested by the latter, in spaces or by technical means intended for that purpose (*megaphones, billboard, etc.*) in locations within the facility where the event takes place or in other facilities where activities are occurring in relation to the event. For those facilities where only the publicity of the sponsor must appear in a maximum of _____ m^2 (*insertions, fences, etc.*), the LICENSEE must pay the stipulated tariff plus an additional _____ per cent to the RIGHTS OWNER for this advertising integration. In such cases, the RIGHTS OWNER will communicate this to the LICENSEE, within a minimum period of _____ days prior to the commencement of the event, whereupon the LICENSEE must respond if it wishes to make use or not of this advertising inclusion and of the characteristics of the advertising within a maximum period of 15 days from the notification. The LICENSEE forfeits this right if it fails to respond within 15 days of notification.

11. The RIGHTS OWNER guarantees that in any audiovisual contract it may sign, a clause stipulating that the LICENSEE will have a preference over the other advertisers will be included, with exception for the sponsors of the event and other subjects who hold licences for television advertising slots which are, or which may be, subject to a special provision of time or preferences by the organizer. For these purposes, the RIGHTS OWNER will communicate to the LICENSEE, within a minimum period of _____ days prior to the commencement of the event of such possibility by providing him the details of the time slots and the characteristics of open advertising spaces. The LICENSEE must respond if it wishes to make use or not of this advertising inclusion and of the characteristics of the advertising, within a maximum period of 15 days from the notification. The LICENSEE forfeits this right if it fails to respond within 15 days of notification.

Eighth: Commitments and guarantees of the LICENSEE

1. If the LICENSEE registers patents for inventions, for a certificate of inclusion, for brands or distinctive symbols of the production or the business, for the usefulness of prototypes, for models or industrial designs, for artistic or commercial names, or for certain rights of the subjects and individuals referred to in this contract, it will then be obligated to amend them in any drawing, slogan, logo or pattern inspired by creations, with the characteristics, of the individuals, logos, emblems and names to which this contract refers.

2. The LICENSEE is obligated, if physically possible, to secure the label of the licensed product for each unit according to the authorization, which it will have to obtain from the RIGHTS OWNER or the specialized company which designed it, as a guarantee for the ultimate consumer. In all occurrences, the LICENSEE guarantees that the price of the label per unit or the system to secure or the authorization will not exceed € _____. (*It is not always possible to have this guarantee. Undeniably, it is difficult to have a place for a label on a keyring when it is sold without packaging.*)

3. The LICENSEE, with direction from the RIGHTS OWNER, agrees to assist all the companies sponsoring the event, the sponsors and any other collaborators by providing them with the number of units of product they need within one month from their solicitation and at the best selling price offered by the LICENSEE to any distributor or salesperson within the entire territory where the product will be distributed. If the request of product units is higher than _____ (*for example: 50,000 keyrings, badges, hats, shirts, etc., and 10,000 pens, umbrellas, etc.*), the time limit will be extended to three months.

4. The LICENSEE shall purchase a policy for civil liability insurance with a reputable insurance company on all the licensed products referenced in this contract and in each territory where the products are directly distributed or by third parties, and is to provide a copy of this insurance policy, as well as any extensions and updates, to the RIGHTS OWNER within the 30 days following the signing of this contract, its renewal, or its replacement. This civil liability insurance policy must have a minimum coverage of € _____ in every country, except for the European Union countries where the minimum coverage is € _____ and in the United States and Japan where it will be US$ _____. Likewise, the LICENSEE commits to extending this insurance obligation to all the individuals or companies to which it may have granted a sublicence for the distribution and the sale of the licensed products to the public.

5. The LICENSEE shall indemnify the RIGHTS OWNER, agreeing to avoid and, according to the situation, to be accountable for all legitimate complaints and further legality interests of prejudice, and, as a general rule, for any disputes being brought forth to the RIGHTS OWNER derived from the event related to the commercial exploitation of the licensed products provided for in this contract. For the purpose of this clause, the term 'RIGHTS OWNER' includes the employees, directors, agents and other personnel dependent upon the RIGHTS OWNER, as well as with its respective subsidiary companies or subsidiaries. In any case, the RIGHTS OWNER retains the opportunity to directly respond to and execute all legal proceedings which it regards as necessary for the protection of its interests. The RIGHTS OWNER assumes the

court expenses in such a case and must inform the LICENSEE beforehand of its intention to act.

Ninth: Causes for cancellation

The parties explicitly consent that this contract will be terminated, without any need for prior notice, when provided with the following circumstances.

1. When the LICENSEE introduces or solicits a legal procedure of recuperation, whether it is during the suspension of payments phase or the bankruptcy phase.
2. When the LICENSEE accepts the dissolution and/or the liquidation of the company; or when the social purpose is modified making the execution of the contract impossible.
3. When the LICENSEE is appointed a legal receiver and/or a trustee.
4. In the event of the transfer of this contract on behalf of the LICENSEE for the benefit of its creditors.
5. In the event of non-fulfilment by the creditor of its payment obligations and those arising out of the Fourth article of this contract.
6. In the event of the manufacture and/or of the distribution of the products without the authorization of the RIGHTS OWNER.

This contract may be cancelled if the RIGHTS OWNER declares it for the non-fulfilment by the LICENSEE of the agreements herein this contract. The RIGHTS OWNER must inform the LICENSEE beforehand by giving him a notice to carry out its obligation. When this communication has remained unsuccessful for a minimum period of 10 days from the receipt of the notification, the contract will become null and void.

In the event of the cancellation of the contract due to the realization of one of the circumstances previously stated, without prejudice to the formal reserve, actions could be started against the LICENSEE for damages and interests in favour of the RIGHTS OWNER. The LICENSEE will not be allowed to carry out any kind of commercial exploitation, beginning from the resolution or from the extinction of the contractual relation, and, consequently, must stop the manufacturing, distribution and direct sale of the licensed products and withdraw all existing products from the market. The RIGHTS OWNER, in the event of non-fulfilment, will retain a share of remission of the products legally put in circulation without prejudice to other legal actions it is entitled to.

In addition, in the case of cancellation of the contract due to one of the causes previously provided, or for the mere expiration of the contractual validity period, the LICENSEE is obligated to return to the RIGHTS OWNER or prove that it destroyed all:

- Stocks of the products existing at this time, such as manufacturing or distribution units like those at the points of sale.
- Moulds, stencils, stampings and other necessary means for the manufacture or the making of the products.

Tenth: Penal clauses and breaches

1. Both parties explicitly consent that if for any reason, except for major cause, the LICENSEE does not manufacture and/or distribute the minimum number of products agreed upon in the Fifth clause, the RIGHTS OWNER will receive a penalty compensation in its favour of € _____ for each month of non-fulfilment with the monthly allowances accumulating in the event of reiterated non-fulfilments. If the duration of the breach lasts more than two consecutive months or for four non-consecutive months over a maximum period of eight months, the RIGHTS OWNER will have the option to choose between the cancellation of the contract, or its maintenance with the right to collect the penalty allowance previously provided for.
2. Both parties also consent that if for any reason, except for major cause, the LICENSEE experiences certain difficulties in the manufacturing and/or the distribution of the licensed products having not met the minimums established in the previous paragraph, if this minimum is 20 per cent lower than those manufactured and/or distributed during the same period the previous year (or if it is during the first year and the minimums are lower than the average of the two previous months), it is established that the sum having to be paid by the licence to the RIGHTS OWNER will be equal to that paid the previous year (or if it is the first year of the contract, equal to the average of the two previous months).
3. Likewise, it is established herein the penalty clause that the LICENSEE is obligated to pay to the RIGHTS OWNER the sum of € _____ in the event the contract is cancelled whereupon the LICENSEE does not return to the RIGHTS OWNER all the stocks and moulds or stencils referred to in the Ninth article within a maximum period of six months from the date of resolution or relinquishment without prejudice to the right of the LICENSEE to be able to claim damages for these actions if they indeed had occurred.

Eleventh: Confidentiality

The parties agree to maintain the confidentiality of the terms and conditions of the contract and will not reveal, directly or indirectly, any type of data or information contained herein, and will adopt necessary measures to effectively guarantee this confidentiality, without prejudice to the legal assumptions imposed in accordance with the regulation in force.

Twelfth: Public accounts

Each party commits to reviewing the public account of this contract at the request of either one of the parties, the expenses being the responsibility of the requesting party.

Thirteenth: Expenses and taxes

Each party of the contract will assume the expenses and taxes resulting from the signing of the contract pursuant to what has been previously established by law.

Fourteenth: Notifications and communications

All the notifications required for this contract will be sent to the following places of residence:

- For the RIGHTS OWNER, address of notification: _____
  _____
- For the LICENSEE, address of notification: _____
  _____

The communications between the parties may be executed by any means for which the reception can be proven; thus, it is allowable to communicate by fax, COD letter, e-mail with acknowledgment of delivery or any other traditional mode of communication.

Fifteenth: Jurisdiction

With regard to the resolution of any divergence derived from the interpretation or execution of the contract, each party agrees to be subject to the arbitration of the Court of Arbitration for Sport (CAS) whose seat is located in Lausanne, Switzerland, while expressly renouncing any other jurisdictional appeal.

As proof of conformity, this contract will be written in as many copies as there are parties, at the place and on the date stated above.

On behalf of PERRIER FLUO BEACH VOLLEYBALL EXPERIENCE SARL

_____

On behalf of PROEVENT SA _____

Notes

Introduction

1 Prior to the design of any sponsorship offer, it is advisable to analyse the rights of the different parties within the system of sports sponsorship to avoid any legal problem. We focus on this topic in Chapter 2.
2 Article 2, Fundamental principles: Olympic Charter. The Olympic Charter is the codification of the fundamental principles, rules and application texts/processes adopted by the International Olympic Committee (IOC). It governs the organization and operations of the Olympic Movement and determines the conditions of the celebration of the Olympic Games.
3 Freeman (1984) initially popularized this concept. 'A stakeholder in an organization is (by definition) any group or individual who can affect or is affected by the achievement of the organization's objectives.'
4 www.canadianheritage.gc.ca/progs/sc/pubs/hosting_policy_2004_e.cfm
5 This aspect will be discussed in Chapter 3 under brand equity management.

Chapter 1

1 This definition is tied to the 1980s. In the 1990s the concept of brand equity was integrated into it.
2 Primary stakeholders are those who are directly affecting or affected by the event organization (i.e. rights owner, sponsors, media, local authorities ...).
3 In the 1980s, sponsors targeted this category of stakeholder with institutional objectives in mind. The current trend is to develop commercial relationships between these organizations within the framework of systemic marketing. We will expand on this aspect later in this chapter.
4 A marketing target refers to the potential customers of a product (i.e. who can I sell to?). A communication target refers to the general public viewed as potential customers (i.e. who should I target?). The communication target is thus more comprehensive than the marketing target, as it includes both the potential customers and the whole set of consumers likely to be interested in a product or a brand, whereby serving as a

communication relay between a company and its customers (e.g. media, market experts, etc.).

5   Cegarra (1987) identifies three approaches to sponsorship, i.e. the passion, opportunistic and strategic approaches. The strategic approach is the only one allowing an integration of the sponsorship operation within the communication strategy of the company.

Chapter 2

1   This does not apply to a recurring event by the same owner.
2   www.olympic.org/uk/organisation/movement/index_uk.asp
3   International and national federations penalize athletes and clubs participating in unauthorized sporting events.
4   www.epha.org/a/2086

Chapter 3

1   'Sporting organization' is a generic term referring to the rights owner of the event who is implementing the sponsorship operation.
2   In some cases, it is a corporation which initiates contact and presents a sponsorship offer.
3   www.olympic.org/uk/organisation/missions/charter_uk.asp
4   www.opengazdefrance.com
5   www.olympic.org/uk/organisation/facts/programme/sponsors_uk.asp
6   The internal reference price is based primarily on the sponsorship experience of the manager and cost of the communication plan required to achieve the sponsorship operation objectives.
7   Referred to as the equivalent opportunity cost.
8   www.fifa.com/en/fairplay/humanitariansection/0,1422,1,00.html
9   www.fivb.com, www.fifa.com, www.iihf.com/index.shtml

Chapter 4

1   www.uncitral.org/uncitral/en/uncitral_texts/arbitration/NYConvention.html
2   http://untreaty.un.org/english/bible/englishinternetbible/partI/chapterXXII/treaty2.asp
3   www.uncitral.org/uncitral/en/uncitral_texts/arbitration/1985Model_arbitration.html
4   www.tas-cas.org/en/present/frmpres.htm
5   Cannibalization occurs when a secondary fact becomes more important than the principal fact on which it depends.
6   Case COMP/C-2/37.214
7   A bumper break is the name given to the brief appearance of a logo before, after or in-between commercial breaks.
8   http://europa.eu.int/eur-lex/en/com/pdf/2004/com2004_0002en03.pdf

9 It could also be defined as a contract of insertion with association. The difference lies in the greater or lesser importance which one attaches to either of these two aspects.

Chapter 5

1 The FFVB received authorization from the French Minister of Sport to organize the official competitions, e.g. French championships.
2 In this scenario, a sports brand is governed by associative law, particularly by the regulations of the FIVB and of the FFVB.
3 www.fivb.ch/EN/BeachVolleyball/Handbook/2006/index2006.asp?sm=18
4 www.fivb.org/EN/BeachVolleyball/Partnership_Opportunities/Forms/Candidature/WT-04b.pdf
5 The rules of the game influence the spectacle presented to the public and the media.
6 www.fivb.ch/EN/BeachVolleyball/Handbook/2006/index2006.asp?sm=18
7 For more information, consult: www.wipo.int/classifications/fulltext/nice8/enmain.htm
8 Article 2: www.wipo.int/treaties/en/ip/paris/trtdocs_wo020.html#P81_6245
9 www.wipo.int/about-ip/en/industrial_designs.html
10 www.wipo.int/treaties/en/general
11 For a WHOIS search on the European Registry of Internet Domain Names, go to: www.whois.eu/whois/GetDomainStatus.htm
12 www.perrier.com/EN/entrezbulle/rubrique10.asp
13 www.perrier.com/en/entrezbulle/rubrique73.asp
14 PET: polyethylene terephthalate
15 www.perrier.com/EN/entrezbulle/rubrique73.asp
16 Note that it is not necessary to set a price to the initial offer. The primary objective is to meet with the prospective sponsor in order to introduce the sponsorship offer and gather the sponsor's feedback and expectations. Thus, the price of the offer can be revealed after that meeting.
17 Plans and models must be used to show the title sponsor where its name and/or products will be displayed and/or sold.
18 Class 32: water, syrups, beers and non-alcoholic drinks.

Conclusion

1 www.solar-impulse.com
2 www.iso.org
3 www.valais-excellence.ch
4 www.omegaeuropeanmasters.com
5 www.grand-raid-cristalp.ch
6 There are 142 sporting disciplines and 25,000 events worldwide each year.

References

Aaker, D.A. (1991) *Managing brand equity: capitalizing on the value of a brand name*, New York: The Free Press.

——(1996) *Building strong brands*, New York: The Free Press.

——(2001) *Strategic market management*, 6th edn, Hoboken, NJ: John Wiley.

Abimbola, T., Saunders, J. and Broderick, A.J. (1999) 'Brand intangible assets evaluation: a conceptual framework', *Proceedings of the Chartered Institute of Marketing Research Seminar, Assessing marketing performance*, Cookham, 1–18.

Abratt, R. and Grober, P.S. (1989) 'The evaluation of sports sponsorships', *International Journal of Advertising*, 8: 351–62.

Ajzen, I. and Fishbein, M. (1980) *Understanding attitudes and predicting social behaviour*, Englewood Cliffs, NJ: Prentice Hall.

Andreasen, A.R. (1994) 'Social marketing: definition and domain', *Journal of Marketing and Public Policy*, Spring: 108–14.

Arthur, D., Scott, D., Woods, T. and Booker, R. (1998) 'Sport sponsorship should ... a process model for the effective implementation and management of sport sponsorship programmes', *Sport Marketing Quarterly*, 7, 4: 49–61.

Bayless, A. (1988) 'Ambush marketing is becoming popular event at Olympic Games', *The Wall Street Journal*, February: 8.

Becker-Olsen, K. and Simmons, C.J. (2002) 'Fortifying or diluting equity via association: the case of sponsorship', *European Advances in Consumer Research*, 5: 32–48.

Bourdieu, P. (1979) *La distinction: critique sociale du jugement*, Paris: Editions de Minuit.

Bowen, H.R. (1953) *The social responsibilities of the businessman*, New York: Harper & Row.

Bowey, S. (1988) 'Sponsorship: effective or extravagant?', paper presented at ESOMAR Congress, Amsterdam.

Brochand, B. and Lendrevie, J. (1989) *Publicitor*, 2nd edn, Paris: Dalloz.

Bromberger, C., Hayot, A. and Mariottini, J.M. (1987) 'Aller l'OM! Forza Juve! La passion pour le football à Marseille et à Turin', *Terrain, Carnet du Patrimoine Ethnologique*, online. Available online: http://terrain.revues.org/document3636.html (accessed 12 November 2005)

Cegarra, J.J. (1987) 'La promotion par l'action: analyse du parrainage de la Course de l'Europe à la voile par la Commission des Communautés Européennes', unplublished thesis, Université Lyon III.

Chappelet, J.L. (2004) 'Strategic management of Olympic sport organisations', in J.L. Chappelet and E. Bayle (eds), *Strategic and performance management of Olympic sport organisations*, Champaign, IL: Human Kinetics.

Chappelet, J.L., Brighenti, O., Clivaz, C. and Favre, N. (2005) *From initial idea to success: a guide to bidding for sport events for politicians and administrators*, SENTEDALPS, Lausanne: Editions IDHEAP. Available online: http://www.sentedalps.org/

Cohen, J.B. and Areni, C.S. (1991) 'Affect and consumer behaviour', in T.S. Robertson and H.H. Kassarjian (eds), *Handbook of consumer behavior*, Englewood Cliffs, NJ: Prentice Hall.

Communication and Business (1988) Time to assess sponsorship impact, *Communication and Business*, 4 April, 8-11.

Cornwell, B.T., Weeks, C.S. and Roy, D.P. (2005) 'Sponsorship-linked marketing: opening the black box', *Journal of Advertising*, 34, 2: 21–42.

Crompton, J.L. (1993) 'Sponsorship of sport by tobacco and alcohol companies', *Journal of Sport and Social Issues*, 17, 3: 148–67.

——(2004) 'Conceptualization and alternate operationalizations of the measurement of sponsorship effectiveness in sport', *Leisure Studies*, 23, 3: 267–81.

Crowley, M.G. (1991) 'Prioritising the sponsorship audience', *European Journal of Marketing*, 25, 11: 11–21.

Dambron, P. (1991) *Sponsoring et politique de marketing*, Paris: Editions d'Organisation.

Davis, K. (1973) *The case for and against business assumption of social responsibilities*, New York: McGraw-Hill.

Derbaix, C., Gérard, P. and Lardinoit, T. (1994) 'Essai de conceptualisation d'une activité éminement pratique: le parrainage', *Recherche et Application en Marketing*, 9, 2: 43–67.

Dominitz, J.C. and Tochon, S. (1988) *La communication promotionnelle*, Paris: Les Editions d'Organisation.

Dussard, C. (1983) *Comportement du consommateur et stratégie de marketing*, Toronto: McGraw-Hill.

Ferrand, A. (1995) 'Contribution à l'évaluation de l'efficacité du sponsoring événementiel d'image', unpublished PhD thesis , Université Claude Bernard Lyon 1.

——(2004) 'Costruire una strategia di comunicazione efficace', *Rivista di Cultura Sportiva*, 62–63: 82–88.

——and Pagès, M. (1996) 'Image sponsoring: a methodology to match event and sponsor', *Journal of Sport Management*, 10: 278–91.

——and Pagès, M. (2004) 'Contribution du Grand Prix de Tennis de Lyon au renforcement de l'identité Lyonnaise', in B. Michon and T. Terret (eds), *Pratiques sportives et identités locales*, Paris: L'harmattan.

——and Nardi, M. (2005) *Marketing dello fitness*, Milan: Alea Edizioni.

——and Torrigiani, L. (2005) *Marketing of Olympic sport organisations*, Champaign, IL: Human Kinetics.

Field, M. (1981) 'Sponsorship: to trust to luck', *Médias*, 11, 32-39.

Freeman, R.E. (1984) *Strategic management: a stakeholder approach*, Boston, MA: Pitman.

Ganassali, S. and Didelon, L. (1996) 'Le transfert comme principe central du parrainage', *Recherche et Application en Marketing*, 11, 1: 37–48.

Gillis, R. (2004) 'Giving something back', *Marketing*, 22 Sept.: 38–39.

Gross, A.C., Traylor, M.B. and Shuman, P.J. (1987) 'Corporate sponsorship of art and sport events in North America', paper presented at ESOMAR Congress.

Hardie, M.E., Charron, C. and Das, A. (1999) *The sport power shift*, Forester Research report.

Henry, I. and Lee, P. (2004) 'Governance and ethics in sport', in J. Beech and S. Chadwick (eds), *The business of sport management*, London: FT/ Thompson.

Holbrook, M.B. and Hirschman, E.C. (1982) 'The experential aspects of consumption: consumer fantasies, feelings and fun', *Journal of Consumer Research*, 9, 2: 132–40.

Hovland, C., Lumsdaine, A. and Sheffield, F. (1945) *Experiments on mass communication*, Princeton, NJ: Princeton University Press.

Howard, J.A. and Sheth, J.N. (1969) *The theory of buyer behaviour*, New York: Wiley.

Howell, D. (1983) *Committee of inquiry into sport sponsorship*, London: Central Council of Physical Recreation.

IEG (2004) Sponsorship report, 24, 12.

IOC (2000) *Marketing fact file*, Lausanne: International Olympic Committee.

IOC (2002) *Marketing fact file*, Lausanne: International Olympic Committee.

IOC (2006) Olympic charter. Available online: www.olympic.org/uk/organisation/missions/charter_uk.asp

Kapferer, J.N. (1988) *Les chemins de la persuasion: le mode d'influence des média et de la publicité sur les comportements*, Paris: Dunod.

—— and Laurent, M. (1983) *Comment mesurer le degré d'implication des consommateurs?*, Paris: IREP.

Keller, K.L. (1993) 'Conceptualizing, measuring, managing customer-based brand equity', *Journal of Marketing*, 57, 1: 1–22.

Kiely, D. (1993) 'Sponsorship: it's a buyers' market', *Marketing*, February: 9–12.

Kotler, P. and Armstrong, G. (2004) *Principles of marketing*, Upper Saddle River, NJ: Pearson/Prentice Hall.

Labro, J.P. (1982) 'Le problème d'image d'une grande compagnie pétrolière: recherche d'une stratégie et résultats', *Communication d'entreprise et communication d'institution*, Paris: IREP.

Lambin, J.J. (2002) *Marketing stratégique: du marketing à l'orientation marché*, Paris: Dunod.

Lehu, J.M. (2004) *L'encyclopédie du marketing*, Paris: Editions d'organisation.

L'événementiel (1994) 'J'usqu'où vont-ils aller?', *L'événementiel*, 32, 8-11.

McCarville, R.E., Flood, C.M. and Froats, T.A. (1998) 'The effectiveness of selected promotions on spectators assessments of a nonprofit sporting event sponsor', *Journal of Sport Management*, 12, 1: 51–63.

Maffesoli, M. (1988) *Le temps des tribus*, Paris: Méridiens Klincksieck.

Meenaghan, T. (1994) 'Point of view: ambush marketing immoral or imaginative practice?', *Journal of Advertising Research*, September/October: 77–88.

Meenaghan, T. (2001) 'Understanding sponsorship effects', *Psychology & Marketing*, 18, 2: 95–122.

Morin, E. (1990) *Introduction à la pensée complexe*, Paris: ESF.

Oliver, R.L. (1997) *Satisfaction: a behavioral perspective on the consumer*, New York: McGraw-Hill.

Otker, T. (1988) 'Exploitation: the key to sponsorship success', *European Research*, May: 77–86.

Parasuraman, A., Berry, L.L. and Zeithaml, V.A. (1988) 'SERVQUAL: a multiple-item scale for measuring customer perceptions of service quality', *Journal of Retailing*, Spring: 12–40.

Pinfield, L.T. (1986) 'A field evaluation of perspectives on organizational decision making', *Administrative Science Quarterly*, 31, 3: 365–88.

Piquet, S. (1985) *Sponsoring*, Paris: Vuibert Gestion.

Pociello, C. (1983) *Sport et société: approche socio-culturelle des pratiques*, Paris: Vigot.

Pracejus, J.W. and Olsen, G. (2004) 'The role of brand/cause fit in the effectiveness of cause-related marketing campaigns', *Journal of Business Research*, 57, 6: 635–41.

Ries, A. and Trout, J. (1981) *Positioning the battle for your mind*, New York: McGraw-Hill.

Rokeach, M. (1973) *The nature of human values*, New York: The Free Press.

Rougé, J.F. (1987) 'It is expensive, and it can bring nothing in return', *L'Expansion*, 6/19 November: 72-73.

Ruth, J.A. and Simonin, B.L. (2003) 'Brought to you by brand A and brand B': investigating multiple sponsors' influence on consumer attitudes toward sponsorship events', *Journal of Advertising*, 32(3): 19–30.

Sahnoun, P. (1986) *Le sponsoring mode d'emploi*, Paris: Chotard et Associés.

Saporta, B. (1985) 'Sponsoring, commandite et parrainage sportif, mode passagère ou technique privilégiée de communication?', *Cahiers de Recherche de l'IAE de Toulouse*, 24: 1–34.

Sandler, D.M. and Shani, D. (1989) 'Olympic Sponsorship vs. ambush marketing: who gets the gold?', *Journal of Advertising Research*, August/September: 44–54.

Schultz, D.E., Tannenbaum, S.I. and Lauterborn, R.F. (1993) *Integrated marketing communications: putting it together and making it work*, New York: McGraw-Hill.

Sheth, J.N. and Parvatiyar, A. (2000) *The handbook of relationship marketing*, Thousand Oaks, CA: Sage Publications.

Shrimp, T. (2003) *Advertising, promotion and supplemental aspects of integrated marketing communications*, 6th edn, Belmont, CA: Thomson South-Western.

Speed, R. and Thompson, P. (2000) 'Determinants of sports sponsorship response', *Journal of the Academy of Marketing Science*, 28, 2: 226–38.

Sport+ Market study (1998) 1998 World Cup survey. Available online: http://www.redmandarin.com/archive/article_ambush.htm

UDA (1986) *Enquête U.D.A. sur le parrainage*, Paris: Union Des Annonceurs.

UDA (1990) *Enquête U.D.A. sur le parrainage*, Paris: Union Des Annonceurs.

UDA (1998) *Enquête U.D.A. sur le parrainage*, Paris: Union Des Annonceurs.

Walsh, K. (1984) 'Despite image, grassroots sports generate excellent marketing results, but don't expect to quantify them', *Advertising Age*, 24: 8.

Wilkinson, D.G. (1993) *Sponsorship marketing: a practical reference guide for corporations in the 1990's*, Toronto: The Wilkinson Group.

Zajonc, R.B. and Markus, H. (1982) 'Affective and cognitive factors in preferences', *Journal of Comparative and Physiological Psychology*, 86: 581–85.

Zeyl, A. and Dayan, A. (2003) *Force de vente: direction, organisation, gestion*, 2nd edn, Paris: Editions d'Organisation.

Bibliography on legal aspects

Abe, M. Trademark issues in cyberspace: the brave new frontier. Available online: www. fenwick.com/pub/ip_pubs/Trademark%20in%Cyberspace%2098trademark_issues_ in_cyberspace.htm.

Agustinoy, A. (2002) *Régimen jurídico de los nombres de dominio. Estudio práctico sobre sus principales aspectos técnicos y legales,* Valencia: Tirant lo blanch.

Blackshaw, I. and Hogg, G. (1993) *Sports marketing Europe: the legal and tax aspects,* The Hague: Kluwer Law International.

Dueker K.S. (1996) 'Trademark law lost in cyberspace: trademark protection for internet addresses', *Harvard Journal of Law and Technology,* 9.

Griffith-Jones D. (1997) *Law and the business of sport,* London: Butterworths.

Landaberea, J. (1992) *El contrato de esponsorización deportiva,* Pamplona: Aranzadi.

Vicente, E. (1998) *El contrato de esponsorización,* Madrid: Civitas.

Wise, A. and Meyer, B. (1997) *International sports law and business,* The Hague: Kluwer Law International.

Index

References to figures and tables are in **bold** type, and titles of documents in *italic*.